Fact and Value

Fact and Value

Essays on Ethics and Metaphysics for Judith Jarvis Thomson

edited by
Alex Byrne, Robert Stalnaker, and Ralph Wedgwood

A Bradford Book
The MIT Press
Cambridge, Massachusetts
London, England

This book was set in Palatino by Best-set Typesetter Ltd., Hong Kong and was printed and bound in the United States of America.

Library of Congress Cataloging-in-Publication Data

Fact and value : essays on ethics and metaphysics for Judith Jarvis Thomson / edited by Alex Byrne, Robert Stalnaker, and Ralph Wedgwood.

   p. cm.

"A Bradford book."

Includes bibliographical references and index.

ISBN 0-262-02498-5 (hc. : alk. paper)

   1. Ethics. 2. Metaphysics. I. Thomson, Judith Jarvis. II. Byrne, Alex. III. Stalnaker, Robert. IV. Wedgwood, Ralph.

BJ1012 .F3   2001

100—dc21

                                               00-048033

Contents

Preface

Judith Jarvis Thomson joined the philosophy faculty at MIT in 1964, four years after completing her Ph.D. at Columbia, and except for an occasional visiting semester away, she has been here ever since. Her arrival at MIT coincided with the beginning of its philosophy graduate program, and her distinctive way of doing philosophy has left a permanent mark on the program's structure and content.

Judy continues to inspire her colleagues and students by showing us how to think about philosophical problems. She teaches us to be problem solvers rather than deep thinkers, to be impatient with pontification, inflated theory, unnecessary apparatus, and fuzzy formulations. She takes on big problems—central issues in metaphysics and moral theory—but her approach to them is straightforward and down to earth. Her philosophical work is not guided by any one "big" idea, or by one conception of philosophical method. The aim is just to make a question as clear as possible, and to find and defend the right answer. Her gift is an ability to make the big issues of metaphysics and ethical theory concrete—to find the examples that make a distinction clear, or that show the consequences of a thesis or an analysis.

Judy has had a legendary influence on students. Although her reaction to a first draft of a term paper is not generally a cause for rejoicing, in retrospect the benefits of her exacting comments are all too obvious. A recent in-house "Philosophical Lexicon" entry says it best:

Thomson effect, n. An increase in philosophical clarity brought on by fear of *adjudycation*.

As is apparent from the bibliography of Judy's work compiled at the end of this volume, she has addressed a wide range of philosophical problems. She has written about metaphysical problems such as the identity of persons and physical objects over time, the individuation of events and actions, and the character of practical reason. In her writings about moral theory, she has been a relentless critic of utilitarianism, and a defender of the central role of rights in a correct moral theory. She sees the abstract issues of moral theory as continuous with issues of public policy, and has applied the same style of philosophical analysis to questions about physician-assisted suicide, government regulation, academic freedom, preferential hiring and, most famously, abortion.

The breadth of Judy's philosophical work is reflected in the diversity of topics that her friends and colleagues have chosen to write about in this collection in her honor. Some of the papers discuss specific moral and political issues, most of which Judy has written about: abortion, the right of self-defense, the rights and obligations of prospective fathers, and the impact of political campaign finance on equality of opportunity. Others concern the foundations of moral theory: hedonism, virtue ethics, the nature of nonconsequentialism, and the objectivity of moral claims. Three of the papers address questions in metaphysics and epistemology: the existence of sets, the structures of conditional statements, and the commitments of testimony.

The papers in this collection also reflect Judy's style. They all aim at the high standard of clarity and concreteness for which her work provides a model. In doing so, they pay tribute to the importance of her contribution to philosophy.

On behalf of her colleagues and students, past and present, we are pleased to dedicate this collection to her with admiration and affection.

Acknowledgments

We are greatly indebted to Tyler Doggett, Roxanne Fay, Josh Flaherty, Ishani Maitra, Sarah McGrath, Carolina Sartorio, and Ásta Sveinsdóttir for expert editorial assistance; to Ulrich Meyer for compiling the bibliography; and to Carolyn Gray Anderson and Judy Feldmann of The MIT Press for their help and advice.

Chapter 1

Conditionals and Explanations

Jonathan Bennett

1 Preliminaries

On what basis should conditionals be sorted into two main groups, and what does each group contain?

A well-known division of English conditional *sentences* puts them into two groups according to whether the consequent has 'would' as its principal operator. 'If he had asked me politely, I would have agreed', 'If you were to give her half a chance, she would complete the job'; contrast with 'If it's high tide now, then the table is wrong', 'If he has an ounce of decency, he will own up'. Philosophers often call these *subjunctive* and *indicative*, respectively. These grammatically suspect terms throw no light on any philosophical issue, but I shall use them, *faute de mieux*, to label those two classes of sentence.

It has usually been thought that the division of conditional sentences into indicative and subjunctive corresponds to the principal division of conditionals—that is, items meant by conditional sentences—but in recent years this has been challenged. V. H. Dudman has argued for dividing conditionals differently, using a certain grammatical-semantical criterion, and has defended the resultant classification on the basis of an intricate theory about how conditionals of the two kinds work. This theory has not won much acceptance; but its placing of the line of division has also been suggested on grounds other than Dudman's—and sometimes before him—by Timothy Smiley, Brian Ellis, and Allan Gibbard. I published a defense of it;[1] but I soon learned that I had been led astray by my ignorance of relevant data. I tried to make good in a repentant second paper arguing that the principal line through conditionals (i.e., items meant) coincides exactly with the line between indicative and subjunctive sentences.[2] The conclusion was right, but I was still rushing to judgment: I had noticed some relevant new facts, but not all of them. I now offer a *complete* survey of the relevant data and, on that basis, definitive answers to the two questions about classification.

In what follows, the phrase 'subjunctive conditional' will mean 'conditional that could properly and naturally be expressed in a subjunctive conditional sentence', and analogously for 'indicative conditional'. (Sometimes I shall abbreviate the phrases to 'subjunctive' and 'indicative', used as nouns.) I shall prove that the best line to draw through conditionals is that corresponding to the so-called indicative/subjunctive line through sentences.

As a dummy reference to any subjunctive conditional I shall use the standard form $A > C$. For indicative conditionals I shall use $A \rightarrow C$.

When we accept If (A,C) we do so on the basis of a movement of the mind from A to C—a thought to the effect that A supports C, makes it probable, or the like. Sometimes we get from A to C purely through general principles:

> (1)   If he had been a cannibal, he would not have been a vegetarian.

> (2)   If that particle is more than a light year from here, it will not reach here nine months from now.

> (3)   If they tormented that child purely for the fun of it, they behaved execrably.

Here one can get from A to C with the sole aid of meanings and logic (1), causal laws (2), and basic moral principles (3). Only someone who was muddled or ignorant or monstrous could think that to get to C he needed matters of particular fact in addition to A. Contrast those three with these:

> (4)   If each time she was pregnant it had been with twins, she would have had six children.

> (5)   If my dinghy had been floated in water and then filled with water, it would have sunk.

> (6)   If he asked her publicly what she had been doing over the weekend, then he behaved execrably.

Here the speaker presumably gets to C from A by means of logic and her having had three pregnancies (4), causal laws and the dinghy's being heavier than water (5), and moral principles and some unstated further fact about the situation (6).

This does not distinguish two kinds of conditional—only two kinds of grounds for accepting one. As Robert Stalnaker has pointed out to me, I might accept on the strength of some matter of particular fact a conditional that you accept as absolute—for example, that if the state put Caryl Chessman to death it acted unjustly. This difference between us does not require the conditional to be ambiguous.

This paper will be fueled by considerations about the grounds for accepting conditionals. I shall focus on the grounds that bring in particular facts, setting aside cases where someone accepts a conditional absolutely, that is, independently of any particular facts. My territory will thus be populated with the likes of (4) through (6), not of (1) through (3). I could stretch my remarks to cover absolute acceptances as well, but it makes things simpler if I set them aside. They are in any case uninteresting. Someone who accepts If (A,C) absolutely can convey his thought more fully and clearly without conditionals: being a cannibal entails not being a vegetarian; it is causally impossible for a particle to travel faster than light; tormenting a child purely for fun is always dreadfully wrong. Absent a dependence on unstated matters of particular fact, the special need for, strengths of, and problems concerning conditionals are also absent.

2 *Three Bases for Accepting Indicative Conditionals*

Many of us accept Frank Ramsey's views about the acceptance of indicative conditionals. The so-called Ramsey Test says that to evaluate $A \to C$ for acceptability you must do this:

> Pretend to be sure that A is true, adjust the rest of your belief system to accommodate that change, and see what your resulting belief level is with respect to C.

If $A \to C$ passes this test, that means that C is probable relative to a trio of propositions:

> A, the antecedent of the conditional;
> E (for 'evidence'), conjoining all that you believe about particular matters of fact, minimally adjusted to make it consistent with A;
> P (for 'principles'), containing whatever basic doctrine you need to infer C from A & E.

The principles always include some logic, taking this to include mathematics, abstract probability theory, and other a priori aids to the movement of the mind. Sometimes they contain nothing more. 'If that child had lived, the family would have had as many boys as girls' could be accepted on the strength of an E consisting in 'That child was a boy, and the remainder of the family consisted of one boy and two girls'. More often P combines logic with causal doctrine ('If you put one more block on that girder, it will bend') or with moral principles ('If he paid for the child's upkeep, that was noble of him') or with both ('If you give him that injection, you will be behaving wrongly').

Let us ask two questions about the movement of one's mind when one accepts an indicative conditional, being led to C by A & E. (1) Does it involve a sufficient basis for a thought about something's explaining something? (2) If so, what is being explained? The idea of asking these questions came to me from Mark Lance; most of what I shall say by way of answer is mine.

The answer to (1) is yes—usually and perhaps always, though I shall present two possible no's. Any novelties that I have to offer come from my answer to (2), namely, that the person's thought may support any one of three patterns of explanation:

> A and E explain C.
>
> E and C explain A.
>
> A and C and part of E explain something else in E.

E is always essential to the story I shall tell: in two cases as helping to explain, and in the third not only doing that but also supplying what is to be explained. In the first two cases, if E were not helping to explain, it would have no role and so the person would be accepting the conditional absolutely rather than in dependence on particular facts; and I am setting those cases aside.

Some examples will put flesh on these abstract bones. In each of the three categories, the speaker thinks of the truth of A and E as bringing with it the truth of C; but the reasons for this differ.

3 Explaining-C

Here the thought is of A and E leading to and explaining C. Example: 'If Checkit Inc. conducted the audit, the audit report is accurate', said by someone whose E includes propositions about Checkit's competence, honesty, and so on. Another: 'If Stauffenberg used his bomb, Hitler is dead'. In these examples, the speaker envisages a state of affairs in which A helps to explain C: the report is accurate because Checkit wrote it; Hitler is dead because Stauffenberg used his bomb.

Cases will vary in how natural it is to pick on A as "the explanation" for C, rather than picking on some elements in E. But that is only pragmatics, and we need not attend to it here.

In one species of this category, A has no explanatory role: the speaker regards C as true, and his thought in accepting $A \rightarrow C$ is just that elements in his E lead to and explain C, whether or not A is conjoined with them. The word 'even' can naturally be used here: 'Even if I study from now until the time of the exam, I'll fail'; 'Even if the inspector didn't check it out, the work is up to code'. The two special features of these cases—A does not help to explain C, and the speaker accepts C unconditionally—are of course linked.

I assume that the speaker bases 'I'll fail' upon (E) his not having worked all semester long, and bases 'The work is up to code' upon (E) the workers' being competent and conscientious. But what if the person accepts C as a *basic* truth, not supported by any E and thus not explained by any? He might say 'Even if A, C', and his grounds for this will not include the makings of any thought about evidence or explanation. If there are such basic acceptances (perhaps: 'Even if an omnipotent Deceiver is at work, I exist'), then there can be "even if" conditionals that do not fit any of my three patterns. For them, the answer to my question (1) at the end of section 2 is no, that being the first 'no' of the two that I mentioned.

4 Explaining-A

The thought here is of C and E explaining A's supposed truth better than anything else would. 'If my umbrella is not in the coat closet, then I took it to campus this morning'. Here, A has no tendency to explain C; but C helps to explain A. That supports $A \rightarrow C$ only if C is needed for the best available explanation for A, and it gets that status with the help of E. That is how the truth of A and of E bring with them the truth of C.

An element in E may have either of two roles in this. (1) It may help to explain A, as does my belief that I did not bring my umbrella home from campus today. (2) It may instead serve to block other potential rivals for the title of best explanation, as does my belief that the umbrella was in the coat closet when I awoke this morning. That does not explain its not being there now, but it helps to make C ('I took it to campus this morning') the best explanation for its not being there now. Another example: I say 'If Joe died, he had an accident', partly because my E includes the belief that Joe has been in excellent health. His good health does not help to explain his supposed death, but it eliminates some rival explanations. (The explaining-C category has no such bifurcation of roles for elements in E, because the concept of "best explanation" has no place in it.)

The two roles that elements in E may play in explaining-A are not both open to C. For an explaining-A conditional to be acceptable, C must be involved in the explaining of A, not merely in eliminating a rival. This follows from C's being the consequent of the conditional: it is what one is pushed to, not what helps in the pushing.

When a conditional is accepted on an explaining-A basis, it is always idiomatic to use 'must' in the consequent: 'If the umbrella is not in the coat closet, I must have taken it to campus this morning'; 'If Joe is dead, he must have had an accident'. This 'must' expresses a sense of being forced to settle for a C-involving explanation because one knows or believes things that knock out a possibly better rival; and this, I have contended, is always the case when C is regarded as the best explanation for A.

I have implied that in an explaining-A basis, C is always thought of as at least part of the explanation; but that is not so. Sometimes C enters the picture not as explanatory of A but in a *dependent* role, as following from and being explained by whatever explains A. James Thomson invented this beauty:

> If there is a copy of *Moby-Dick* on that table, then there was at least one very large Great Dane with a solid gold collar in Paddington Station yesterday.

This could be accepted on the grounds that the best explanation for (A) the book's being on the table is that Mary came here from London yesterday and left it there, and her doing that would almost certainly involve (C) her coming via Paddington and (as always) bringing her Great Dane, which . . . etc.[3] This speaker thinks that the conjunction of A with something he knows is best explained by something (Mary came up from London yesterday) which leads to (and explains) C. This has an explaining-C element in it, but it gets to C through an explaining-A move, and I choose to classify it as a special case of Explaining-A, namely, one where C occurs dependently, resulting from the explanation rather than being part of it.

Notice that like other explaining-A bases, this also involves some thought of being driven to something (Mary's trip from London) as the best explanation, so that again the 'must' is appropriate: 'If there is a copy [etc.], then there must have been at least one [etc.]'.

5 Explaining-E

The ruling thought in the third category concerns an explanation for some element in E (call it E_1)—specifically, the best explanation for E_1 given the remainder of E (call that E_2) and also given the hypothesis A. The thought is simply that this explanation includes C. In this kind of conditional as in the others, then, a thought about *explaining* is at work; but here, uniquely, the explained item is not expressed in the conditional. 'If the umbrella is not in the coat closet, my memory is failing'. In accepting this I have no thought of explaining either A or C. Rather, I think this: I have a seeming memory of putting my umbrella in the closet and no memory of removing it (E_1). This could be because I did put it there and leave it there; but the hypothesis that it is not there (A) eliminates that, and the best remaining explanation is that my memory is failing (C).

This pattern deserves another example. I feel the cold ashes of what has been an enormous fire, and I say, pointing to some drab plants growing nearby, 'If those are desert verbena, then this fire is many days old'. Initially the best explanation for the coldness of the ashes is that there has been heavy rain; but when rain falls on desert verbena it flowers immediately, which those plants have not done. If they are desert verbena, therefore, there has not been rain recently; that rules out that explanation, leaving standing the cold-because-old one. In accepting this reasonable conditional I have no thought of explaining either A or C.

Here, as always, the knocking out of a rival makes it idiomatic to use 'must' in the consequent: 'If the umbrella is not in the coat closet, my memory must be failing'; 'If those plants are desert verbena, this fire must be many days old'.

In every explaining-E basis for accepting a conditional, A serves to eliminate rival explanations for E_1. That is to be expected: when A and C both belong to the unconditionally best explanation for E_1, the speaker has reason to assert A & C rather than the weaker $A \rightarrow C$.

In explaining-E bases, as in explaining-A ones, C may enter the story dependently, not as helping to explain E_1 but as an explained consequence of whatever explains E_1. 'If those plants are desert verbena, we'll have no trouble crossing the stream'—the plants have no flowers, as desert verbena always do soon after rain; so if they are desert verbena there has not been recent rain, which implies that the stream will be low and we'll have no trouble crossing it. As with explaining-A, 'must' can always come into play here: 'If those plants are desert verbena, then the stream must be easy to cross'.

I shall mostly ignore the species of explaining-A and explaining-E where C has a dependent role, being a consequence rather than a part of what does the explaining. This is just for simplicity's sake and will not blunt any of the points I shall make.

Some familiar examples fit snugly into the explaining-E frame. Having become convinced that the gate was unlocked either by the porter or by the secretary, I accept 'If it wasn't unlocked by the porter, it was unlocked by the secretary'. In this case, the gate's being unlocked by the secretary (C) is my best explanation for the evidence (E) I have for my disjunctive belief, on the supposition that it was not unlocked by the porter (*A*). And I can have that thought even if I have forgotten what the evidence was. What if the whole story is just that someone told you 'Either the porter or the secretary unlocked the gate' and you just believed him? If I believed him because I trusted him to have good evidence for what he said, that trust will lead me to think of *C* as the best explanation, given not-*A*, for that evidence of his, whatever it was. What if you believed him absolutely, for no reason, with no lurking thought of his being believable because he would have evidence for the disjunction's truth? In that case you would accept 'If *A*, *C*' in a manner that does not involve explanation in any way at all. I agree. If there are such cases, they fall outside my three-part schema, and thus support a negative answer—the second such—to my question (1) in section 2.

6 Are Indicative Conditionals Ambiguous?

So we have three species of case in which $A \rightarrow C$ is acceptable to someone. His basis may be of any one of the types, Explaining-*C*, Explaining-*A*, or Explaining-*E*. A single conditional sentence might be accepted on any of the three bases. That points to three situations, not three conditionals: if there were three conditionals, the sentence in question must be ambiguous, and I will now argue that it is not.

Consider the old familiar sentence:

(S) If Booth didn't shoot Lincoln, someone else did.

(1) Someone might accept (S) on the grounds that, while not knowing whether Booth succeeded, he believes that reliable plans were made for someone else to take over if Booth failed. His basis for accepting (S) is of the explaining-*C* type. (2) Someone else might accept (S) for reasons of the explaining-*A* type. His thought is that nothing could have deterred Booth from his assassination attempt except his finding that Lincoln had already been shot by someone else. So this person gets from *A* to *C* on the grounds that *C* would best explain the truth of *A*. (3) You and I accept (S) because of all the evidence we have (E_1) that Lincoln was shot by someone. Our basis for the conditional is then of the explaining-*E* type: *C* is our best explanation for E_1, given the hypothesis, *A*, which eliminates the chief rival.

Thus we have the sentence (S) with three possible bases for its acceptance. It is implausible to suppose that because it can have any of those bases the sentence is ambiguous.[4] All three conform to Adams's theory of indicatives, which is the best we have: an indicative conditional serves purely to express the speaker's high conditional probability for C given A.[5] That does not require the speaker to say or even hint at what this conditional probability is based on. Its basis could belong to any of the three types I have delineated.

A conditional's content may point to some kind of basis. When A pertains to a later time than C does, that pretty well settles it that the speaker does not have an explaining-C basis for accepting $A \rightarrow C$; and when A predates C the basis can hardly be of the explaining-A type. Far from showing the conditional to be ambiguous, however, this reinforces the idea that it has only one meaning and that further news about what the speaker has in mind can be gathered from further facts about it. Consider an analogous case. George is Helen's uncle if he is a brother of either her mother or her father; some contexts could make clear which ('George is Helen's uncle; having never had any sisters, he feels especially close to her'); but in those contexts 'George is Helen's uncle' does not have a narrowed meaning.

Suppose that you have seen good evidence that someone has shot Lincoln, which leads you to accept

> If Booth didn't shoot Lincoln, someone else did,

on an explaining-E basis. I, on the other hand, am one of the conspirators; I don't yet know exactly what happened, but I firmly believe that plans were in place for someone else to take over in the event that Booth failed. So I too am in a position to assert:

> If Booth didn't shoot Lincoln, someone else did,

but this time on an explaining-C basis. Now, if either of us asserts the conditional and asks 'Don't you agree?' it would be excessively odd for the other to say 'It depends on what you mean'. It seems more natural to take the sentence as the vehicle for an agreement between us and to think that we differ only in our reasons for accepting it.

Compare that case with one in which two people agree that *Lincoln has been shot*—one because he believes that people planned to shoot Lincoln and trusts them to have succeeded, the other because he found the bullet in the body. Nobody would say that these speakers mean different things by 'Lincoln has been shot'.

Here is another argument against ambiguity. The sentence 'If Booth didn't shoot Lincoln, someone else did' clearly has a sense in which it implies nothing about the speaker's basis for it; this is the sense of it—common to all three types of basis—that has been the subject of Adams's classic analysis of the sentence-*form* 'If A, C' in the indicative. The claim of ambiguity says that some instances of that form have a stronger meaning, in which their asserted content entails that the sentence is accepted on an explaining-C basis. Now, what a sentence-token means is linked to what a competent speaker can reasonably hope to communicate by asserting it, which raises the question: What could make it reasonable for a speaker to expect to communicate that stronger meaning?

He must be relying on some feature of the context: perhaps we have been discussing reliable causal structures; or your conditional needs an explaining-C basis if it is to respond to a question I have just asked; or nobody in our society would normally accept this conditional on any basis but an explaining-C one; or the like. The speaker who knows such contextual facts can rely on them to get across his message, for example, that he accepts his conditional on an explaining-C basis. But because this help is contextual, it removes any need to load extra meaning into the sentence itself. And because we *can* handle the data without postulating ambiguity, we *ought* to do so. I say this on the strength of the semantic occamism—the thesis that meanings ought not to be multiplied beyond necessity—which H. P. Grice defended by argument and made irresistible by his best uses of it.[6] Crucially: if you put too much into the meaning of a word in some of its uses, you will have to plead ambiguity—multiplying senses—to cope with other uses where some of that meaning is absent.

Perhaps I do not need to press this no-ambiguity claim. No one has ever suggested in the literature that indicative conditionals are ambiguous in the way in question here. Although I have not seen the three kinds of basis pinpointed before, many writers must have been half-aware of them; yet nobody has even hinted at a corresponding triple ambiguity in indicatives. So my denial of ambiguity is probably safe, at least until I build on it in section 13 below.

If someone wants to assert $A \rightarrow C$ while making clear which kind of basis she has for it, there are ways to do so—two of them fairly simple. Explaining-C: 'If Booth did not shoot Lincoln, that will have led to someone else's shooting him'. Explaining-A: 'If Booth did not shoot Lincoln, that will be because someone else had shot him'. Explaining-E: 'If Booth did not shoot Lincoln, then the best explanation for the evidence I have is that someone else shot him'. These and other verbal resources are available; I deny only that one can properly assert 'If Booth didn't shoot Lincoln, someone else did' and mean by that what one of those more explicit conditionals means.

7   Starting to Sort Indicatives from Subjunctives

Let us turn now to the view that the important line dividing conditionals does not correspond to that between indicative and subjunctive conditional sentences. Friends of that view wanted to relocate indicatives with a present-tense antecedent and a future-tense consequent, such as:

Does-will: If the ruble falls below twenty to the dollar, the government will intervene in the market.

This had been classified as indicative—it has no 'would'—and yet it seemed right to think that any adequate basis for asserting the above Does-will at a given time will also support:

Had-would: If the ruble had fallen below twenty to the dollar, the government would have intervened in the market

at a later time, if in the interim the antecedent proves false. This supposed fact, together with some others, encouraged us to think that Does-will conditionals differ from corresponding Had-would conditionals only in tense (and perhaps in the speaker's attitude to the truth-value of the antecedent), from which we inferred that Does-will belongs along with Had-would in the hopper containing all the subjunctives. The other bin was to contain only indicatives that lacked the Does-will distribution of tenses.

A more thorough scrutiny of the data, however, points to a different story. Here are its two principal theses:

1. Does-will conditionals can have bases of any of the three types described above; so can indicative conditionals that are not of the Does-will form.
2. The basis for an indicative conditional also supports the corresponding subjunctive if it is of the explaining-A or explaining-C type, but not if it is of the explaining-E type.

These imply that support for a conditional of the Does-will form does not always support the corresponding subjunctive, and that some supports for indicatives that are not of the Does-will form do also support the corresponding subjunctives. So the announced reason for reclassifying the Does-will form does not apply to all Does-will conditionals and does apply to many that lack that form. I now defend and illustrate all this.

8 Support for Subjunctives, Not Does-will

Explaining-C   A member of the Booth conspiracy knows that the assassination attempt (if there was one) is over. Confident that Booth's only chance of failure was his not getting into the theater, he thinks to himself 'If Booth got into the theater, Lincoln is dead', accepting this on an explaining-C basis. His support for this involves trust in Booth's nerve and his aim, Lincoln's presence there, and so on; and this obviously would also entitle him, if he became sure that Lincoln had survived, to say 'If Booth had got into the theater, Lincoln would be dead'. Thus, the explaining-C support for a conditional that is not of the Does-will form also supports the corresponding subjunctive.

Explaining-A   Another conspirator knows what Booth planned to attempt, and how; and he is confident that there were no other threats to Lincoln's life (something the previous man did not need for his conditional). He thinks 'If Lincoln is dead, Booth got into the theater', his basis for this being an explaining-A one. If this person became sure that Booth had failed, he could accept 'If Lincoln were [or: had been] dead, Booth would have to have got into the theater,' a backward subjunctive conditional, on a par with 'If Stevenson had been President in February 1953 he would have to have won the election in the previous November'. (The 'have to' is not essential, but backward conditionals always sound better with it. It does not imply an internal necessity, but only the necessity of being driven to *A* as the best explanation. This might be made clearer by writing that 'it would have to have been the case that' Booth succeeded or Stevenson won.) Quite generally, explaining-A bases for indicatives support temporally backward subjunctives.

An explaining-E basis for accepting $A \rightarrow C$ usually or always supports some subjunctive conditionals, but never $A > C$—that is, the corresponding one, with the same *A* and *C*. You and I accept 'If Booth didn't shoot Lincoln, someone else did', because we have evidence that Lincoln was shot by someone. This is an explaining-E basis: supposing (*A*) that Booth didn't shoot Lincoln, the best explanation for (E_1) a lot of things we believe about Lincoln's end is that (*C*) someone else shot him. (Because *A* serves to eliminate a rival, we can naturally say 'If Booth didn't shoot Lincoln, someone else must have done so'.) Our basis for accepting that conditional supports *some* subjunctives—perhaps 'If there had been a conspiracy to fake Lincoln's death, it would have been revealed by now'—but it could never support 'If Booth hadn't shot Lincoln, someone else would have'.

Again: the subjunctive 'If Booth had not shot Lincoln, someone else would have' gets no support from *an explaining-E basis for* 'If Booth didn't shoot Lincoln, someone else did'. The latter sentence in itself can go hand-in-hand with the corresponding subjunctive, if it is accepted on a basis of one of the other types.

9 Does-will, No Support for Subjunctives

Having presented indicatives that *are not* of the Does-will form but *do* support the corresponding subjunctives, I turn to ones that *are* of that form but *do not* support the subjunctives because they have explaining-E bases. For minor reasons, I switch from Booth examples to the following one. Nearing the time of departure for our holiday, I think about the need for someone to check that all the windows have been latched. I hear Gillian ask someone (probably Sara, but possibly Guy) to do this, and I am sure that whomever she asked will comply; so I think 'If Sara doesn't check the windows, Guy will'.

In this example, C occurs dependently; my thought of Guy's doing the job does not occur as explaining anything, but as a consequence of what explains what I heard, given that it didn't involve Sara. I heard Gillian telling someone to check the windows (E); the best explanation for my auditory experience, given that Sara won't check the windows (A) (which I take to imply that Gillian didn't ask her to), is that Gillian asked Guy to do so (which I take to imply that he will (C)). In a Does-will conditional with an explaining-E basis, C will have to occur in a dependent role. For C itself to help to explain E in such a case, there would have to be temporally backward causation.

This basis for this indicative conditional does not support the corresponding subjunctive. If Sara does check the windows, then the closest world where she doesn't is one where she is asked to but forgets, or where she is not asked to; but nothing in the story as I have told it implies that at those worlds Guy is asked to check the windows and does so. So no basis has been provided for 'If Sara had not checked the windows, Guy would have done it'.

A second example: We watch a black earth-to-sky pillar of cloud approaching your villa outside Marrakesh; I ignorantly remark 'I hope it doesn't rain—that would make our picnic uncomfortable', and you—knowing more—reply sardonically: 'If it doesn't rain, the picnic will be impossible'. Your E is what you see to the east, along with some general views implying that the two best explanations for what you see are that a rain-cloud approaches and that a sandstorm approaches; that, conjoined with the hypothesis that it will not rain (A), implies that the best explanation for the cloud part of E is that a sandstorm is coming our way, which implies that we cannot have a picnic (C). Here again, as always in Does-will conditionals with explaining-E bases, C is a consequence of the explanation of E, not a part of it. And here again, the corresponding subjunctive conditional has no support. If it does rain, none of us will think 'If it hadn't rained, the picnic would have been impossible'. If it does rain, then the closest worlds where it doesn't rain contain no dark cloud that has that trajectory; they don't contain one with that trajectory but carrying sand.

Summing up these two sections: A subjunctive conditional must be either:

> a forward one, making a claim about A's power to lead to and explain C; which connects with the explaining-C basis for $A \rightarrow C$;

or

> a backward one, making a claim about C's power to lead to and explain A; which connects with the explaining-A basis for $A \rightarrow C$.

There is no room for the explaining-E basis here, because in that basis A and C collaborate in explaining something else; there is no explanatory relation *between* them, which there must be in subjunctive conditionals. (Except for "even if" ones, where the speaker unconditionally accepts C as true at the relevant worlds, and is making the point that if A were true that would not block C from being true. I sketched the indicative analogue of this early in section 3 above.)

When philosophers adduce examples to show how greatly indicatives differ from subjunctives, they always illustrate the former with ones that we naturally think of as accepted on an explaining-E basis. Now it is clear why. While not explicitly aware of the three types of basis, they are subliminally guided to examples where the most likely type of basis for acceptance is the one that does not support the corresponding subjunctive.

10 Subjunctive Conditionals Are Zero-tolerant

Given that someone's belief system supports both $A \rightarrow C$ and $A > C$, how does asserting one differ from asserting the other? This question arises when $A \rightarrow C$ has an explaining-C or explaining-A basis, but I shall confine our discussion to the former. The explaining-C basis goes with temporally forward subjunctives, while explaining-A goes with backward ones, which I find convenient to ignore from now on.

Well, then, how does accepting 'If Booth got into the theater, Lincoln is dead' on an explaining-C basis differ from accepting 'If Booth had got into the theater, Lincoln would be dead'? As well as Had-would there are also Were-would subjunctives: 'If Booth were to have got into the theater, Lincoln would be dead'. This is virtually synonymous with the other, and I shall lump the two together. If they differ in some way that I have overlooked, I hope it will not affect any of my points.

Some philosophers have denied that a subjunctive conditional signals the speaker's disbelief in A;[7] but it is essentially true. Someone who is pretty sure that A is true needs a special reason for saying 'If A were to be true, so would C be', for example, he is adjusting his speech to make it acceptable to his hearer, as in:

North: "Why do you think he is hostile to you? I'm sure he is not."

South: "Well, you'll agree that if he were hostile to me, he would behave toward me with unpleasantly formal courtesy. That's his style—right?"

North: "Agreed."

South: "Well, that's just how he does behave; and that's my evidence for his hostility."

In this exchange, South asserts a subjunctive whose antecedent he believes; but that is merely to conform his speech to North's beliefs. If he were explaining his reasons to someone who had no opinion on the matter, it would be more natural for him to say 'If he is hostile to me, he will behave . . .', or 'Because he is hostile to me . . .', etc.

So it is basically right to connect subjunctive conditionals with the speaker's disbelief in the antecedent. This distinguishes them from indicatives, though not sharply; for ordinarily one has no reason to say or think $A \rightarrow C$ unless one has significant doubts about A's truth. Perhaps $A \rightarrow C$ does not signal as strong a doubt, or does not signal doubt as strongly, as $A > C$ does, but I shall not spend time on this. Another property of subjunctive conditionals, relating to A's falsity in a different way, marks them off from indicatives more sharply and powerfully than the foregoing.

Every subjunctive conditional is *zero-tolerant*, meaning that someone could have a serious use for it in a context where everyone presupposes that A is false, that is, there is no question of considering its possible truth. This will often be because all concerned accord A a probability of zero; hence the label "zero-tolerant." Initially I thought of this purely in terms of the speaker's probability for A, but Stalnaker has cured me of that: (1) The attitude to A of the hearers is also relevant; and (2) What counts is A's being excluded as a candidate for truth, not merely its being thought to be certainly false. (Point 2 will be important in explaining the zero-*in*tolerance of indicative conditionals.)

Example: You know that I skimmed the broth while it was still hot, and I know that you know; neither of us would call this in question; but it remains sensible for you to say to me 'If you had cooled the broth before skimming it, you would have got all the fat'. Try this out also on the other subjunctives that I have used as examples.

Future-tense subjunctive conditionals are also zero-tolerant. Given what you and I know about the rain that has fallen so far and the geology of the catchment area, we assume that the river will rise by at least two feet in the next two days; we do not consider whether we might be wrong about this. In this context I can properly remark 'If the river were to stay at its present level for the next two days, the salmon would be trapped in the rapids'. If you comment: 'But the river won't— it can't—stay at its present level for the next two days', I can reasonably reply: 'I know that. I spoke only of what would happen if it *were* to stay level . . . ', etc.

Frank Jackson has pointed out to me a fact about subjunctives that follows—presumably I need not explain how—from their zero-tolerance. When I assert the conditional about the river and the salmon, in a context where everyone presupposes its antecedent to be false, I can also sincerely say: 'If the river were to stay at its present level for the next two days, things would work out differently from how they actually will'. And someone who accepts 'If Booth hadn't shot Lincoln, Andrew Johnson would never have become president' should also be willing to say: 'If Booth hadn't shot Lincoln, events would have unrolled differently from how they actually did'. To this Dorothy Edgington has added that it makes sense—logically if not historically —to say 'If Booth hadn't shot Lincoln, American history would have continued just as it actually did', whereas the indicative cousin of this is nonsense.

Because a subjunctive conditional is zero-tolerant, one can properly accept it while knowing that one would not be willing to use it in modus ponens. In 1998 I went to Turkey; I am pretty sure that *if I had not visited Turkey in 1998 I would have visited Sicily*. However, if I consider the implications of my discovering to my amazement that I did not visit Turkey in that year, they do not lead to the conclusion that I went to Sicily. On the contrary, if I add 'I did not visit Turkey in 1998' to my belief system with its multitude of memories and other evidences of my having done so, the resulting system generates an unwillingness to have any opinion about what I did in 1998. In contrast with this, it would be improper to assert—and impossible to accept—an indicative conditional while knowing that one's present belief system would not make one willing to apply modus ponens upon coming to believe its antecedent.

You can accept an indicative conditional even though *in fact* if you came to believe its antecedent you would not infer its consequent— perhaps because coming to believe the antecedent would shock you into handling all sorts of evidence differently. You might even believe that this would be the effect of coming to accept *A*. The Marquis reflects that *if his wife has a lover, that is a secret known only to three people*. This passes the Ramsey test: putting together everything else he believes about the circles in which he moves—who can be relied upon to blab, who can be trusted not to—the supposition of his wife's infidelity (*A*) generates the conclusion that there has been this three-person secret (*C*). Yet if he actually comes to believe his wife to be unfaithful, this will drive him into unhinged conspiracy fantasies involving half of France; *and he knows this*. But his present attitude must be that this, if it happens, will be deplorable and pathological. Within the framework of his actual present intellectual character and system of beliefs (*E*), the hypothesis that his wife is unfaithful (*A*) leads to the conclusion that only three people know that she is (*C*). Within that framework, then, modus ponens holds. The corresponding thing is not necessarily true for a subjunctive conditional.

11 Indicative Conditionals Are Zero-intolerant

Indicative conditionals are zero-intolerant. They are devices for intellectually managing states of partial information, and for preparing for the advent of beliefs that one does not—or that one's hearers do not—currently have. In a context where nobody regards *A* as a candidate for truth—that is, where everyone presupposes its falsity—no work can be done by $A \rightarrow C$ for any *C*.

Two scholars differ about a certain text: One holds that if Eusebius didn't write it, a medieval forger did; the other thinks that if Eusebius didn't write it, Lactantius did. This is a sober topic of contention; but when they become sure that Eusebius *did* write the text—or when for any reason they come to regard his not having written it as excluded, off the table, no longer in consideration—neither scholar has any use for either conditional. They could still disagree about which of their bases had been sounder (whether the text resembles a medieval forgery more closely than it does Lactantius's work), but for them the competing conditionals themselves have died.

In this matter, Stalnaker's revision of my initial idea is important. What disqualifies $A \rightarrow C$ is not the speaker's complete confidence that not-*A*, but rather a context in which everyone presupposes *A*'s falsity. Stalnaker has written to me (pers. comm.):

> If the speaker is in a situation where it is in dispute whether *A* is true, then even if he is certain that *A* is false, he cannot presuppose that it is false. I think one can often use indicatives with *A* as antecedent in such a situation. . . . The potential belief revision that one is preparing for, in using indicatives, might be the

addressee's rather than one's own. Your interlocutor expresses some skepticism about your claim to have visited Turkey last year. You reply, with some irritation, 'If I didn't visit Turkey, then I am obviously a shameless liar, so if you doubt me, why should you believe anything I say?' You are not saying that you are yourself disposed to conclude that you are a liar were you to discover (to your amazement) that you didn't make this visit. The subjunctive would, of course, be all wrong in this circumstance.

I am convinced, so I replace speaker's belief with Stalnaker's contextual presupposition.

Extending the notion of zero-intolerance to quantified conditionals, I submit that 'If any F ϕs, it πs' is useless in a context where there is no question of allowing that any F ϕs. I would almost never have any use for this: 'If any member of the Roman Curia admires the Rolling Stones, he will never become Pope'. I believe the corresponding subjunctive; but the indicative would have a place in my life only in a context where someone was taking seriously the possibility that at least one member of the Curia admires the Rolling Stones.

Logic can take us outside the bounds of conversational propriety. A conditional whose A is presupposed false in a given context may nevertheless be acceptable—or anyway unexcludable—there because it follows from something that is more directly acceptable. In a context where it is absolutely all right for me to say 'If any Catholic bishop admires the Rolling Stones he will never be Pope' because my hearers and I have open minds about whether there are any such bishops, there is a warrant of a kind for 'If any member of the Curia admires the Rolling Stones he will never be Pope', even if we all presuppose that there are no such members of the Curia.

This is what I call the *inferential exception* to zero-intolerance. The thesis that indicative conditionals are zero-intolerant should be confined to ones that stand on their own feet, so to speak, and not applied to ones that someone accepts only because they are entailed by a general conditional that he accepts.[8]

12 *What Subjunctive Conditionals Are For*

Having written about what indicatives are for, I want to do the same for subjunctives. The uses we have for them explain not only their zero-tolerance, but also their having something I have not yet mentioned, namely, *impossibility-intolerance*: in general, $A > C$ is useless, pointless, if A is intrinsically causally impossible.

This is doubly unlike the zero-intolerance of indicatives. The two differ as impossibility from falsehood, and as fact from presupposition. The impossibility-intolerance of subjunctives concerns what *is the case* at *all* the causally possible worlds, while the zero-intolerance of indicatives concerns what *some people presuppose* about *one* world, the actual one.

Someone constructing a logic of subjunctive conditionals might find it convenient to rule that when A is impossible $A > C$ is vacuously true; but the fact remains that the purposes for which we have subjunctives are not met by any whose antecedent is causally impossible. What about counterlegals? I have argued elsewhere that they can survive only with special propping-up; I choose not to go through that again here.[9] Counterlegals—subjunctives whose antecedents are intrinsically causally impossible—do not figure in the ordinary daily life of subjunctives. We can safely set them aside.

The three roles of subjunctive conditionals in our lives help to explain their being impossibility-intolerant and zero-tolerant. (1) We use them where A concerns someone's behavior, for broadly moral purposes. They may be guides to ourselves in future practical problems, and bases for applauding or reproaching the person in question because of his causal relevance to some upshot. For example, 'I know that he didn't do anything; but if he had done something—the right thing— the disaster wouldn't have occurred. So don't tell me that because he was inactive he had nothing to do with the disaster'. (2) Whatever A is about, a subjunctive can sketchily report facts about how the world was, is, or will be causally hooked up. 'Although we don't yet understand the mechanisms, we are convinced that if the Pacific Ocean had been cooler last year there would have been fewer hurricanes'. (3) Subjunctives can be used to express, and perhaps also to shape and sharpen, our elations and regrets. 'If just five of my colleagues had forgotten to vote, I would have lost the election'. 'If that deer hadn't bounded in front of the car right at the start of an oil-slick on the road, my niece would be alive today'. Some people frown on regret; perhaps some frown on elation too; but both belong to the human estate, and we voice them in subjunctives.

These roles that such conditionals play for us go naturally with zero-tolerance and with impossibility-intolerance. That, I submit, is obvious.

I have been discussing antecedents that are *intrinsically* causally impossible, not ones that are causally ruled out *in the circumstances*. 'If the deer hadn't . . .' I think; but it may have been causally inevitable that the deer would, and that does not deter me from accepting the conditional. David Lewis has correctly described our handling of such matters: we take as the relevant A-worlds ones that are just like the actual world until shortly before the A-time and then part company from actuality in a humanly inconspicuous manner—a different outcome of an indeterministic process, or else what Lewis calls a "small miracle." In practice, we do not go into those details with ourselves; we allow ourselves the thought of the deer's not leaping in front of the car, and think vaguely of this as coming about *somehow*; but if pressed we might postulate a small miracle in the deer's brain.[10]

13 The Reclassification Is Wrong

At last we can look at how an indicative conditional accepted on an explaining-C basis relates to the corresponding subjunctive. Let us take two Booth conspirators, one of whom (indicative Ike) has no idea whether Booth succeeded while the other (subjunctive Sam) has been told that he did. Each has faith in the arrangements that were made for a back-up shooter in the event of Booth's failure. Now, Ike accepts (I) 'If Booth didn't shoot Lincoln, someone else did', while Sam accepts (S) 'If Booth hadn't shot Lincoln, someone else would have'. The two conditionals may differ in that (S) signals confidence that not-A more strongly than (I) does; but I have nothing to say about that. What other differences are there?

(S) is zero-tolerant, which (I) is not; but that feature of subjunctive conditionals is far from being the whole truth about them. They have many other properties, which have been studied by Goodman, Stalnaker, Lewis, and others—ones that seem to most of us to invite analysis in terms of possible worlds. The best work on indicatives and subjunctives points to there being these two *root differences* between them:

> indicative conditionals are subjective, not truth-valued, and essentially matters of interrelations within individual people's systems of belief;

whereas

> subjunctive conditionals are objective, truth-valued, and essentially concerned with causal and other principled interrelations within worlds.

I cannot defend all that here. From now on I shall assume that indicatives and subjunctives differ in those two ways. Observe that zero-tolerance has no role in them.

One might think that although Ike's conditional differs from Sam's in being zero-tolerant, the two are not separated by either of the root differences. I agree that Ike and Sam have the very same thought about how the world is causally hooked up, but I deny that their two conditionals mean the same thing. If they do, then what Ike means by (I) is what Sam means—what anybody would mean—by (S) , namely, something of the subjunctive type. But then you also accept (I) on the explaining-E basis of good evidence that someone shot Lincoln. So you and Ike are willing to assert the very same sentence; it is proposed that this is tantamount to a subjunctive; but, because yours is patently not so, the proposal implies that that sentence is ambiguous. There is nothing special about that sentence, however. If it is ambiguous for that reason, then *every indicative conditional sentence is ambiguous*: someone who asserts such a sentence means one thing if he has an explaining-C basis for it and a different thing if his basis is an explaining-E one.

I have shown in section 6 that indicative conditionals are not systematically ambiguous in that way, and that refutes the proposed reclassification. There, I kept the question internal to indicative conditionals, leaving subjunctives out of the discussion. But the supposed ambiguity that was in question is exactly what has to be postulated by someone who puts Ike's and Sam's conditionals into one category and yours into another. So the earlier discussion serves again here.

To give us relief from Does-will, I chose to argue the point out in terms of an indicative that is not of that form. My entire discussion applies just as well to Does-will conditionals, and therefore refutes the popular reclassification of conditionals in which the Does-will ones are lumped in with the subjunctives.

14 A Gap in Our Language

Consider someone who believes that because of the existence of certain reliable causal structures, she has a good explaining-C basis for accepting $A \rightarrow C$. She would like to assert $A \rightarrow C$ while

(i) implying that she has an explaining-C basis for it, and

(ii) saying something that is not zero-tolerant, that is, that can appropriately be said only in a context where someone regards A as an active candidate for truth.

Because of (i), a plain indicative will not serve her purposes; because of (ii), no subjunctive will serve either. No simple conditional wording will enable this speaker to do what she wants.

As I noted at the end of section 6, she can do it by augmenting an indicative conditional: 'If A, then that will lead (or will have led) to C's being the case'. She may also (I repeat) convey the facts about her basis through contextual clues. But our language contains no form of conditional that does, just through its meaning, precisely what she wants done. The only plain conditionals we have which imply that A's truth leads causally to C's *also* are zero-tolerant: the conventional meaning of such a conditional ensures that it can appropriately be asserted in a context where everyone presupposes A to be false. An indicative conditional lacks that feature, but at the price of silence about causal structures. I do not know why no conditional unaided does both jobs.

This gap in our language is not unique. Derek Parfit showed me another, and I'll bet there are many. I had (I now pretend) a good friend with whom I quarreled and from whom I was then estranged for many years. Hearing that he was far away and dying, I recently sent him an affectionate and conciliatory letter. I know that he either died recently or will die soon, and I invest no hopes or wishes in that. But I do earnestly hope that

> either he received my letter before he died, or he does or will receive it before he dies.

That is clear but clumsy; we have no clear and elegant way of saying this simple, normal, natural thing.

15 Speaker's Meaning and Sentence Meaning

The thesis that all indicatives are zero-intolerant has been challenged on the grounds that I may accept and have a use for 'If I touch that stove, I will be burned' in a context where it is presupposed that I will not touch that stove.[11] I once took this as further evidence that this Does-will conditional belongs with the subjunctives: to one already convinced that the main line through conditionals should be shifted, this little argument was irresistible. I now resist it.

First, the easy bit. Someone who asserts *touch* → *burned* when it is presupposed that he will not touch the stove may be inferring it from 'If anyone touches that stove he or she will be burned', which he accepts without being perfectly sure that nobody will touch the stove. In that case, his conditional about himself is an inferential exception to zero-intolerance (see the end of section 11).

That does not exhaust the power of examples like this one, however. Zero-tolerance aside, one is powerfully tempted to hear 'If I touch that stove, I will be burned' as meaning '. . . that will lead to my being burned'; that is to hear it as declaring its explaining-C basis, and thus approaching equivalence to 'If I were to touch that stove, I would be burned'. That temptation should be resisted, for reasons I briefly recapitulate here.

The crucial fact is that *touch* → *burned* could be accepted on an explaining-E basis by someone who doesn't know that the stove is hot and thus has no reason to accept *touch* > *burned*. The only stories of this kind that I can devise are fanciful; that is why it is so natural to construe *touch* → *burned* as having an explaining-burned basis. Still, the job can be done by a tale such as the following. Henry is being subject to a mysterious series of ordeals; he does not know why. He has a strong seeming-memory of being told that he will be subject to a horrible burn (E_1); he is sure that whatever he has been told is true; but he thinks the best explanation of this seeming-memory is that it was hypnotically induced in him, in which case he has no reason to think it is veridical and thus no reason to expect to be burned. He is also sure that if he has been subjected to any hypnotism in the course of this ordeal he has, among other things, been given the famous *noli id tangere* procedure in which the hypnotist causes the subject to be utterly unwilling to touch any household items. His touching the stove would knock out the hypnotism explanation for his seeming-memory, leaving it best explained by the hypothesis that it is veridical, which he thinks implies that he will be burned. Nothing in all this helps to explain—even conditionally—the burning; all that gets explained is the seeming memory (E_1). So it would be absurd for Henry to accept 'If I touch that stove, that will lead to my being burned' or 'If I were to touch that stove I would be burned'. Yet he can reasonably accept 'If I touch that stove, I will be burned'. And if he becomes mercifully sure that he will not touch the stove, that conditional dies in his mind.

The contrived nature of the story does not detract from the lesson it teaches about the meaning of indicative conditional sentences.

Now, if any of those sentences can sometimes conventionally mean the corresponding subjunctive, then they are ambiguous. I claim to have shown that they are not. It remains true that a sensible person might well say 'If I touch that stove, I will be burned' and intend to convey the message that touching the stove would lead to his being burned; and of course he may well succeed. We know about stoves and burning, and explaining-E scenarios for that conditional—all of which are bizarre, it seems—are far from our minds; so of course we assume he has an explaining-C basis, and we may even think that he has told us so. None of this discomfits my thesis that the conditional itself means nothing about the basis for its acceptance.

Compare this with something that Grice explained to us. You ask me when the meeting will be held, and I say 'They scheduled it either for

the second or the third of the month'. Seeing no reason for my withholding information (I seem not to be joking, teasing, or conducting an
intelligence test), you infer that I am not certain of the date. You may
even think that I have told you so; and so I have, in a way, but not
in a way that puts my uncertainty into the meaning of my sentence.
Some philosophers used to think otherwise, but Grice's work on pragmatics, and his use of it to defend semantic occamism, has cured everyone of that error. All the facts that might be explained by attributing
that rich meaning to *some* occurrences of 'either . . . or . . .' can be perfectly well explained by combining a thin truth-functional meaning to
'either . . . or . . .' and attending to what generally goes on in civilized
discourse.

Final challenge: What if someone asserts *touch* → *burned* in the belief
that he is not merely conveying but asserting *touch* > *burned* or at least
is declaring that his conditional has an explaining-C basis? This person,
I say, is in error about what he is doing—in error about the conventional meaning of his utterance. Similarly with someone who says 'I
could care less' to express indifference, or who says 'No head-injury is
too trivial to ignore' meaning that every head-injury, however minor,
should be taken seriously. Mistakes like these can be widespread yet
still be mistakes, and we know how to demonstrate this.

16 The Stand-off Property

Allan Gibbard has convinced many of us that a conflicting pair of
indicative conditionals—relating as $A \rightarrow C$ to $A \rightarrow$ not-C—can be
equally good, in the sense that neither of the people who accept them
has made any error.[12] I shall illustrate this first with a variant on an
example of his:

> In a hand of poker everyone but Pete and one other player have
> folded. Two onlookers leave the room at that point, and a few
> moments later each sees one player leave the gaming room.
> William sees Pete without the scowl and the trembling cheek
> that he always has after calling and losing, and concludes that *if
> Pete called he won*; Lucinda sees Pete's opponent caressing more
> money than he owned when she left the room, and concludes
> that *if Pete called he lost*.

Neither person makes any mistake. Given that *Pete called* (A), a subset
E_w of William's evidential beliefs leads him to *Pete won* (C), for which
he has a sound explaining-E basis. Given that *Pete called* (A), a subset
E_l of Lucinda's evidential beliefs leads her to *Pete lost* (C), for which she
also has a sound explaining-E basis. They accept different conditionals

because they are explaining different things on the hypothesis that Pete called.

This stand-off between the two conditionals contributes to the case for saying, as Gibbard and Adams do, that conditionals like these are subjective and thus—since they demonstrably do not express truth-valued propositions *about* the speaker's beliefs—lack truth-values.[13]

There can be such a stand-off because the situation can be symmetrical in a certain way. It need not be the case that as William and Lucinda learn more, facts will eventually transpire that will condemn one of their conditionals as improbable or false, leaving the other as the winner. If, as the facts pour in, they do not favor either conditional, they will instead establish A's falsity. (If A is true, then as between $A \rightarrow C$ and $A \rightarrow$ not-C there is just one clear loser.) The discovery of A's falsity even-handedly makes each conditional useless to its author in that context, because each is zero-intolerant. Their fitness for a stand-off does not, therefore, mean that they could stand up against the world indefinitely, but only that they may relate to it symmetrically: it can happen that as the facts come in the members of the opposing pair survive equally well until at last they both collapse into inutility.

Although each conditional becomes useless to its author when it comes to be presupposed that A is false, the conditionals themselves are beyond reproach. They are equally good, not equally bad. As Gibbard has noted, someone who trusts both speakers may infer that Pete folded; and that is a sound procedure—not a mere fluke in which two falsehoods happen to imply a truth.

That is an established result. There remains a question, however, about whether the stand-off property of indicative conditionals depends upon what type of basis they have. In the example I have given, each conditional is accepted on an explaining-E basis. Of course if Pete calls and wins, his calling does explain his winning, and analogously if he calls and loses. But that is an irrelevant accident of the example. What drives each conditional is the thought not of A's explaining C but rather of A & C's explaining E. Lucinda cannot claim to know things which imply that Pete's calling would lead to his losing, but only things that are best explained, if Pete called, by supposing that he lost. Analogously for William.

In Gibbard's original version of the story one conditional has an explaining-C basis: Lucinda has seen both hands and believes that Pete's was the losing one; so her thought is that A, when conjoined with something she believes, leads to and explains C. The other conditional has an explaining-A basis in which C occurs in a dependent role of the sort I described in section 4 above. William has seen Pete getting a good look at his opponent's hand; he believes Pete to be relentlessly dedicated to not losing; so after leaving the room he announces 'If Pete called, he won'. His thought is that the conjunction of *A* with something he knows is best explained by something (Pete has a winning hand) that leads to and explains *C*. This has an explaining-*C* element in it, but it gets to *C* through an explaining-*A* move.[14]

Some commentators on Gibbard's story prefer Lucinda's conditional to the other, but that must be because they are judging the two as though they were the corresponding subjunctives. In that scenario,

> If Pete had called he would have lost

and, before the time in question,

> If Pete were to call, he would lose

are simply true, for Pete had the losing hand. We evaluate this conditional by considering Pete-calls worlds that diverge inconspicuously from the actual world shortly before the time in question; and those are worlds where events in Pete's brain run a little differently from how they do in actuality, not ones where the cards are differently distributed. So the would-lose subjunctive is true and the would-win one false; but Lucinda's and William's indicative conditionals are equally good.

The same holds for a conflicting pair of conditionals each with an explaining-*C* basis, though poker games do not illustrate this well. Here is a fresh example:

> Top Gate holds back water in a lake behind a dam; a channel running down from it splits into two distributaries, one (blockable by East Gate) running eastward and the other (blockable by West Gate) running westward. The gates are connected as follows: if east lever is down, opening Top Gate will open East Gate so that the water will run eastward; and if west lever is down, opening Top Gate will open West Gate so that the water will run westward. On the rare occasions when both levers are down, Top Gate cannot be opened because the machinery cannot move three gates at once.

Now, just after the lever-pulling specialist has stopped work, Wesla knows that west lever is down, and thinks 'If Top Gate opens, all the water will run westward'; Esther knows that east lever is down, and thinks 'If Top Gate opens, all the water will run eastward'. Each has an explaining-*C* basis for her conditional; each basis is perfect; someone might rightly trust both speakers and soundly infer that Top Gate will not open.

This is a Gibbardian stand-off between conditionals accepted on explaining-C bases. Because the bases are of that type, the standoff requires that A be not merely false but impossible in the circumstances. (Where at least one conditional has an explaining-E basis, mere falsity of A can suffice.)

Now try it with the subjunctive conditionals. Although both levers are down, so that Top Gate cannot open, its opening is not intrinsically causally impossible (like its opening faster than the speed of light); so the impossibility-intolerance of subjunctives does not kick in, and there may be truths of the form 'If Top Gate had opened, . . .'. Their truth requires a recent inconspicuous divergence from actuality. This needs to be understood fairly vaguely, and there will often be no clearly best candidate; but that need not disqualify the conditional we are interested in. Suppose that in evaluating $A > C$ we find that several A-worlds are about equally close to actuality: each diverges inconspicuously from exact likeness to the actual world shortly before the time to which A pertains. If C obtains at all those worlds, the conditional is true. But there might instead be several suitably close worlds with C obtaining at only some of them; and in that case neither $A > C$ nor $A >$ not-C is true. Do not try to rescue one of them by fine-tuning: at one world the divergence from actuality occurs a few minutes later, or is a shade less conspicuous, than at any of the others. Examples trading on this sort of thing have been used against Lewis, and the precisions in his official theory have perhaps invited them. But we do not play the game in that way; our actual practice with subjunctives uses a broader brush.

Return to Top Gate. If west lever has been rusted into the down position for months, while someone pulled east lever down at 11:55 A.M., the conditional 'If Top Gate had been opened at noon, all the water would have run westward' comes out as true. It is easy to tell a story in which 'If Top Gate had been opened at noon, all the water would have run eastward' is true instead; or one where neither is true. But never can both be true or fully acceptable, as can conflicting indicatives in a stand-off.

Notes

1. Jonathan Bennett, "Farewell to the Phlogiston Theory of Conditionals," *Mind* 97 (1988), pp. 509–527.
2. Jonathan Bennett, "Classifying Conditionals: The Traditional Way is Right," *Mind* 104 (1995), pp. 331–354.
3. James F. Thomson, "In Defense of '⊃'," *Journal of Philosophy* 87 (1990), pp. 57–70, at p. 64. The paper was written in about 1963, and published posthumously.

4. I was once disposed to claim ambiguity in this area, and Dorothy Edgington pulled me back from that precipice. Now that I have assembled all the data, I am not tempted to go near that edge.

5. Ernest W. Adams, *The Logic of Conditionals* (Dordrecht, Holland: Reidel, 1975).

6. H. P. Grice, "Logic and Conversation" and "Further Notes on Logic and Conversation," in his *Studies in the Way of Words* (Cambridge, MA: Harvard University Press, 1989), pp. 22–57. Those best uses do not include Grice's treatment of indicative conditionals in ibid., pp. 58–85. Incidentally, if my argument in this paragraph is sound, then it proves that no sentence in a natural language is ambiguous through having two conventional meanings of which one is stronger than the other. I accept that.

7. Following the lead of Alan Ross Anderson, "A Note on Subjunctive and Counterfactual Conditionals," *Analysis* 12 (1951), pp. 35–38.

8. Thomas McKay and John Hawthorne alerted me to the existence of this class of exceptions.

9. Jonathan Bennett, "Counterfactuals and Temporal Direction," *Philosophical Review* 93 (1984), pp. 57–91, at pp. 82–85.

10. David Lewis, "Counterfactual Dependence and Time's Arrow," in his *Philosophical Papers*, vol. 2 (New York: Oxford University Press, 1986), pp. 32–52.

11. Simon Blackburn, "How Can We Tell Whether a Commitment has a Truth Condition?" in Charles Travis (ed.), *Meaning and Interpretation* (Oxford: Blackwell, 1986), pp. 201–232, at p. 222.

12. Allan Gibbard, "Two Recent Theories of Conditionals," in W. Harper et al. (eds.), *Ifs* (Dordrecht: Reidel, 1981), pp. 211–247, at pp. 231f.

13. Dorothy Edgington disputes this in her magisterial "On Conditionals," *Mind* 104 (1995), pp. 235–329, at pp. 295–299. I have not fully grasped her reasons for dissent, and I am not yet converted by what she writes there.

14. There can also be a stand-off between two indicative conditionals of which one has an explaining-C and the other an explaining-E basis.

Chapter 2

A Question about Sets

Richard L. Cartwright

1

In an article[1] published several years ago, I said:

> It is one thing for there to *be* certain objects; it is another for there to be a *set*, or set-like object, of which those objects are the members.

And in an unhelpful note, I added:

> When Aquinas said, cagily, that the angels exist in exceeding great number (*Summa Theologiae* 1, 50, 3), he did not mean that there is a set-like object of large cardinality of which the members are the angels. He meant just what he said.

No doubt he did. But what did *I* mean? (The question will spill over into, What *could* one mean by such a remark? For I won't try very hard to recall now what I meant then.)

Well, consider the negation of what I there said: it is not the case that it is one thing for there to be certain objects and another for there to be a set of which those objects are the members. One proposition that seems to be implied by this negation is a certain version of the naive principle of set existence. Benson Mates puts the principle this way: "Any thing or things whatever constitute the entire membership of a class; in other words, for any things there are, there is exactly one class having just those things as members."[2] So it might be supposed that at any rate one thing I meant to assert was that the naive principle of set existence is false. And in fact I did say in the article:

> But this . . . principle is false. There surely are objects that do not together constitute, as its members, some one object: surely *some* objects are not members of themselves, and there is nothing the members of which are precisely the things that are not members of themselves.

But I think that even if this is part of what I meant, it is not the whole. I think I meant to imply also that, for instance, even if the cookies in the jar constitute a set, it is one thing for there to be the cookies in the jar and another for there to be a set of which the cookies in the jar are the members. Apparently I thought that there are two "things": there being certain objects, and there being a setlike object of which those objects are the members. What exactly *are* these "things" of which I thought there were two?

A natural suggestion is that they are propositions—in the example given, the propositions:

>   (1)   There are some cookies in the jar

and

>   (2)   There is a set the members of which are the cookies in the jar.

Evidently these are distinct propositions; but perhaps my idea was not only that they are two but also that the second does not follow from the first. But how is *this* to be understood?

If someone says that (2) does not follow from (1), and says this in the absence of any special context, it is natural to suppose that the relevant consequence relation is strict implication. The claim then would be that there is a possible world at which (1) is true but (2) is false—in other words, that the proposition

>   (3)   In every possible world in which there are some cookies in the jar, there is a set the members of which are the cookies in the jar

is false. But when it is said that it is one thing for there to be the cookies in the jar and another for there to be a set of which those cookies are the members, a different claim may be being made, one that concerns the cookies themselves that are as a matter of fact in the jar, a claim to the effect that it is not essential to them that they be the members of a set, that is, that they might have existed and yet not have been the members of a set. The claim would then be that the proposition

>   (4)   The cookies in the jar are such that in every possible world in which they exist, there is a set of which they are the members

is false.

Peter van Inwagen thinks that "nearly everyone" would instead take (4) to be true. He speaks of "a position about sets that nearly everyone holds," namely, that "In every possible world in which, for instance, Tom, Dick, and Harry exist, there also exists a set that contains just them."[3] One wonders who the dissenters are. An unsystematic search of some recent literature turned up two passages that seem relevant. One is from an essay by Charles Parsons, and reads this way:

> Given the elements of a set, it is not necessary that the set exists together with them. If it is possible that there should be objects satisfying some condition, then the realization of this possibility is not as such the realization *also* of the possibility that there be a set of such objects.[4]

The other occurs in an essay by George Boolos. In it he says that "it doesn't follow just from the fact that there are some Cheerios in the bowl that, as some who theorize about the semantics of plurals would have it, there is also a set of them all."[5] These passages *suggest* dissent, but I think one can't be certain that dissent is intended. I cannot be sure that Parsons is speaking *in propria persona*, and Boolos's 'follows from' may stand for the converse of a relation narrower than strict implication. However that may be, the question I want to discuss is: Who is right, van Inwagen's overwhelming majority or his minority of dissenters, whoever they may be?

Opposition to (4) is apt to be indirect, focusing on a certain one of its consequences, namely,

(5) If there is a set of which the cookies in the jar are the members, then in every possible world in which the cookies exist there is a set of which they are the members.

The reason is that (4), but not (5), implies

(6) There is a set of which the cookies in the jar are the members.

In fact, (4) is equivalent to the conjunction of (5) with (6), and dissent from (4) can be based on rejection of either conjunct. Dissenters like Boolos and Parsons, if indeed they are properly so called, do not deny that there is a set of which the cookies in the jar are the members. Their view is, or seems to be, that although there is as a matter of fact a set of which the cookies in the jar are the members, this only happens to be the case; in some possible worlds the cookies exist but the set does not.

Van Inwagen's "Tom, Dick, and Harry" hints at some generality. And of course so does my example of the cookies in the jar. For there is nothing special about them: other Fig Newtons, or even Oreos, would do as well. And there is nothing special about cookies: baked goods of any sort would do, as would for that matter any artifacts, or indeed natural objects, concrete or abstract. Just any old objects, we may be inclined to say. But of course we know better. For we know that not just any old objects are the members of a set: the nonselfmembered things, for example, are not. The brakes must thus be applied somewhere; but it is unclear where, and to that extent unclear just how to generalize (4). On the other hand, (5) easily generalizes to:

> (7)   If there is a certain set, then in every possible world in which the members of the set exist there is a set of which they are the members.

It might be thought that (5) admits of a further generalization, namely,

> (8)   If there is in some possible world a certain set, then in every possible world in which the members of the set exist there is a set of which they are the members.

But I'm not sure this will do, for I'm not certain how to rule out the possibility that there should have been a set of which the non-selfmembered objects of this world are the members.

2

Throughout the discussion that follows, I assume that sets are, as the books commonly say, "determined by" their members. Sometimes this slogan seems to be understood simply as an informal statement of, or perhaps an informal statement of a consequence of, the Principle of Extensionality, the proposition that no two sets have the same members.[6] Now I take that proposition to follow from the stronger proposition that it is not *possible* for there to be two sets that have the same members, and indeed from the following still stronger proposition:

> (9)   It is not possible for there to be a set A such that it is possible for there to be a set other than A that has the same members as A.

And when it is said that a set is fully determined by its members, I think two further propositions are implied, namely,

> (10)   It is not possible for there to be a set A and an object x in A such that it is possible for A to exist and yet not have x as a member

and

> (11)   It is not possible for there to be a set A and an object x not in A such that it is possible for A to have x as a member.

From these two propositions it follows that a set could not but have precisely the members it does have—in other words, that it is essential to a set to have just the members it does in fact have.

Does the thing go the other way? Is it essential to the members of a set that they be the members of the set? Well, given (9), that's just the question whether (5) is true. But without begging that question, something may be said, namely, that it is not in general true that if an object x is a member of a set A, then it is essential to x that it be a member of A. Consider again the cookies in the jar. I take them to be contingent and independent objects, so that any one of them might have existed even though the others did not. Suppose, then, that there are just three of them—x, y, and z—and that they are the members of a set A. Then x might have existed even though y and z did not, in which case there would have been no such set as A. Thus it is not essential to x that it be a member of A. Similarly for y and z. So to no one of x, y, and z is it essential that it be a member of A.

It might seem to follow that it is not essential to the cookies that they be members of A, and hence by (9) that (5) is false. But it does not. It is indeed true of each cookie that it is not essential to it that it be a member of a set of which the cookies are the members. But it may nevertheless be true of *the cookies* that it is essential to *them* that *they* be the members of a set. Just so, it may be true of each man from Acme Movers that he didn't carry the piano upstairs, but nevertheless true of the men from Acme that they carried the piano upstairs; it may be true of each horse in the team that it didn't draw the king's carriage, but nevertheless true of the horses in the team that they drew the carriage;[7] and so on, and so on. Here, as in ever so many other cases, something is true of the so-and-sos that is true of no one of the so-and-sos.

Another cautionary word: From the fact that in no possible world in which one or more of the cookies fails to exist is there a set of which the cookies are the members, it does not follow that in no possible world in which one or more of the cookies fails to exist is there a set correctly describable as $\{x{:}x$ is a cookie in the jar$\}$. For that matter, even if it is assumed that 'a', 'b', and 'c' are names of the three cookies in the jar, '$\{x{:}x = a \lor x = b \lor x = c\}$', of which '$\{a,b,c\}$' is sometimes taken to be an abbreviation,[8] will with respect to some possible worlds denote a set the members of which are not the cookies: if, for instance, a does not exist in possible world w but b and c do, then with respect to w '$\{x{:}x = a \lor x = b \lor x = c\}$' denotes the set of which the members are just b and c. So the question whether (4) is true must not be confused with the question whether

> (12)   In every possible world in which the cookies exist there exists a set describable as {x:x is a cookie in the jar}

is true, or with the question whether

> (13)   In every possible world in which the cookies exist there exists a set describable as {x:x = a ∨ x = b ∨ x = c}

is true.

3

Let us try to suppose, with the minority, that (5) is false, so that there does exist a set of which the cookies in the jar are the members, but in some other possible world the set doesn't exist, though the cookies do. Possible worlds in which the cookies exist would thus come in two varieties: those in which the set exists, and those in which it doesn't. Let $w+$ be a world of the first kind, and let $w-$ be of the second kind. Now $w+$ and $w-$ may be expected to differ in other ways as well, consequent on various conditional principles of set existence. If, for instance, the following commonly accepted principle of set theory holds at $w+$:

ADJUNCTION   If A is a set and x is any object whatever, there is a set the members of which are x and the members of A

then there will exist at $w+$, but not at $w-$, a set the members of which are the cookies and the set of which the cookies are the members. But it would seem that the two worlds must differ in some other way as well, some way that is not simply a set-theoretic consequence of the existence in $w+$ of the set of cookies in the jar; something must *explain* the set-theoretic differences between $w+$ and $w-$. But it is not easy to see what this could be. Imagine a baker who produces the cookies in $w+$ and in $w-$. He follows the same recipe in both worlds—indeed, his ingredients and mixings and stirrings in the two worlds are precisely the same; and yet somehow a set results in $w+$ but not in $w-$. One suspects an Invisible Hand. So consider:

> And God said, Let us make man in our image, after our likeness: and let them have dominion over the fish of the sea, and over the fowl of the air, and over the cattle, and over all the earth, and over every creeping thing that creepeth upon the earth. So God created man in his image, in the image of God created he him; male and female created he them.

And at the end of the sixth day, "God saw every thing that he had made, and, behold, it was good."[9] But what if God had noticed on that day that he had neglected to see to it that there was a *set* the members of which were Adam and Eve? What could he have done other than what he did do? The set was surely not to have been made from "the dust of the earth," or indeed *from* anything at all. There would seem in fact to be nothing God could have done except the kind of thing he had already done on the first day: "Let there be light," he had said then, and of course there was light. Just so, he might have said at the end of the sixth day: "Let there be a set of which Adam and Eve are the members," and of course there would have been such a set. Now creation out of nothing is pretty hard to understand in any case. But in this case it is utterly mysterious. I suggest that it is equally mysterious how $w+$ and $w-$ could differ only in that the former has in it a set of which the cookies are the members, and such further sets as may be consequent on that, whereas the latter does not. The supposed set-theoretic difference between $w+$ and $w-$ thus appears inexplicable. It is simply a fact, an ultimate fact, about the two worlds that in the one there is a set of which the cookies are the members whereas in the other there is not.

Connected with this metaphysical difficulty is an epistemological one. On what ground can one say, as someone who denies (5) would say, that our world is of the $w+$ variety? If it is possible for the cookies to exist though the set does not, how can we be sure that that possibility is not in fact realized? It is no good just looking in the jar. Maybe, as some think,[10] sets, some of them anyhow, can be seen. Even so, how is an observer to know whether what he sees when he looks is the set of cookies or just the cookies? Perhaps there is a certain *look* that the cookies have got in a world of the $w+$ kind that they haven't got in a world of the $w-$ kind. But what is an observer to make of the look? Could he know that it goes with the existence of a set of which the cookies are the members? Could he be sure that the look does not signify absence of a set?

4

The negation of (5), and hence of (4), is sometimes urged on the strength of the alleged general principle that a set is something over and above its members. Oddly, those who affirm (4) and (5) are apt to use the same turn of phrase: the set of cookies in the jar, they say, is nothing over and above the cookies. The problem is to say what this means, and to do so in particular without simply posing anew the question whether (4) and (5) and their ilk are true.

Let me try to cast some light by commenting on a certain use of words such as 'multitude', 'plurality', 'multiplicity', and 'collection'.

The use I have in mind is exemplified in Cantor's explanations of the concept *set*. At the very beginning of his "Beiträge" of 1895, Cantor wrote:

> By a 'set' we are to understand any collection into a whole . . . of definite and well-distinguished objects of our perception or thought . . . .[11]

This explanation is often quoted only to be dismissed as uninformative. I think in the end it is uninformative, but I also think it is worth attending to.

The explanation can be understood as one in which 'collection' is presumed to have a wider application than 'set', in such a way that sets are to be only some among collections. As to what a collection is, Cantor has nothing to say; but he has a good deal to say about the circumstances under which a collection is a set.

First, a collection is to qualify as a set only if the objects in it are "definite," by which Cantor means that it must be determinate, for any object whatever, whether that object is in the collection. It need not be known with respect to each object whether it is in the collection, nor need there be ready to hand some effective means for determining which objects are in the collection. As Cantor remarked elsewhere, it is required only that

> in consequence of its definition and of the logical principle of the excluded third, it be intrinsically determined whether an object . . . belongs to the set or not. . . . We cannot in general effect in a sure and precise manner these determinations with the means that we have at our disposal; but here it is only a question of *intrinsic* determination, from which an actual or extrinsic determination is to be developed by perfecting the auxiliary means.[12]

Second, a collection is to qualify as a set only if its members are "well-distinguished," by which Cantor means that, for any objects x and y in the collection, it must be fully determinate whether x is identical with y.[13]

A collection satisfying these conditions is said by Cantor to be "well-defined."[14] Is every well-defined collection a set? No, for there is an additional condition that must be met, namely, that the collection be "into a whole," by which Cantor seems to have meant that the collection be—or perhaps be capable of being consistently conceived as being—a single object in its own right. This is a point that is difficult to be clear about, but evidently Cantor attached a great deal of importance to it. Already in 1883 he had written:

> By an "aggregate" [*Mannigfaltigkeit*] or "set" [*Menge*] I understand generally every many [*Viele*] which can itself be thought of as one, i.e. every totality [*Inbegriff*] of definite elements which can be bound together by a law into a whole.[15]

And in his famous letter to Dedekind of 28 July 1899, Cantor wrote:

> If we start from the notion of a definite [i.e., well-defined] multiplicity (a system, a totality) of things, it is necessary, as I discovered, to distinguish two kinds of multiplicities (by this I always mean *definite* multiplicities).
>
> For a multiplicity can be such that the assumption that *all* of its elements "are together" leads to a contradiction, so that it is impossible to conceive of the multiplicity as a unity, as "one finished thing." Such multiplicities I call *absolutely infinite* or *inconsistent multiplicities*.
>
> As we can readily see, the "totality of everything thinkable," for example, is such a multiplicity; later still other examples will turn up.
>
> If on the other hand the totality of the elements of a multiplicity can be thought of without contradiction as "being together," so that they can be gathered together into "*one* thing," I call it a *consistent multiplicity* or a "set."[16]

Some will regard this, perhaps rightly, as a model of obscurity. But there may seem to be a more fundamental difficulty: how can there be something (*a* collection, *a* multiplicity) that cannot be thought of as one thing? And the difficulty seems even more striking if we excise Cantor's anthropomorphic talk of what can be "thought of" as one thing and what can be "gathered together" into one thing, so as to obtain simply: an absolutely infinite, or inconsistent, multiplicity is a multiplicity that cannot be one thing.

I think the difficulty can be got round, though at some cost to what I take to be Cantor's explanation of *set*. There is, as we know, no one thing (object, entity) of which, for example, all and only the nonselfmembered objects are the members: it is a contradiction to say there is. But one can nevertheless speak, as I just now did, of "the nonselfmembered objects." As George Boolos pointed out,[17] the proposition:

> (14)   There are some things that are nonselfmembered and every nonselfmembered thing is one of them

is plainly true, and that is enough to legitimize the plural definite description. I suggest that it is enough as well for there to be a collection, in Cantor's sense, consisting of the nonselfmembered objects—enough, that is, for the truth of

> (15)   There is a collection of things that are nonselfmembered and every nonselfmembered thing is one of them.

Notice that (14) and (15) differ only in that where the former has 'are some', the latter has instead 'is a collection of', and this brings out the fact that, as Helen Cartwright has said, 'collection', in this use, "serves *only* to singularize a plural nominal" and thereby "affords means of referring in the singular to what can also be referred to in the plural."[18]

It thus seems right to say that a collection of so-and-sos, in Cantor's sense, is nothing over and above the so-and-sos it consists of. And if, as Cantor thought, every set is a collection, then sets too are nothing over and above the things that constitute them—nothing over and above what are called their members. But there is good reason to say, with Russell[19] and contrary to Cantor, that no set is a collection. Like 'is one of', the phrase 'is a member of', when it translates the set-theoretic use of the Greek letter epsilon, demands a genuinely singular subject. And unlike 'is one of', the blank in a phrase of the form 'is a member of____', or, in the usual notation, the position to the right of epsilon, must be filled by a genuinely singular noun phrase. As Russell said,

> $\in$ cannot represent the relation of a term to its class as many; for this would be a relation of one term to many terms, not a two-term relation such as we want. This relation might be expressed by e.g. "Socrates is one among men"; but this, in any case, cannot be taken to be the meaning of $\in$.[20]

Thus the cookies in the jar cannot be said to be *a* member of anything at all (though, of course, one can say that the cookies in the jar are members of this or that set, for that is only to say that *each* cookie is a member). And though each cookie in the jar is one of the cookies in the jar, none of them can be said to be a member of the cookies in the jar. The collection (multiplicity, class as many) of cookies in the jar is not the set of which they are the members.

Although no set is a collection, every set *represents* a collection, in the sense that its members are precisely the things each of which is one of the collection.[21] On the other hand, not every collection is represented by a set: witness the nonselfmembers. Standard set-theoretic axioms can sometimes be understood as principles concerning the representation of collections by sets.[22] For instance, corresponding to Zermelo's *Aussonderungsaxiom* is:

SUBCLASS AXIOM   If a collection is represented by a set, every sub-collection of it is represented by a set.

Again,

POWER AXIOM   The collection of subsets of a set is represented by a set

corresponds to his Power Set Axiom (for which see (20), below).[23]

Are there collections? It is certainly true to say that there is a collection of which each cookie in the jar is one; for that is only to say, in a pompous way, that there are cookies in the jar. And it may be true to say that there is a collection of men who moved the piano upstairs, for that would only be to say that there are some men who moved the piano upstairs. But the cases differ, as in effect already noticed: although each object that is one of the first collection is a cookie in the jar, it is not true that each object that is one of the second collection is a man who moved the piano upstairs. The cookies in the jar are the things x such that x is a cookie in the jar, but the men who moved the piano upstairs are not the things x such that x is a man who moved the piano upstairs. As Helen Cartwright has shown, a phrase of the form

the so-and-sos

may denote a collection even though not of the form

the things x such that x is a so-and-so.

It does not follow that some collections altogether elude specification by phrases of the second form. The men who moved the piano upstairs are not the things x such that x is a man who moved the piano upstairs; but they may be the things x such that x is a ten-year veteran of Acme Movers, or such that x participated in the moving of the piano upstairs, or such that x is Tom or Dick or Harry. But is there *always* a specification of this kind?

Certain problematic cases derive from the Axiom of Choice, one form of which is:

CHOICE   Given any pairwise disjoint collection of nonempty sets, there is a collection that consists of exactly one member of each of the sets of the collection.

(A collection of sets is pairwise disjoint just in case no two of them have a member in common.) Consider Russell's famous example of an infinite collection of pairs of socks. By the Axiom of Choice (and on the assumption that each pair is a set) there exists a collection that consists of exactly one sock from each pair. Yet, since "manufacturers adhere to the regrettable custom of producing equal stockings for both feet,"[24] it might seem to be sheer luck were the collection to be specifiable as, say, the collection of things x such that x is a sock with a hole where the big toe should go. If it is not to be sheer luck, every collection must have what McTaggart called an "exclusive common quality,"[25] by which he meant that something must be true of each one of a collection that is not true of anything not one of the collection. Whether that principle is true, as McTaggart thought, is a controversial question well beyond the scope of this paper.

5

It must be conceded that in everyday talk 'set' often means *collection*, in Cantor's sense, and is accordingly eliminable in favor of plural noun phrases. Thus there is on the label a set of instructions for washing if and only if, I suppose, there are on the label instructions for washing. Much set talk is in fact just puffery, indulged in especially by certain academics: a subset of the students favor (favors?) a longer reading period, we hear at a faculty meeting, and we know that the speaker means only that some of the students, maybe quite a few, are in favor.

Sometimes, however, set talk serves a serious purpose, even though eliminable; for plural noun phrases quickly become unwieldy, and paraphrase in terms of sets simplifies and exploits a familiar idiom. Consider, for example, the logical law known as *Cut*:

> (16)   If certain propositions together imply p, and if each of those propositions is implied by certain other propositions taken together, then the latter propositions together also imply p.

So expressed, this is awkward, to say the least. Some improvement results from introducing variables 'X', 'Y', and so on, understood as ranging over sets of propositions. Thus the above formulation would give way to:

> (17)   If the members of X together imply p, and if each member of X is implied by the members of Y taken together, then the members of Y together imply p.

This is more perspicuous, but the ratio of length to content is still high. A more compact notation is wanted.

One is at hand, suggested already by the introduction of variables 'X', 'Y', and the like: replace the homogeneous but multigrade relation of implication with a dyadic but inhomogeneous relation that takes a *set* of propositions to a proposition just in case the members of the set together imply the proposition. If 'imps' is understood to signify that relation, Cut comes to be succinctly expressed thus:

(18)   If X imps p and Y imps q for every q in X, then Y imps p.

Within set theory itself, talk of sets is never puffery and not always a matter simply of convenience. An instructive example is the proposition often called Cantor's Theorem, which in its usual formulation is:

(19)   Every set is cardinally smaller than the set of all its subsets.

Reference here to the set the members of which are the subsets of a given set enables one to infer at once that given any set A, there is a set B that is cardinally larger than A. The reference is justified by the Power Set Axiom:

(20)   Given any set A, there is a set the members of which are the subsets of A.

But if one's purpose is only to establish that the subsets of a set outrun its members, that is, to prove

(21)   Given any set A, the subsets of A exceed in cardinality the members of A,

or, more simply,

(22)   There are more subsets of a set than there are members,

then there is no occasion to invoke (20). But one cannot infer from (22) that for every set there is a set of greater cardinality; for that, (20) is required. It might be thought that one can in any case take a step beyond (21), or (22), to:

(23)   Given any objects whatever, there are fewer of them than there are sets the members of which are some of them.

Unfortunately, however, (23) is false: the objects there are are *not* fewer in number than the sets the members of which are some of them.[26]

6

Perhaps it has been evident that I side with van Inwagen's majority. But such argument as I can give falls far short of demonstrating the truth of (4) and hence (5). In fact, I shall argue for the weak conclusion that *either* (4) is true *or* in some possible world there are no sets at all.

The argument is quite simple. It proceeds from two premises:

(24)   Necessarily: If A is a set and x is any object, there exists a set the members of which are x and the members of A

and

(25)   Necessarily: Any members of a set are themselves the members of a set.

And it goes as follows. Let w be any possible world in which the cookies in the jar exist (though perhaps not in that jar) and in which there also exists at least one set. Assuming A to be one such set, three (or fewer) applications of (24) will establish the existence of a set the members of which are the cookies and the members of A. A single application of (25) will then yield the conclusion that there exists in w a set the members of which are the cookies. So if there is a possible world in which the cookies exist but in which the set of them does not, then in that possible world there are no sets at all. And thus either (4) and hence (5) are true or in some possible world there are no sets at all.

Of the premises appealed to, (24) is the necessitation of what I earlier called Adjunction, and (25) is the necessitation of a proposition equivalent to the Subclass Axiom. I don't know how to demonstrate either principle, and no doubt one or the other, or both, would be denied by someone convinced of the falsity of (4) and (5). All I can do in the face of this is to assert that neither Adjunction nor the Subclass Axiom seems to me a contingent truth and that I know of no reason to think either false.

So if it is possible for the cookies to exist and yet for there to be no set of which they are the members, then it is possible for there to be a world in which there simply are no sets—a world in which no collection is "represented." Perhaps that would not be worrisome were we sure that this world, the actual world, is not such a world. But I know of no way of demonstrating that. It is in effect a set-theoretic axiom that there are sets. And some set-theoretic axioms seem to me to be necessary truths. But I cannot see that this one is. In somewhat similar circumstances, Russell said, "In this unsatisfactory state, I reluctantly leave the problem to the ingenuity of the reader."[27]

Appendix: Cantor's Theorem

1. Cantor's Theorem is usually said to be the proposition that every set is cardinally smaller than its power set, i.e., the set of all its subsets. To prove the theorem one must show that, for any set x, x is cardinally equivalent to a subset of $P(x)$ but $P(x)$ is not cardinally equivalent to any subset of x. It is easy to see that x is cardinally equivalent to a subset

of P(x): the function that assigns {a} to each a in x is one-one from x into P(x). To show that P(x) is not cardinally equivalent to any subset of x, one may invoke reasoning that derives from Cantor and prove:

LEMMA   There is no function that has in its range every subset of its domain.

Proof   Assume, contrary to the theorem, that f is a function that has in its range every subset of its domain. Put

$$d = \{x \in \mathrm{dom}(f): \text{not } x \in f(x)\}.$$

Obviously d is a subset of the domain of f. Now let z be any member of the domain of f. Then

$$z \in d \text{ iff not } z \in f(z).$$

So d is not identical with $f(z)$, and hence not in the range of f.

And of course there follows:

COROLLARY   For any set x and any subset y of x, it is not the case that P(x) is cardinally equivalent to y.

Proof   Suppose that P(x) is cardinally equivalent to y. Then of course y is cardinally equivalent to P(x), in which case there is a one-one function f from y onto P(x). But every subset of y is in P(x). Hence every subset of the domain of f is in the range of f, contrary to the lemma.

The proof of Cantor's Theorem is complete.

2. The proof just given is to be thought of as carried out in ZF. It is of some interest to see how in Bernays's set theory,[28] and related systems, one can prove:

THEOREM   Every set is cardinally smaller than the class of all its subsets.

Proof   Supposing x to be any set, and letting Px be the class of subsets of x, we need to show that there is a one-one function from x into Px but no one-one function from Px into x. Obviously the function that assigns {y} to each y in x is one-one from x into Px. Now there is a one-one function from Px into x only if there is a one-one function from a subclass of x onto Px. Suppose, if possible, that f is a one-one function from a subclass Y of x onto Px. Put

$$D = \{z\eta Y: \text{not } z \in f(z)\}.$$

(I follow Bernays in using $\in$ for the relation of set to set and η for the relation of set to class.) Evidently D is represented by a set d, for D is a subclass of Y and hence of the set x. So d is in Px. But, for an arbitrary u in Y:

$u\eta D$ iff not $u \in f(u)$

and hence

$u \in d$ iff not $u \in f(u)$.

So d is not identical with $f(u)$, and thus not in the range of f, contrary to the supposition that f is onto Px. It follows that there is no one-one function from Px into x.

Employed in the proof are Class Existence (roughly, every formula that contains no bound class variables determines a class of sets),[29] Extensionality, the so-called Axioms of the Small Sets, and the Subclass Axiom. Notice in particular that the Power Axiom is not used.

And notice that (unless the Bernays theory is inconsistent) it is *not* a theorem that every class is cardinally smaller than the class of all its subsets. For V is identical with the class of all its subsets.

3. Nothing in the foregoing requires that "classes" be understood to be other than collections, or classes as many. But the following definitions may help to allay certain doubts.

> A *function* is a collection of ordered pairs (i.e., sets of the form $\{\{x\},\{x,y\}\}$) no two of which have the same first term.
> The *domain* of a function is the collection of things x such that for some y, $\langle x,y \rangle$ is one of the pairs of which the function consists.
> The *range* of a function is the collection of things y such that for some x, $\langle x,y \rangle$ is one of the pairs of which the function consists.
> A function is *from* a collection X *into* a collection Y iff X is the domain of the function and Y is some of its range; and the function is *onto* Y just in case Y is its range.

Notice that the domain and range of a function, though themselves collections, consist of sets (and perhaps *urelemente*). Collections are neither arguments to nor values of functions.[30]

Notes

1. "Speaking of Everything," p. 8.
2. *Skeptical Essays*, p. 43. George Boolos called the quotation to my attention. To separate issues, it would be preferable to have 'a' in place of 'exactly one'; extensionality is not in question. And I take Mates's 'class' to be synonymous with my 'set'.
3. *Material Beings*, p. 74.
4. *Mathematics in Philosophy*, p. 294.
5. *Logic, Logic, and Logic*, p. 72.

6. See, e.g., Abraham A. Fraenkel, Yehoshua Bar-Hillel, and Azriel Levy, *Foundations of Set Theory*, p. 27; Thomas Jech, *Set Theory*, p. 4; and Azriel Levy, *Basic Set Theory*, p. 5.

7. Contrary, I take it, to Frege: see *Die Grundlagen der Arithmetik*, section 46. See also Michael Dummett, *Frege's Philosophy of Mathematics*, p. 93.

8. See, e.g., Kurt Gödel, *The Consistency of the Axiom of Choice and of the Generalized Continuum Hypothesis with the Axioms of Set Theory*, p. 3.

9. *Genesis* 1:26–7 and 31, King James version.

10. See Penelope Maddy, *Realism in Mathematics*, chapter 2.

11. Georg Cantor, "Beiträge zur Begründung der transfiniten Mengenlehre, 1."

12. "Über unendliche, lineare Punktmannigfaltigkeiten, 3." Reprinted in *Gesammelte Abhandlungen*. The quotation is on p. 150 of that volume.

13. See *Gesammelte Abhandlungen*, p. 150.

14. *Gesammelte Abhandlungen*, p. 150.

15. *Gesammelte Abhandlungen*, p. 204.

16. *Gesammelte Abhandlungen*, p. 443; English translation in J. van Heijenoort (ed.), *From Frege to Gödel*, p. 114.

17. *Logic, Logic, and Logic*, pp. 70–71.

18. "On Plural Reference and Elementary Set Theory," p. 213.

19. Russell's "collections" are his "classes as many," and are accordingly distinguished from what he calls "classes as one." See *The Principles of Mathematics*, pp. 68–69 and especially p. 76, where he speaks of "an ultimate distinction between a class as many and a class as one."

20. *Principles*, p. 78.

21. The empty set, if there is one, and singletons present problems that cannot be addressed here.

22. Here, and at several other places, I lean heavily on Paul Bernays, "A System of Axiomatic Set Theory."

23. It is perhaps of some interest to notice that if the Power Axiom is strengthened to:

> For every set x, there is a set y such that for every class Z, $Z < x$ iff Z is represented by a member of y

(where $Z < x$ iff everything that is one of the collection Z is a member of the set x), the Subclass Axiom follows.

24. Fraenkel, Bar-Hillel, and Levy, *Foundations of Set Theory*, p. 63.

25. J. M. E. McTaggart, *The Nature of Existence*, vol. 1, chapter 17.

26. In the discussion of (20)–(23) I have drawn on Bernays, "A System of Axiomatic Set Theory, 4."

27. *Principles*, p. 368.

28. That is, the theory expounded in "A System of Axiomatic Set Theory." The theory is sometimes referred to as VNB, on the ground that its leading idea derives from John von Neumann, "Eine Axiomatisierung der Mengenlehre."

29. I follow Levy (in Fraenkel, Bar-Hillel, and Levy, *Foundations of Set Theory*) in taking as an axiom-schema what Bernays proves from finitely many class-existence axioms.

30. An earlier version of this paper was presented as part of a symposium, held at Tufts University in September 1998, honoring the work of Helen Cartwright. Other participants were Sydney Shoemaker and Judith Thomson.

In thinking about the topics discussed in the paper, I have benefited from conversations with Gabriel Uzquiano; and to those who know their work, it will be obvious that I have benefited enormously from reading papers by the late George Boolos and by Helen Cartwright. I am especially indebted to Helen, with whom I have discussed these matters at great length. I am very grateful to Ralph Wedgwood for pointing out a mistake in the early version.

References

Bernays, Paul. "A System of Axiomatic Set Theory," *Journal of Symbolic Logic* 2 (1937): 65–77; 6 (1941): 1–17; 7 (1942): 65–89, 133–145; 8 (1943): 89–106; 13 (1948): 65–79; 19 (1954): 81–96. Reprinted with minor alterations in Gert H. Muller, ed., *Sets and Classes* (Amsterdam: North-Holland, 1976), pp. 1–119.

Boolos, George. *Logic, Logic, and Logic* (Cambridge, MA: Harvard University Press, 1998).

Cantor, Georg. "Beiträge zur Begründung der transfiniten Mengenlehre, 1," *Mathematische Annalen* 46 (1895): 481–512. Translated into English by P. E. B. Jourdain as *Contributions to the Founding of the Theory of Transfinite Numbers* (New York: Dover, 1952).

———. "Über unendliche, lineare Punktmannigfaltigkeiten, 3," *Mathematische Annalen* 21 (1882): 113–121. Reprinted in E. Zermelo (ed.), *Gesammelte Abhandlungen*.

———. *Gesammelte Abhandlungen* (Berlin: Springer, 1932). Excerpts in English translation in J. van Heijenoort (ed.), *From Frege to Gödel* (Cambridge, MA: Harvard University Press, 1967).

Cartwright, Helen. "On Plural Reference and Elementary Set Theory," *Synthese* 96 (1993): 201–254.

Cartwright, Richard L. "Speaking of Everything," *Noûs* 28 (1994): 1–20.

Dummett, Michael. *Frege's Philosophy of Mathematics* (Cambridge, MA: Harvard University Press, 1991).

Fraenkel, Abraham A., Yehoshua Bar-Hillel, and Azriel Levy. *Foundations of Set Theory*, second edition (Amsterdam/New York/Oxford: North-Holland, 1973).

Frege, Gottlob. *Die Grundlagen der Arithmetik: Eine logisch-mathematische Untersuchung über den Begriff der Zahl* (Breslau: W. Koebner, 1884). Translated as *The Foundations of Arithmetic: A Logico-mathematical Enquiry into the Concept of Number* by J. L. Austin (Oxford: Basil Blackwell, 1950).

Gödel, Kurt. *The Consistency of the Axiom of Choice and of the Generalized Continuum Hypothesis with the Axioms of Set Theory* (Princeton: Princeton University Press, 1940).

Jech, Thomas. *Set Theory* (New York/San Francisco/London: Academic Press, 1978).

Levy, Azriel. *Basic Set Theory* (Berlin/Heidelberg/New York: Springer-Verlag, 1979).

Maddy, Penelope. *Realism in Mathematics* (Oxford: Clarendon Press, 1990).

Mates, Benson. *Skeptical Essays* (Chicago: University of Chicago Press, 1981).

McTaggart, J. M. E. *The Nature of Existence*, vol. 1. (Cambridge: Cambridge University Press, 1921).

Neumann, John von. "Eine Axiomatisierung der Mengenlehre," *Journal für die reine und angewandte Mathematik* 154 (1925): 219–240.

Parsons, Charles. *Mathematics in Philosophy* (Ithaca: Cornell University Press, 1983).

Russell, Bertrand. *The Principles of Mathematics* (Cambridge: Cambridge University Press, 1903).

Van Inwagen, Peter. *Material Beings* (Ithaca and London: Cornell University Press, 1990).

Chapter 3

Money, Politics, Political Equality

Joshua Cohen

---

1 Introduction

In this paper, I discuss and criticize the current system of electoral finance in the United States and the constraints on the reform of that system imposed by the Supreme Court.

1. I begin by stating and discussing a three-part principle of political equality (sec. 2), which I present as a partial statement of a normative ideal of democracy.

2. I argue that the current system of campaign finance conflicts with the principle of political equality, in particular its requirement of equal opportunity for political influence. Current arrangements establish, in effect, a framework of inequalities of opportunity (secs. 3, 4).

3. I discuss the constitutional limits on reform initially set down by the Supreme Court in the 1976 case of *Buckley v. Valeo* and reinforced in a number of cases decided since then. These decisions substantially limit the role that the value of political equality can play in shaping our system of campaign finance. A regulatory scheme that gave weight to that value by aiming to equalize opportunities for political influence would (barring special assumptions about diminishing returns to political investment) reduce the overall quantity of electoral speech. But the Court has held that fundamental constitutional principles preclude any restrictions on the amount of speech in the name of equalizing opportunities for political influence (secs. 5, 6).

4. I argue that the limits imposed by the Court reflect an unduly narrow conception of democracy and the role of citizens in it, a conception that—like the elite theories of democracy that trace to Joseph Schumpeter—casts citizens exclusively in the role of audience for the messages of elite competitors rather than political actors, as listeners rather than, so to speak, content-providers.[1] And I suggest that alternatives to the current system, founded on a less narrow conception of democracy and the role of citizens in it—a conception that does not treat the elite-mass distinction as the central fact of political sociology—

might achieve a better reconciliation of expressive liberty and political equality (sec. 7). In short, my central point is that the current system is deeply troubling not simply because it subordinates democracy to something else—to property, or to an abstract and absolutist view of freedom of expression—but because it can be seen as founded on and as constitutionalizing a narrow conception of democracy and citizenship, and thus as precluding experimentation aimed at more fully realizing democratic values.

I will not defend a particular proposal for reforming the system of campaign finance, though for purposes of illustration, I will, from time to time, refer to the voluntary public financing scheme recently adopted by Maine voters in 1996, a variant of which was adopted in Massachusetts in 1998. In essence, that scheme—whose constitutional standing remains uncertain (though it has been upheld thus far)[2]—finances candidate campaigns through a public fund, on condition those candidates not raise or spend private money. So it combines public subsidy with voluntary spending limits, incentives to accept the limits as condition for receiving the subsidy (therefore incentives to reduce the overall quantity of speech), some constraints (in the form of reasonably low contribution limits) on private money nonparticipants, and additional support for public money candidates who face large private spending by opponents or large independent expenditures.[3]

One final prefatory note: as I was adding final touches to this paper (in January 2000), the Supreme Court announced its decision in *Nixon v. Shrink*, in which it upheld Missouri's statutory limits on campaign contributions. Were I rewriting the paper now, I would make two changes in light of the opinions in *Nixon*. First, I would change the discussion in section 6 to take notice of the fact that *Nixon v. Shrink* rejects the idea that restrictions on the size of campaign contributions should be subjected to the most demanding level of scrutiny. Second, and more important, I would underscore that the vast majority of the Court now seems willing to uphold campaign finance regulations enacted to ensure a more fair democratic process. This willingness is explicitly stated in Justice Breyer's concurrence, and is suggested as well by Justice Souter (writing for the Court), who indicates that corruption of democratic process is not confined to the financial quid pro quo. The implications of this shift remain to be seen. But the apparent departure in constitutional philosophy is cause for hope.

2 A Principle of Political Equality

In a democratic society, the members are conceived of as free and equal persons. A principle of political equality for a democracy presents norms that are suited to persons thus conceived; it articulates values that apply to democratic arrangements for making binding—authoritative and enforceable—collective decisions; and it aims to provide guidance about the appropriate design of such arrangements. In particular, the norms are to guide judgments about voting rights, rules for organizing elections and aggregating votes (ballot access, systems of representation, electoral finance), and the organization of legislative and executive decision making.[4] Thus, a principle of political equality applies to the framework for making authoritative and enforceable collective decisions and specifies, inter alia, the system of rights and opportunities for free and equal members to exercise political influence over decisions with which they are expected to comply and that are made in their name. It does not apply to the dispersed networks of political-cultural discussion, founded on the associational life of civil society—what Habermas calls the "informal public sphere," and Rawls calls the "background culture."[5] It presents, and is framed for the purpose of presenting, an account of, inter alia, demands that free and equal members can legitimately make on the highest-level systems of authoritative collective decision making.

The principle of political equality I rely on here has three components. It states that arrangements for making binding collective decisions are to accommodate the following three norms:

1. *Equal rights of participation*, including rights of voting, association, and office-holding, as well as rights of political expression, with a strong presumption against restrictions on the content or viewpoint of expression, and against restrictions that are unduly burdensome to some individuals or groups;

2. A strong presumption in favor of *equally weighted votes*; and

3. *Equal opportunities for effective political influence*. This last requirement, what Rawls has called "the fair value of political liberty," condemns inequalities in opportunities for holding office and influencing political decisions (by influencing the outcomes of elections, the positions of candidates, and the conduct of interelection legislative and administrative decision making).[6]

To be sure, a principle of political equality is not the only requirement on the authoritative system of collective decision making. Decisions should also be substantively just, according to some reasonable conception of justice, and effective at advancing the general welfare. But a principle of political equality states norms that will normally override other considerations, apart from the most fundamental requirements of justice. To be sure, conflicts may emerge between and among the norms comprised by the principle. So the force of saying that arrangements for making binding collective decisions are to accommodate all three components is that, when conflicts emerge, we can't say a priori which value is to give way. In particular, if we accept this three-part principle then we allow that we may need to regulate speech to avoid certain kinds of inequalities in opportunities for political influence.[7]

This third requirement is modeled on the familiar norm of equality of opportunity. Stated intuitively and abstractly, that norm says that one person ought not to have greater chances than another to attain a desirable position because of some quality that is irrelevant to performance in the position. Using some familiar jargon, I will say that this expresses the *concept* of equal opportunity, and that different *conceptions* of equal opportunity are distinguished by the interpretations they give to "irrelevant to performance." For the sake of discussion here, I rely on Rawls's *conception* of equal opportunity, which specifies "irrelevant to performance in the position" as follows: that people who are equally motivated and equally able ought to have equal chances to attain the position.[8]

When this conception of equal opportunity is applied to the political system, the relevant position is *active citizen* in the formal arrangements of binding collective decision making. The requirement, then, is that people who are equally motivated and equally able to play this role, by influencing binding collective decisions, ought to have equal chances to exercise such influence.[9] The constitution and surrounding rules governing elections as well as legislative, executive, and administrative decision making establish this position. When suffrage was restricted to property owners, economic position was a formal qualification for holding that position. We now agree that economic position is not a relevant formal qualification. But if economic position is not a relevant formal qualification for voting and other forms of political influence, how could it be acceptable to organize the highest-level system for exercising political influence in a way that makes the opportunity for such influence dependent on economic position? How could it be acceptable to organize the framework so that greater opportunity comes with greater resources?

I do not propose here to defend this principle (though see pp. 72–73 for some relevant considerations), but will confine myself to four comments on the idea of *equal opportunity for political influence*. Three of the comments bear on the content of the principle—why equal *opportunity* for political influence; why *equal* opportunity for political influence; and why equal opportunity for *political* influence—and one on its status as "autonomous" or independent.

First, then, political equality demands equal *opportunity* for effective political influence rather than equality of effective influence itself. Inequalities of effective influence are sometimes acceptable, on any reasonable view of political equality. Some citizens may be more influential because, for example, they care more about politics. Differences of influence that trace to such differences in values and choices seem unobjectionable. Similarly if a person is more influential because her views are widely shared, or her judgment widely trusted, and others are therefore likely to be swayed by her position on the issue at hand: the differences of influence trace to the distribution of political values and commitments in the population, not to the organization of the structure of collective choice. The requirement of equal opportunity for effective influence condemns certain kinds of effective exclusion or dilution, but it does not support charges of objectionable exclusion or dilution merely because I am unwilling to make reasonable efforts to persuade others, or because others regard my views as ridiculous, or because they lack confidence in my judgment.

What about inequalities due to differences in persuasiveness, or in physical attractiveness? In neither case are the greater opportunities for influence due to aspects of the design of arrangements for making collective decisions that we can permissibly control. To be sure, we could make collective efforts to reduce the importance of differential persuasiveness, for example, by investing more in civic education. But the legitimacy and importance of making such investment do not imply that it would ever be permissible to regulate the activities of the persuasive in order to achieve greater equality of opportunity. To regulate those activities would go to the core of the free speech guarantee, by establishing regulations that control viewpoint and are unduly burdensome. Moreover, it would defeat the point of political discussion. After all, differences in persuasiveness are not irrelevant to performance in the position. Similarly, we could try to control the power that flows from being attractive (such as it is), but only by measures that would keep people from appearing before one another (only radio spots, no TV). And such regulations would, on their face, be damaging to political judgment.

Underlying this focus on opportunity is the idea that it is unreasonable to demand influence irrespective of one's own actions or of the considered convictions of other citizens. That demand is unreasonable because a compelling interpretation of the idea of political equality must ensure a place for individual responsibility. Members of a democratic society are represented as free and equal. As free, they are to be treated as responsible for their political judgments and conduct. So if I demand influence irrespective of the judgments of other citizens, then I deny the importance of such responsibility. Once we accept it, then we accept, too, that a regime with equal opportunity for effective influence is almost certain to be associated with inequalities of actual influence.

Second, the norm of equal opportunity for political influence assigns *autonomous* importance to political equality, rather than merely *dependent* or *derivative* importance.[10] Thus, suppose we eliminate all inequalities of political influence due to causes that we can identify as unjust apart from their effects on political influence. Assume in particular that the distribution of economic resources is fair, and that effective participation is not impeded by stereotype or group hostility. Still, unequal opportunities for effective influence might result from inequalities—assumed by stipulation to be fair—in the distribution of resources. In condemning these unequal opportunities, the principle assigns autonomous importance to political equality. It does not require political equality simply as a way to discourage independently cognizable forms of injustice.

Third, the principle requires *equal* opportunity for political influence, not simply that we ensure a certain threshold level of opportunity—a principle of sufficiency or adequacy of opportunity[11]—or a maximin level of opportunity.[12] Thus, consider a public auction the winners of which get free television time to present their political views, in particular their electoral views. But the proceeds of the auction go to a fund that subsidizes political activity by low-income citizens: perhaps it subsidizes media access, or internet access with assistance for content provision. So holding the auction expands general opportunities for political influence, but the opportunities are unequal in that greater opportunities for influence are available only to those who have the resources to win the auction.

One response is to deny the premise that underlies the distinction between equalization and the alternatives: that it is possible to improve everyone's opportunity for influence. But that seems mistaken. If we establish a lottery the winners of which get free television time for presenting their political views, then everyone has greater opportunities for influence (anyone can win the lottery).

Putting this zero-sum response to the side, then, I note two points about the merits of a limit on inequality of opportunity that is more modest than the one I endorse here. First, from the point of view of the issue that motivates this essay, the distinction between equality of opportunity and, say, maximin opportunity is idle. I am concerned here with the issues about liberty, equality, and democracy raised by the (in)famous sentence in *Buckley*: "the concept that government may restrict the speech of some elements of our society in order to enhance the relative voice of others is wholly foreign to the first amendment." Whether the restrictions would serve to equalize opportunity, "adequatize" opportunity, or maximin it, the same issues emerge—unless it could be shown that the need for restrictions emerges only when we are concerned to achieve equal opportunity for political influence.

Second, part of the reason for thinking that a maximin (or sufficiency) view of opportunity is reasonable is that such a view makes sense when it comes to the distribution of economic resources. Although the equality of citizens as moral persons imposes some pressure to reduce socioeconomic inequalities—as a way to express the respect owed to equals—that pressure is limited by the mutual benefits that can flow from inequalities. A parallel case can be constructed, so it may seem, for inequalities of political opportunity. Although the equality of citizens as moral persons imposes some pressure to reduce inequalities of political opportunity—as a way to express the respect owed to equals—that pressure is limited, it might be argued, by the mutual benefits that can flow from inequalities of opportunity. But this parallel is in part illusory. One reason that resource inequalities are not troubling in a world of moral equals is precisely that their equality is already expressed through the equal standing of individuals as citizens in the system of authoritative collective decision making: "The basis for self-respect in a just society is not . . . one's income share but the publicly affirmed distribution of fundamental rights and liberties. And this distribution being equal, everyone has a similar and secure status when they meet to conduct the common affairs of the wider society. No one is inclined to look beyond the constitutional affirmation of equality for further political ways of securing his status."[13] But if inequalities of opportunity extend to the political system itself, as the authoritative system for making collective decisions, then the public basis of mutual respect is less secure. To be sure, an explanation might be given for the inequalities that does not depend on the idea that citizens are unequal (namely, that the inequalities of political opportunity benefit all). But when citizens lack assured equal standing, that explanation may itself provoke suspicion.

Coming back to the principle of political equality, then, my final observation is that the principle requires equal opportunity for *political* influence. To clarify the force of this condition, I distinguish three interpretations of the idea of political equality, each of which supplements the requirement that votes not be diluted. Thus, equal opportunity for *electoral* influence condemns inequalities in chances to hold office or influence the outcome of elections, but is confined to the electoral setting.[14] Equal opportunity for *political* influence (the requirement I endorse here) extends beyond equal opportunity for electoral influence by condemning inequalities in chances to influence decisions made by formal political institutions. Thus, it condemns conditions in which citizens have equal chances to influence the outcome of elections, but unequal chances to form or join groups that influence the outcome of legislative decisions. Equal opportunity for *public* influence requires equal opportunities to influence the formation of opinion in the wider, informal public sphere, as well as decisions taken by formal political institutions.

The principle of political equality requires equal opportunity for political influence and is thus more stringent than the norm of equal opportunity for electoral influence. But it does not go as far as the requirement of equal opportunity for public influence. Why not endorse this wider requirement?[15] After all, just as political influence is more important than electoral influence (because of the nonelectoral ways to influence legislative or executive decisions), public influence is arguably more important than political influence. Thus, make the assumption that public opinion is translated into legitimate law. Surely, then, it seems especially desirable to have opportunities for shaping public opinion. So we might suppose that a case for ensuring equal chances for political influence would support equal chances for public influence as well.

I think, however, that we should resist this conclusion and reject the wide interpretation of the principle of political equality.

First, the content of the requirement of equal opportunity for public influence is obscure. The informal process of opinion-formation is not at all well defined or bounded: it extends throughout life, spreads through all its spheres, and the processes involved are not at all well understood. So it is not clear what the requirement demands: not clear, that is, when opportunities for influence are suitably equal—when individuals who are equally motivated and equally able have equal chances to influence the formation of public opinion. To be sure, effective chances to persuade others and discuss cultural and political issues are important, but those chances are ensured by the protections of expressive and associative liberties that fall under the first part of the principle of political equality, and by a fair distribution of resources. Here, I am asking whether there is a further, *independent* requirement of equal opportunities for public influence. To be more precise, I am asking whether such a requirement ought to be included in a principle of political equality, as a fundamental political value to be accommodated along with equal rights of participation and equally weighted votes. If it is not included, it may still be legitimate to reduce inequalities of opportunity for public influence by subsidizing opportunities for people with limited resources: through ensuring more traditional public fora, and expanding access to the new fora by, for example, subsidizing internet access (addressing the so-called digital divide) and opportunities for content provision. But the obscurity of the norm speaks against including it in a first principle of political equality, for such inclusion might lead to excessive restrictions on expression.

Second, part of the reason for requiring equal chances for political influence is that the state speaks in the name of citizens, claiming authorization for its binding collective decisions from its equal members; moreover, its decisions are enforceable. So we want to be sure that that claim is founded on arrangements that manifestly treat citizens as equals. But in the wider public sphere, we have no such authoritative statement of results. Although citizens have fundamental interests in chances for public influence, the equality requirement is less compelling.

Third, part of the reason for ensuring equal opportunities for political influence is to establish, in a visible, public way, the respect for citizens as equal members of the collective body that authorizes the exercise of political power. Given the uncertain content of the wider principle of equal opportunity for public influence, it is perhaps unnecessary for ensuring such mutual respect.

3 Facts and Trends

I want now to shift attention in two ways: from political equality in general to the particulars of campaign finance, and from political norms to facts and trends about current campaign finance in the United States. The current system of financing, then, has four fundamental features:

Increasing costs   In the 1996 election cycle, $2.4 billion was raised and $2.2 billion was spent on candidate campaigns.[16] In addition, another $175 million was spent on independent expenditures and issue advocacy. *Independent expenditures* are funds—roughly $25 million for the 1996 elections—used expressly to advocate the election of one candidate or defeat of another, but not spent in explicit coordination with a candidate's campaign. In *issue advocacy*, money—roughly $150 million for the 1996 elections—is spent supporting or opposing the stand of an elected official or a challenger on some issue, but without expressly advocating the election or defeat of the candidate. These aggregates nearly doubled the previous record.

Who gives?   Though spending is growing steadily, the number of contributors remains small. In 1996, for example, just 0.1 percent of the population gave more than $1000 to candidates and parties. Altogether, the $1000+ contributors accounted for $638 million for the 1996 elections: $477 million to candidates and parties, and another $161 in soft money and PAC contributions.

Moreover, business spending continues to dominate the scene. "In 1996 . . . the biggest source of campaign money—by far—was the business community. Overall . . . business outspent labor by a factor of 11 : 1 and ideological groups by 19 : 1. Looking strictly at contributions to candidates, business gave nine times as much money as organized labor, and fifteen times as much as ideological donors."[17]

In *Voice and Equality*, Verba, Schlozman, and Brady provide two findings that bear on our understanding of this relatively small pool of citizens who participate in American politics by making financial contributions, and who are responsible for a large share of contributions and spending. First, willingness to contribute money is largely explained by income—by the capacity to contribute—and not by political interest. Whereas every other political-participatory act—voting, talking, giving time to a campaign—is substantially explained by the participant's general interest in politics, contributing is explained very little by general political interest and very strongly by income.[18] Second, the pool of contributors is unrepresentative of the citizenry: for example, they tend to be more conservative on economic issues.[19]

Unregulated flows   The current system of finance is complex, and contributions to candidate election campaigns are regulated. But here I want to emphasize that certain areas of growing importance are entirely unregulated:

> • *Soft money*: soft money given to political parties for activities allegedly unrelated to federal elections—for example, get-out-the-vote campaigns by a state Democratic or Republican Party— is entirely unrestricted by federal law.[20] Such soft money contributions grew by 206 percent between 1992 and 1996, to the current level of $262 million. Whereas corporations and unions are prohibited from contributing money from their treasury to a candidate, they can contribute soft money, with no restrictions on amounts.
> • *Issue ads:* spending on issue ads is also unregulated by federal law, because such advocacy is not explicit in its endorsement of candidates. So corporations and unions can spend as they wish on issue advocacy, with no disclosure requirements. Absent such requirements, the estimate of $150 million in 1996 is inevitably

speculative, but everyone agrees that issue ads are growing in importance.

· *Candidate spending*: out-of-pocket spending by candidates is unregulated: the cases of Ross Perot, Steve Forbes, and Michael Huffington are the most famously large doses of such spending.

· *Independent expenditures*: whereas contributions to organizations that engage in independent expenditures are regulated, the extent of such expenditures cannot be regulated. The importance of such spending has grown—fourfold between 1994 and 1996, to $22 million—because the Supreme Court decided that spending by parties on candidate elections cannot be regulated unless that spending is expressly coordinated with the candidate. But contribution limits for donations to parties are much higher than limits on giving to individual campaigns: individuals can give $40,000 to a party in an election cycle (half during the primary season, and half for the general election), and only $2000 to a candidate. So I can give $20,000 to the Democratic Party to spend on vote-for-Kennedy ads promoting Ted Kennedy over other Democratic hopefuls for Senator, and then another $20,000 to support Kennedy in the general election. So long as the Democrats don't ask Kennedy how to spend the money, there is no problem.

Money Matters   In 1996, the candidate who outspent his or her opponent won 92 percent of the House races and 88 percent of the Senate races. These high correlations of spending and winning are typical. But they leave open questions of fact and interpretation about the political difference that money makes, even in the relatively well-defined arena of candidate elections, much less in the wider arena of political influence. For three things are true:

i. The bigger spender tends to win.
ii. Incumbents tend to win.
iii. Incumbents tend to be better fund-raisers.

The trick is to provide a consistent and empirically tenable interpretation of these facts. For example, the correlation between spending and electoral advantage may be spurious, as incumbency may directly confer both. Or perhaps, instead, incumbency confers some fund-raising advantage, and the money in turn directly confers electoral advantage—apart from any direct, nonpecuniary incumbency advantage. The truth appears to be the latter: whereas incumbency makes it easier to raise money and independently easier to win elections, the money itself confers electoral benefit, as we see in open-seat races. Moreover, challengers who spend more than incumbents do have considerably greater chances of winning than challengers who spend less.[21]

Second, if incumbents are good at raising money (which confers electoral benefit), that might be because incumbents are a survivor population of especially talented candidates and talent attracts money. Or it might be that the powers of officeholding confer an advantage in fund-raising, because contributors (individuals and particularly organized groups) want to curry favor with officeholders as a result of the powers associated with offices, and/or because reelection-seeking officeholders need to please potential contributors, and have a capacity to please according to the powers of their office. On this issue, the answer seems not to be that officeholders are a survivor population of high quality candidates, but that officeholding itself creates an advantage in fund-raising. Contributors care about the capacity to deliver results; they therefore pay attention to the offices held by elected officials, and invest in those who, by virtue of their official positions, have that capacity.[22]

Putting the complexities to the side, what seems undeniable is that candidate success depends on fund-raising success, that the capacity to raise money depends on performance, that candidates must therefore be especially attentive in their conduct to attract support from the groups that give, and that, by providing such support, contributors gain some measure of influence over electoral outcomes.

To summarize these four observations, then: formal politics is getting more expensive, just as the flow of money unregulated by sum or source is increasing. Because of these increasing costs, and because money is important to electoral success, candidates must be especially—arguably increasingly—attentive to the interests and concerns of the relatively small and unrepresentative group of citizens who spend money on politics and thus provide essential resources for running a modern campaign.

4 Getting the Problem Right

Contemporary discussion of reform tends to focus on one of three issues: that too much money is being spent in the aggregate; that candidates are spending too much time raising money and courting donors; and that donors get political favors in return for their contributions or other forms of spending. I don't think that any of these three concerns get to the heart of the problem.

The first strikes me as weightless: if campaigns were well run, debated real issues, genuinely reached most citizens, and provided them with essential information, why would we think that $2 billion

over a two-year election cycle is too much to spend? Perhaps we are
not spending enough.

Are candidates spending too much time fund-raising? Perhaps.
Dick Morris reports that President Clinton complained "bitterly" about
time spent fund-raising: "I can't think. I can't act. I can't do anything
but go to fund-raisers and shake hands."[23] And Vincent Blasi has made
a forceful case that time devoted to fund-raising injures the democratic process by limiting the capacity of representatives to do their
principal work—information gathering, constituency service, deliber-
ating, legislating.[24] But the case for reducing the sheer time spent
raising funds is not so clear. Suppose, once more, that we had a system
of campaign finance in which each citizen could spend up to $250
on a candidate election, and that candidates were required to raise
all their resources from such contributions. If they spent lots of time
fund-raising, perhaps that would be a good thing: they would be
required to meet with large numbers of potential contributors, and
might learn from those discussions, but without the current bias in the
pool.

Are contributors getting favors in return for their money? Perhaps;
but even if they are not, a large problem of political fairness remains.

The idea of political fairness is captured by the requirement in the
principle of political equality mandating that citizens have equal
opportunities for political influence. The vote is one form of influence,
and the one-person/one-vote requirement is an important implication
of the idea of equalizing opportunities for effective political influence.
But when money is as important a political resource as it is in our
current system, control of it is an important source of political influence. It enables people to run for office, to support electoral efforts
financially, and to join together with like-minded others with the aim
of persuading fellow citizens on some issue of public concern. A system
that does not regulate the flow of money—or provide (as in a system
of public finance) alternatives to relying on private money—provides
unequal opportunities for political influence. It provides channels of
influence to wealthier citizens that are effectively unavailable to others,
who are equally motivated and equally able, but lack the resources
required for using those channels. Do these channels of influence over-
whelm others? Do they establish decisive forms of power? Clearly they
are not always decisive. But it seems clear, too, that we will never have
conclusive answers to questions about the relative importance of different avenues of influence. What we can say is that the current legal
structure establishes a channel of influence that is effectively open to
some and not others. That is itself the problem, however precisely this
opportunity translates into power over decisions.

So the principle of political equality—in particular, the norm of equal opportunity for political influence—raises serious troubles for the current system of finance.

5 Constitutional Landscape

What might be done to remedy this situation? To answer this question, I start with the constitutional landscape.

In the 1976 case of *Buckley v. Valeo*, the Supreme Court heard a challenge to the Federal Election Campaign Act (FECA) of 1971, as amended in 1974.[25] The Court's assessment was mixed: some parts were upheld, some not. But the details of the decision matter less than the framework of analysis and argument announced in it. That analytic framework comprises two key elements.

First, the *Buckley* Court held that "money is speech": meaning that spending money on politics—both contributions to campaigns and expenditures (by candidates or individual citizens or organizations)— has First Amendment protection. Indeed, as political speech, it lies at the core of the First Amendment. For the First Amendment is centrally (though not exclusively) about protecting political speech from regulation, as a necessary condition for assuring the popular sovereignty— rather than governmental sovereignty—that defines the American constitutional system.

The argument that spending is, for constitutional purposes, protected political speech proceeds as follows: "contribution and spending limitations impose direct *quantity restrictions* [emphasis added] on political communication and association. . . . A restriction on the amount of money a person or group can spend on political communication during a campaign necessarily reduces the quantity of expression by restricting the number of issues discussed, the depth of their exploration, and the size of the audience reached. This is because virtually every means of communicating in today's mass society requires the expenditure of money. . . . The electorate's increasing dependence on television, radio, and other mass media for news and information has made these expensive modes of communication indispensable instruments of effective political speech."[26]

So sending messages requires money, and restrictions on money therefore restrict such sending: they limit the "quantity" of speech. The quantity of speech is an important constitutional value not simply because speakers have an interest in advancing their views, but because audiences—citizens, as the ultimate political authority— have an interest in the fullest airing of issues, without control by government over what is said or how much is said. Citizens may of course tune the messages out, but because of the audience/ citizen interest, state restrictions on the quantity of speech face a chilly reception.

More particularly, the Court held that contributions and expenditures both have First Amendment protection, but that regulations of contributions are less offensive to the First Amendment than regulations of expenditures. Contributions are lower in the constitutional scale in part because the principal value of a contribution lies in the fact that it is given, quite apart from its size. Though contributing more reveals greater intensity of support, it does not itself add to the content of the basic message, which is "I support Jones." This claim—here I plead against interest—strikes me as preposterous. Giving lots of money might well express a different belief than giving a smaller amount: namely, the belief that the candidate I contribute to is a *much* better candidate than the competitor, and that it is *very* important that he or she be elected. Apart from this implausible consideration about the independence of the content of the message sent by a contribution from the magnitude of that contribution, the Court also noted that if contributions are regulated, citizens still have other ways to get their message out—by spending in ways that are not coordinated with a campaign.

Neither in *Buckley* nor elsewhere does the Court contemplate the possibility that electoral speech—though assuredly political—should be, as a general matter, easier to regulate than political speech more generally, easier, say, than nonelectoral, political speech in the public sphere. This possibility might have been defended along the following lines:[27] the Court might have treated speech in the electoral setting generally along the lines that it has treated speech in the setting of ballot access law. Thus the Court has generally taken the view that restrictions on ballot access—say, restrictions on write-in ballots that prevent voters from writing in Daffy Duck or restrictions on fusion candidates that prevent third parties from cross-nominating major party candidates—are permissible because the point of ballots is to select officeholders, not to have open-ended debate of political ideas: "the purpose of casting, counting, and recording votes is to elect public officials, not to serve as a general forum for political expression."[28] Similarly, the Court might have said that the principal forum for political expression is the informal public sphere, not the electoral setting in particular. The latter is a specific institution, designed for a particular purpose—the selection of officials—and can permissibly be regulated in light of that purpose. So if the purpose of elections is to translate public opinion into an authorization to exercise power—to provide an accurate register of the state of collective opinion, rather than to form public opinion itself—then regulations designed to ensure such translation would be permissible, even if they have the effect of reducing the quantity of speech, in just the way that it is permissible to restrict write-in candidacies in light of the institutional purpose of ballots.

One reason for rejecting this approach is that—particularly in a world of virtually permanent campaigning—it would require difficult line-drawing exercises to distinguish electoral speech from other forms of political speech. Those distinctions are much crisper in the ballot setting, where the issue is whether and how a particular person's name will appear on a well-defined ballot. Moreover, some ways of drawing the line and regulating electoral speech might end up providing excessive protection for incumbents. Still, I don't think this criticism is compelling. After all, line-drawing is already necessary, as for example in the area of issue advocacy.

More fundamentally, I suspect that the Court would—and should—reject the idea that electoral speech performs a mere "translation function," and would also reject the conception of democracy associated with that idea. Elections, they might say, are important not only to translating an antecedently articulated collective opinion into political power but to crystallizing such opinion in ways that enable the exercise of power to take guidance from it.[29] So we ought not to treat electoral speech as narrowly institutional speech, with a well-defined purpose, or to make the permissibility of regulation turn on such treatment.

Returning to *Buckley*: the second main idea is that the state has a compelling interest in avoiding the appearance and reality of *quid pro quo*—dollars for votes—corruption. "Corruption," the Court says in 1985, "is a subversion of the political process," and the "hallmark of corruption is the financial *quid pro quo*: dollars for political favors."[30] The essential point is that the corruption rationale is narrowly understood—in effect, as a generalization of bribery law.

The Court allows that there *may* be other compelling rationales for regulating spending, but insists that none has yet been identified. In particular, the state is said not to have a compelling interest in "leveling the playing field"—ensuring equal opportunity for political influence. FECA, the Court says, was "aimed in part at equalizing the relative ability of all voters to affect electoral outcomes by placing a ceiling on expenditures for political expression by citizens and groups." But the majority opinion rejects this rationale: "the concept that government may restrict the speech of some elements of our society in order to enhance the relative voice of others is wholly foreign to the First Amendment."[31] In this important remark, the Court does not dispute that restricting the voice of some may enhance the relative voice of others—indeed, that it might be necessary to enhancing their voice. Nor does it deny that such enhancement would be a very good thing, a legitimate and perhaps substantial governmental objective. Instead, the majority asserts that the First Amendment bars the door to achieving equalization through restriction on First Amendment liberties.

With those two elements in place, the rest of the system follows pretty straightforwardly. Because contributions merit lesser First Amendment protection, and because restrictions on "large contributions" are well designed to avoid the appearance and reality of political quid pro quo, restrictions on such contributions are permissible, though only if they are addressed to quid pro quo corruption, and that means only if the regulated contributions are sufficiently large to pose a genuine threat of such corruption. Because expenditures merit especially stringent protection, and because restrictions on expenditures do not advance the one concededly compelling interest in the arena of electoral finance—the interest in avoiding the appearance or reality of quid pro quo corruption—expenditure restrictions are impermissible, unless they are voluntary, as under the public financing scheme for presidential elections that was part of FECA.

6 Persisting Constraints

In the period since *Buckley*, the two fundamentals of this framework have been restated and reinforced, but not changed.

Thus, the Court continues to hold that the First Amendment protects both contributions and expenditures, and has continued to emphasize the importance of spending in contributing to the *quantity* of speech, and thus to the interest of the audience, even more than it has emphasized the importance of protecting the interests of speakers. Because of this emphasis on quantity of speech, the Court has held that the identity of the speaker is not especially relevant to the permissibility of regulation. Particularly important and revealing in this connection is the 1978 *Bellotti* decision, in which the Court held that states could not regulate corporate spending on ballot initiatives. The fact that the speakers were not individual citizens but corporations did not matter because the protected value was not the corporation's interest in speaking but the audience's interest in a full airing of views.[32] This is "the type of speech indispensable to decision making in a democracy," and its value "in terms of its capacity for informing the public does not depend upon the identity of its source, whether corporation, association, union, or individual."[33] "The Constitution," according to the Court majority, "often protects interests broader than those of the party seeking their vindication. The First Amendment, in particular, serves significant societal interests," in particular the interest in the "free discussion of governmental affairs." So the Court vindicated the expressive liberty of the corporation (in this case, the bank) not because of any special concern for the corporation's interests, or because of a judgment that the regulation was especially burdensome to those interests, but because of a concern for the wider public interest in informed decision making. The essential idea is captured in a paraphrase of Mill's reason for thinking that it is as bad to silence one as to silence all: "Were an opinion a personal possession of no value except to the owner; if to be obstructed in the enjoyment of it were simply a private injury, it would make some difference who the injury was inflicted upon. But the peculiar evil of silencing the expression of an opinion is, that it is robbing the human race"[34]—or if that seems excessively high-minded, let's just say "that it is robbing the voters of relevant information."

As to the second element, the Court shows virtually no disposition to break from *Buckley's* claim that there is no such thing as a process being corrupt because it is unfair, because it provides citizens with fundamentally unequal chances to influence the political process—more precisely, that even if such inequality is a form of unfairness, it is not of the same constitutional magnitude as quid pro quo corruption, and therefore does not justify restrictions on expenditures.[35] Put otherwise, the Court continues to be very solicitous of the interests of citizens as spectators, information gatherers, observers—as consumers of information and argument who can decide for themselves which messages to listen to—but to show much less concern for the interests of citizens as activists and participants, seeking fair chances to influence others in the political arena.

In one post-*Buckley* case, the Court majority has acknowledged concerns about fair access—about a corruption extending beyond quid pro quo. In *Austin v. Michigan Chamber of Commerce*, the Court upheld a Michigan law prohibiting corporations from using general treasury funds for independent expenditures in connection with state candidate elections.[36] They upheld it because of concerns about the "corrosive and distorting effects of immense aggregations of wealth that are accumulated with the help of the corporate form and that have little or no correlation with the public's support for the corporation's political ideas." This talk about "corrosive and distorting effects" acknowledges a corruption of democratic process that extends beyond quid pro quo. But the case, which drew a strongly worded dissent from Justice Scalia, has been virtually without impact on subsequent decisions, largely because it has been interpreted as arising specifically from traditional concerns about corporations and wealth accumulated with the help of the corporate form, and not as standing for a more general proposition about the effects of "aggregations of wealth that have little or no correlation with the public's support for the political ideas of the holders of that wealth."

With the two fundamentals of the Court's analysis remaining essentially fixed, proposed regulations continue to face very stringent, in practice nearly insuperable hurdles.

The situation with contribution regulations has not changed fundamentally, though it may be somewhat stricter than it appeared after *Buckley* because the Court, as mentioned, has focused principally on the importance of an anticorruption rationale, and not on the lesser First Amendment importance of contributions. Because of its focus on corruption, the Court has said that states cannot limit contributions to groups running ballot initiatives: because there is no danger of quid pro quo with a candidate, there is no problem.[37] Similarly, lower courts have been overturning laws with "low limits" on contributions ($100 for state contests). Contribution limits cannot, for example, be justified by "level playing field" arguments, or the importance of enabling most people to play, or bringing more citizens into the process. The limit must be set such that there is a plausible concern about quid pro quo: because it seems implausible that you can buy many favors from the mayor of St. Louis for $100, a low limit of that kind provokes suspicion that the aim is to level the playing field, not to fight corruption. In addition, there may well be an emerging Court majority for the view that party contributions to candidates are, as it were, born pure: because political parties are coalitions of candidates, those parties cannot be corrupting candidates by directly supporting their campaigns. According to this view, party contributions are to be treated on a par with the candidates' own expenditures, which cannot be regulated because there is no threat of corruption. Justices Rehnquist, Scalia, Thomas, and Kennedy have recently taken this position, and it may eventually win support from Breyer, O'Connor, or Souter.[38]

The situation with expenditures is similarly crisp, largely stable, with a few signs of increased hostility to anything that suggests limits. Apart from the special case of independent corporate expenditures on candidate campaigns (as in *Austin*), the Court has not upheld mandatory expenditure restrictions, nor are there signs that they will.

Thus, in 1985 the Court held that "independent" expenditures cannot be regulated, even if the candidate supported by those expenditures has accepted public money with associated voluntary limits.[39] Moreover, it has adopted a pretty broad interpretation of "independent." The key point is "uncoordinated": if spending is not explicitly coordinated with a candidate, then quid pro quo concerns are absent. So in *Colorado Republican Federal Campaign Committee v. FEC*, the Court opinion held that spending by the Republican Party to defeat Senator Tim Wirth was an independent expenditure because Wirth's Republican opponent candidate had not yet been chosen, and no exchange of support for favors could have been in play. In short, party spending in support of a candidate is not, as such, coordinated, and may therefore be protected.

Finally, as the definition of "independent" is capacious, so, too, the solicitude for independent spenders, thus defined, is very great. In a 1994 Eighth Circuit decision, the circuit court rejected a provision of a Minnesota public financing law that would have provided increased support for publicly financed candidates facing opposition from independent spending by PACs.[40] Efforts by the state to match that spending would have amounted, in effect, to chilling the speech of those independent opponents. The theme here is potentially very important: the trouble with this regulation is that it puts the state in the position of trying to reduce the quantity of speech, and that is objectionable.

One case that looks different is a decision in the Eighth Circuit upholding a provision of a Minnesota public financing law that removes expenditure caps from candidates who have accepted such caps as a condition for receiving public money, but who face opponents who do not and who spend more than a specified amount.[41] The challengers said that the state's incentives were too good to be voluntary: that the state was in effect coercing people into the public system, and trying to reduce the quantity of speech—likely to be the chief objection to waivers on expenditure limits in public financing schemes. Similarly, the District Court for the Maine District has upheld provisions of the Maine law that provide additional support for clean money candidates facing high-spending challengers.[42]

7 Democracy and Campaign Finance

The current system of campaign finance appears to be at odds with the principle of equal opportunity for political influence. In the name of a constitutionally basic liberty of speech, however, the Court has resisted reform efforts that appeal to that principle. It is essential to understand exactly what is—and what is not—being said by the Court and allied critics of reform. To reiterate: the Court has not said that the current system already ensures equal opportunity, or that equal opportunity for influence is a trivial or illegitimate political concern, or that all policies aimed at promoting it are constitutionally infirm, or that proposed reforms would be ineffective at advancing that value. Thus it is not true, as one recent discussion states, that *"Buckley* outright rejected the legitimacy of the asserted interest in equalizing the relative ability of individuals and groups to affect election outcomes."[43] *Buckley* speaks to the magnitude of the asserted interest, not its legitimacy. It is hard to see what, in *Buckley,* would stand in the way of a redistributive voucher scheme with benefits targeted on low-income citizens, so long as the scheme was not accompanied by expenditure restrictions.[44] Instead the Court has said that neither governments nor citizens themselves acting directly through initiative can legitimately seek to equalize opportunities for political influence *by means of regulations that reduce the quantity of speech.* Such reduction conflicts with the First Amendment's free speech guarantee. In the name of equality, it puts illegitimate restrictions on freedom of speech.

I want to focus on this claim about illegitimate restrictions. But before getting there, I need to consider an argument to the effect that there is no deep conflict between liberty and equality in this area, and that the *Buckley* framework is not a hurdle to achieving fair equality. Thus it might be said that an ideal scheme of financing would accommodate both expressive liberty and political equality by providing subsidies to all eligible candidates (or to political parties) while attaching no conditions to the receipt of those subsidies—no restrictions on expenditures by candidates who accept them (the current system of financing of presidential elections does attach conditions to the acceptance of public money). By establishing *floors* that enable candidates to compete without having to appease the interests of contributors, the scheme would go some way to equalizing opportunity for influence. By excluding *ceilings,* it would achieve that equalization without reducing the level of speech, thus eliminating worries about conflict with the first part of the principle of political equality. Worries about public subsidies because they prompt concerns about incumbency protection, or other forms of official manipulation, could be addressed by using alternative strategies for providing floors: for example, tax credits, deductions, or vouchers that enable individual citizens to finance elections, while eliminating the cost to them of contributing.[45]

Put aside questions about whether such an "all floors/no ceilings" approach, with its focus on candidates, fully addresses the concerns about opportunities for citizen influence. Still, it faces an obvious objection. Private contributions and expenditures may well swamp floors unaccompanied by restrictions, so that no real equalization of opportunities for influence results. In response, the floors-only proponent might say that the benefits of spending more money decline as quantities of money increase; the production function for votes has a negative second derivative. Although this response has some force, it hardly seems sufficient to dismiss the liberty/equality issue. If we take equal opportunity for influence as a basic political value, then we cannot make its satisfaction contingent on a speculative judgment of this kind about the responsiveness of votes to spending.

So a scheme of public financing likely needs to be paired with some limits, and some incentives to accept the limits. Consider, for example, a system of voluntary public financing in which public money goes only to candidates who agree to forgo private money; in which nonpublic candidates face reasonably low contribution limits (say, $250 for statewide offices); and in which additional subsidies go to public money candidates who face independent expenditures or high-spending private money challengers. The Maine system is of this kind, and critics complain that it includes too wide a range of limits. The crux of the worry is that the regulation has the state taking the position that less money, and therefore less speech, is better. And surely they would object still more strenuously to more straightforward limits—for example, a narrower conception of issue advocacy that would result in a widening of regulable expenditures, or expenditure ceilings, or a less capacious conception of an independent expenditure. Though the floors-only idea seems very attractive, then, I don't think we can so easily evade the issue.

Returning, then, to the issue of "illegitimate restrictions of speech," I note first that the phrase is not a pleonasm. We have bribery laws, child pornography laws, and contribution limits; restrictions on the time, manner, and place of speech are widely accepted, and some-times—as with restrictions on campaigning within 100 feet of polling places—those restrictions apply exclusively to political speech: in short, some restrictions of speech are acceptable. Moreover, the kinds of restrictions of speech that are most profoundly objectionable—that offend most directly against the value of freedom of expression—are restrictions very different from those contemplated by campaign finance regulations.[46] First, they are directed against speech with certain contents or viewpoints. Such regulations threaten to freeze the existing state of opinion, and perhaps to insulate the government from popular criticism. But campaign finance regulations are neutral with respect to content and viewpoint.

Second, restrictions are objectionable when they are directed against certain persons or groups. They say in effect that some person or group is not worthy of being heard, or have the objective effect of imposing an undue burden on the expression of some group. Again, the regulations under contemplation appear not to be of this kind.

Suppose, then, that regulations are content- and viewpoint-neutral and do not impose undue burdens on some citizens or groups. Why might they still represent unacceptable burdens on freedom of speech? It might be—third—that they restrict more speech than is necessary for achieving their goal of ensuring equal opportunity for political influence: perhaps, that is, we can find alternative regulations that are less restrictive but more or less as effective. But absent optimistic and highly speculative assumptions about declining marginal benefits of money, I see no reason to suppose that the proposed regulations are, in this way, unreasonable.

Consider, then, a content- and viewpoint-neutral regulation that is not unduly burdensome to any group and no more restrictive of speech than is necessary—given available alternatives—for ensuring equal opportunity for political influence. Why should the sheer fact that it reduces the quantity of speech make it so objectionable? Why does that suffice to trump the importance of equal opportunity for influence?

Two answers come to mind. The first is instrumental and concerns threats to the quality of decisions that might result from restrictions. Recall the Court's statement in *Buckley* that "A restriction on the amount of money a person or group can spend on political communication during a campaign necessarily reduces the quantity of expression by restricting the number of issues discussed, the depth of their exploration, and the size of the audience reached." Here, the restrictions on money, which lead to limits on the quantity of speech, are tied to a threat of making worse collective decisions because the restrictions limit the flow of information and prevent a sufficiently close examination of the issues. In short, the restrictions make the outcomes worse.

This first, instrumental argument against reducing the quantity of expression seems very weak. It is not true that restrictions on money "necessarily" restrict issue range, depth of exploration, or audience size. Though they do limit quantity, the effects of quantity limits—whether they transform into limits on quality—are contingent on the extent and character of the restrictions, and what the money would have been used for: if the money goes to more attack ads, then quantity declines, but not range, depth, or audience size. Indeed, if Steve Ansolabehere and Shanto Iyengar are right, spending on negative ads turns voters off. So an increase in expenditures may produce a decline in audience size.[47]

A second argument is intrinsic and plays a large role in hostility to regulation: it claims that restrictions on the quantity of speech are objectionable not because they worsen political outcomes, but because they worsen the democratic process itself by distorting the proper role of citizens within it. In short, such restrictions conflict with the ideal of democracy itself. The intrinsic argument is founded on an idea about

individual responsibility and its role in democracy. It says that democratic process, properly understood, assigns to individual citizens the
right and responsibility to decide how much information is sufficient,
and to distinguish between reliable and unreliable sources—just as
democracy assigns to individual citizens the responsibility to decide
how much they wish to participate, as indicated by the embrace of an
equality of opportunity rather than equality of influence principle. But
this assignment of responsibility is undermined when collective judgments about appropriate levels and kinds of information replace individual judgments, whether those collective judgments come from
legislatures or citizen majorities acting directly through referenda. It is
incompatible with this idea of democracy to seek to correct, through
collective means, for biases or imbalances in available information,
except perhaps by increasing the level of speech. We cannot restrict the
quantity of speech on the ground that citizens may be misled by what
they hear, or may be put off because they hear too much or because
what they hear is so relentlessly negative. Thus the Court's essential
claim in *Buckley*: "the First Amendment denies government the power
to determine that spending is wasteful, or excessive, or unwise. In the
free society ordained by our constitution it is not the government, but
the people—individually as citizens and candidates and collectively
as associations and political committees—who must retain control
over the quantity and range of debate on public issues in a political
campaign."[48]

"The people," as the passage between the dashes underscores, must
here be understood distributively, as the set of individual citizens and
associations of citizens, not as a single collective authority. The Court
here denies that collective responsibility extends to the issue of how
much should be said in an election, or to the range of issues that ought
to be covered. Though the intrinsic argument emphasizes the role of
individual responsibility, it does not deny the importance of a division
of labor within democracy between collective and individual responsibility. Instead it holds that we discharge our collective responsibility
to uphold democracy by ensuring an open process of communication—
with no restrictions on the flow of information or the content of communications—that enables citizens to act with political responsibility
by making their own judgments about political affairs, including judgments about what to pay attention to.

This intrinsic argument has considerable force. It does not commit
the critic of regulation to saying, for example, that property rights or
private liberties take precedence over democracy. Kathleen Sullivan
correctly observes that "Arguments for greater limits on political contributions and expenditure typically suggest that any claims for indi-

vidual liberty to spend political money ought to yield to an overriding interest in a well-functioning democracy."[49] The critic I have described here turns that argument around. This critic accepts the overriding interest in a well-functioning democracy, but argues that a "well-functioning democracy," properly conceived, does not permit regulation of speech in the name of equal opportunity for political influence. The critic who endorses the intrinsic argument does not say: "Yes, the current regime of campaign finance injures democracy, but this injury is justified by the need to ensure that citizens can freely use their private property" (though of course some critics may say that). Instead, the argument is that the value of democracy itself condemns regulation, because of the conception of responsibility ingredient in the best conception of democracy. The dissent in *Nixon v. Shrink* suggests just this point: "the right to free speech is a right held by each American, not by Americans en masse. The Court in *Buckley* provided no basis for suppressing the speech of an individual candidate simply because other candidates (or candidates in the aggregate) may succeed in reaching the voting public. Any such reasoning would fly in the face of the premise of our political system—liberty vested in individual hands safeguards the functioning of our democracy."[50]

Observing the earlier discussion of equal *opportunity* for influence, the critic argues that a plausible principle of political equality, suited to a political society of free and equal persons, needs to include some account of individual political responsibility. So the argument might be put this way: the principle of political equality includes a right of free political speech and an associated idea of political responsibility, implicit in its hostility to content and viewpoint regulation and the distinction between equalizing opportunity for influence and equalizing influence itself. That's part of what is involved in treating democratic citizens as free. But once we embrace this notion of political responsibility, we must accept, too, that collective regulation of the quantity of speech is incompatible with democracy.

Though forceful, this argument is doubly deficient. First, it misconceives the case for regulation by representing it as dependent on a judgment about who is entitled to decide whether the quantity and kind of information are sufficient. The argument for regulation based on the principle of equal opportunity for influence is not of this kind. Though it leads to restrictions on the quantity of speech, those restrictions are the by-product of a principle of political fairness, not of the claim that the legislature or the majority of citizens are better judges of the value of political messages than citizens and their associations acting separately. The problem that the regulations are designed to address is not that citizens may be misled or put off by what they hear, but that they have a powerful objection to a process whose organization does not even make an effort to ensure equality of opportunity for influence among citizens who are said to be equal. No insult to the freedom of citizens, or to their capacity for responsible judgment, is implied or suggested.

Second, though the intrinsic argument against restrictions stakes its case on the value of democratic process, it neglects an essential point about that process. The point might be put in terms of the different interests of citizens in a democracy or in terms of roles associated with those interests.[51] The *Buckley* framework—like much democratic theory in the "elite" tradition associated with Schumpeter—casts citizens principally in the role of audience. As participants in democratic process, they have a fundamental interest in listening to debates, acquiring information through both formal political communications and more informal processes of discussion,[52] arriving at judgments about policies and candidates, and acting as political agents when they express those judgments at the polls, making informed judgments among competing candidates. But in a democracy, citizens are also agents, participants, speakers, who may aim to reshape both the terms of political debate and its results, by running for office or seeking to influence the views of candidates, the outcomes of elections, and the interelection conduct of politics.[53] A requirement of equal opportunity for political influence aims to ensure that they are in a position to play that role, should they wish to take it on. Of course, they may also wish to influence politics through conduct in the informal public sphere. But, once again, the principle of political equality is confined to the organization of the arrangements of authoritative collective decision making.

The claim that "democracy" casts citizens in this role and respects their expressive-participatory interests might appear to depend on some special philosophical view, whether Aristotelian or Rousseauean, about the value of political participation in a well-lived human life. But it need not be presented as so dependent. The idea that citizens have a fundamental interest in bringing their conceptions of justice to bear on the conduct of political life is common to a range of philosophies of life.[54] A characteristic feature of different philosophies—different comprehensive doctrines, in Rawls's phrase—is that they assign to us strong reasons for exercising responsible judgment about the proper directions of collective life and aiming to correct those directions particularly when they are unjust; and those reasons are all the more compelling when authoritative collective decisions are made in the name of those over whom they are the enforced. Aristotelians found those reasons on the central role of civic engagement in a flourishing human life; Rousseaueans on the fundamental value of individual autonomy and the connection of such autonomy with political participation in a democratic polity; and some religiously based philosophies on the commanding personal obligation to ensure social justice and respect human dignity. These alternative philosophies of life each acknowledge that citizens have substantial, sometimes compelling reasons for addressing political affairs, and a correspondingly fundamental "expressive" interest in favorable conditions for forming judgments about the proper directions of policy and acting on those judgments— by presenting them to others, and seeking to correct for injustices by acting in the political arena. Failure to acknowledge the weight of those reasons for the agent and to acknowledge the claims to opportunities for effective influence that emerge from them reflects a failure to respect the democratic idea of citizens as equals.

The weight of these reasons is reflected in part by the first component of the principle of political equality, which requires equal rights of political speech, association, and participation. But these reasons do not simply support a right to participate. They also yield a right to opportunities for effective influence on the political environment. Moreover, because claims for effective influence reflect the standing of citizens as equals, those claims are for an equal chance to influence: a failure to provide such is a failure to acknowledge that equal standing.

More particularly, the aim must be to mitigate the impact on effectiveness in the role of citizen of irrelevant facts about economic position—particularly when that impact is a result of the design of arrangements of binding collective decision making. And that means a different understanding of the division of individual and collective labor. Individuals remain responsible for finding the signals in the political noise that surrounds them, and for judging how far they wish to go in taking on the role of participant, agent, speaker. Thus we keep free political speech, without content or viewpoint restrictions, and maintain the influence/opportunity-to-influence distinction. When it comes to acquiring the information needed to play this role, collective responsibility is to ensure open communication and perhaps encourage, in the familiar Brandeisian phrase, "more speech." But collective responsibility extends to ensuring that when citizens do decide to operate as political agents, they have a fair chance for influence. We cannot reasonably expect people to respect the results of a political process whose basic organization effectively assigns greater opportunities for political influence to those who are economically advantaged.

What makes the current constitutional framework so disturbing is that it says that the people cannot permissibly adopt this conception of democracy and citizenship and experiment with ways to secure equal opportunities for political influence while also protecting political speech. It says that the constitution enacts Joseph Schumpeter's *Capitalism, Socialism, and Democracy*.

To underscore the point, I conclude by contrasting the framework of constitutional reasoning described here with the framework presented by the *European Court of Human Rights* in the case of *Bowman v. The United Kingdom* (1998).[55] The case involved a challenge to a 1983 British law (the Representation of the People Act) that prohibited individuals from spending more than five pounds either favoring or opposing the election of a particular parliamentary candidate in the period immediately preceding an election. The case was decided under Article 10 of the European Convention on Human Rights, which states that the exercise of freedom of expression "may be subject to such formalities, conditions, restrictions or penalties as are prescribed by law and are necessary in a democratic society." More particularly, the court needed to decide whether the regulation was more stringent than necessary to foster a democratic society, where such fostering was understood to comprise three legitimate aims: establishing fair conditions for competing candidates, ensuring the independence of candidates from interest groups, and preventing political debate around election time from focusing on single issues rather than matters of broad concern. The court found the five-pound limit excessive. The crucial point here, however, is not the conclusion, but the court's recognition that the three aforementioned values are aspects of democracy, and that promoting them provides an entirely legitimate reason for restricting the quantity of speech in the period just prior to an election. Whatever the wisdom of the court's judgment in the *Bowman* case, the framework—with its recognition that political fairness and freedom of expression are both ingredients of democracy—is more suited to a democracy than the *Buckley* framework.[56]

8 Conclusion

A fundamental proposition of democratic thought is that our collective decisions should reflect our judgments (the judgments of individual citizens), formed through open processes of communication, unconstrained by collective judgments about what and how much we should hear. But this important principle must not lead to the undemocratic proposition that citizens are equals only when we sit in the audience, listening to what others say, and unequals when we take to the political stage. The principle of political equality requires that we accommodate the interests of citizens as audience and actor. We need to preserve a system of open political communication that enables citizens to exercise their deliberative responsibilities by forming their views against a background of adequate information and rich debate, and also ensures equal access to the public arena: we should not organize the political arena as a system of unequal opportunities. Designing a regulatory scheme that promises both will be hard: we need some experimentation. But we do not solve the conundrum by throwing out half the democratic ideal.[57]

Notes

I am delighted to include this paper in a volume dedicated to Judith Thomson. In this, as in everything I write, I aspire to meet her high standards of clarity. I am sure that I have not succeeded, but am deeply indebted to Judy for demonstrating in all her work that it is possible to say important things without sacrificing clarity. Readers may wonder why a paper that emphasizes the importance of equality belongs in a volume in honor of Judy, who has not written on this subject. Observing Judy Thomson up close over many years, I see someone dedicated in her bones to eradicating the indefensible privileges that disfigure public life. I know she has some hesitations about the line of argument in this paper, but she breathes an egalitarian sensibility.

1. See *Capitalism, Socialism, and Democracy*, pp. 21, 22. Not that Schumpeter himself was especially concerned about ensuring more informed electoral judgments. What comes from him is the thesis that we should think of democracy as a particular way of organizing competition for political leadership—that instead of using "birth, lot, wealth, violence, co-optation, learning, appointment, or examination" to resolve the contest for political power, democracies resolve it through voting in regular elections—and think of the role of citizens as analogous to that of consumers in the product market.

2. See *Dagget v. Webster*, U.S. District Court, District of Maine, slip op. (November 5, 1999 and January 7, 2000).

3. More precisely, the system allows no private funds beyond the initial seed money required to qualify for public funds. For discussion, see Ellen Miller, David Donnelly, and Janice Fine, "Going Public." This article is published along with responses in Joshua Cohen and Joel Roger (eds.), *Money and Politics: Financing Elections Democratically*.

4. For illuminating discussion of the terrain, see Charles Beitz, *Political Equality*.

5. I return to this limitation, and note some reasons for it later, at pp. 53–55. On the informal public sphere, see Jürgen Habermas, *Between Facts and Norms*; on the background culture, see John Rawls, *Political Liberalism*, pp. 14, 382n. 13.

6. See *Political Liberalism*, pp. 327–330. The general idea is familiar. For example, in the 1986 case of *Davis v. Bandemer*, which concerned political gerrymandering, the Supreme Court indicates that equal protection problems emerge when an "electoral system is arranged in a manner that will consistently degrade influence on the political process as a whole," *Davis v. Bandemer* 478 US 109, 132 (1986). Notice the importance attached to "influence on the political process as a whole," and not simply electoral influence. Lani Guinier refers to the norm that "each voter should enjoy the same opportunity to influence political outcomes," *The Tyranny of the Majority: Fundamental Fairness in Representative Democracy*, p. 152. She emphasizes "the importance of an equal opportunity to influence public policy, and not just to cast a ballot" (p. 134).

7. To use the standard constitutional jargon, equality of opportunity would provide a compelling interest.

8. John Rawls, *A Theory of Justice*, p. 63. Similar requirements of equal political opportunity are found in a variety of accounts of democracy. See, for example, Robert Dahl, *Democracy and Its Critics*, who attaches considerable importance to equal opportunities to express preferences and citizen control over the political agenda. I am indebted to Chappell Lawson for underscoring the consistency with Dahl's view.

9. *Theory of Justice*, p. 197.

10. Here, I disagree with Dworkin's account of political equality in "What Is Equality? Part 4: Political Equality." Dworkin there rejects the idea that political equality has autonomous importance.

11. In discussions of equal opportunity in the context of education, the focus is often on adequacy, in part because a number of state constitutions in the United States guarantee an adequate level of education.

12. David Estlund explores these concerns in his excellent paper, "Political Quality."

13. Rawls, *Theory of Justice*, p. 477. In "The Natural Goodness of Humanity," I trace this idea to Rousseau.

14. Bruce Cain and Kathleen Sullivan both accept equal voting influence, but reject equal opportunity for electoral influence in "Moralism and Realism in Campaign Finance Reform." At p. 136, Cain indicates that equalizing electoral influence through restrictions on political expenditures threatens excessive responsiveness to "ill-formed majoritarian preferences." The basis for that presumption is unclear, but appears to derive from the idea that spending limits restrict the flow of information, and thus give too much sway to uniformed preferences. Sullivan's case is far more plausible. See Kathleen M. Sullivan, "Political Money and Freedom of Speech," esp. pp. 674–675. She points out, rightly, that the equalizing opportunities for electoral influence will require some regulations of election-related expression, but that no such regulations are required by equally weighted votes, however broadly we interpret the range of unacceptable gerrymanders. So we will need to draw some lines between electoral and the political speech that occurs in informal political discussion. The result may be either unacceptable restrictions of political speech in the informal public sphere, if the boundaries around electoral speech are loosely drawn, or only minimal correction for unequal chances for influence, if those boundaries are drawn more crisply. For if we know one thing from our experience with regulation in this field, it is that every regulation represents an invitation to invest in political strategies that are equally effective but circumvent the regulation. One might have thought that these "practical difficulties," as Sullivan calls them, would prompt efforts at legal invention. Sullivan puzzlingly treats them as insuperable hurdles.

15. To be sure, the boundaries are vague, as is amply demonstrated by the problem of regulating issue advertising.

16. I use the 1996 numbers because they come from the most recent presidential election. The $2.4 billion comprises public money for the Presidential campaign ($211m), small donors contributing less than $200 ($734m), larger donors contributing more than $200 ($597m), PACs ($234m), "soft money," which is contributed to the parties but not to be spent in connection with federal elections ($262m), and candidates themselves ($262m, led by Steve Forbes's $37m).

17. From an online publication by Center for Responsive Politics.

18. Level of political interest is measured by responses to survey questions that ask about the respondent's interest in local and national affairs. See Sidney Verba, Kay Lehman Schlozman, and Henry E. Brady, *Voice and Equality*, p. 553. The finding is striking, but not surprising. Someone with little political interest, thus measured, might be

highly motivated to give to a candidate because of a concern about some particular issue, and assuming a declining marginal utility of money the cost to the contributor is very small. Moreover, people with high capacity but low interest are more likely to give than people with low capacity and comparably low interest because the former are more likely to be asked for money. My guess is that the finding that financial contributions (unlike other forms of activity) are largely explained by capacity rather than interest is probably true for a wide range of activities, and almost certainly true of any activity in which professional fund-raisers are involved because they target capacity, not motivation. Perhaps contributions to religious organizations are an exception.

19. *Voice and Equality*, pp. 303, 358, 361–364, 477, 512, 516.

20. Federal candidates are, however, permitted to solicit soft money. For discussion of the complexities of soft money, see Note in *Harvard Law Review*, "Soft Money: The Current Rules and the Case for Reform."

21. The literature is vast. See Gary Jacobson, *Money in Congressional Elections*; Jonathan Krasno and Donald P. Green, "Preempting Quality Challengers in House Elections"; Stephen Ansolabehere and James M. Snyder, "Money, Elections, and Candidate Quality."

22. If the capacity to raise money (especially from organized groups) reflects the powers of office, we should not conclude that power is therefore a source of money *rather than* money a source of power—as Ansolabehere and Snyder suggest in "Money and Institutional Power." After all, it is not implausible that greater decision-making capacity (due to greater powers associated with office) is associated with greater fund-raising capacity because funders are interested in influencing the exercise of official powers and target their investments accordingly. So powers of office beget money because money is a source of influence (over the exercise of powers).

23. *Behind the Oval Office*, pp. 150–151.

24. "Free Speech and the Widening Gyre of Fund-Raising: Why Campaign Spending Limits May Not Violate the First Amendment After All," 94 *Columbia Law Review* 1281 (1994).

25. *Buckley v. Valeo*, 424 US 1 (1976).

26. *Buckley v. Valeo*, 424 US 1, 19 (1976).

27. See C. Edwin Baker, "Campaign Expenditures and Free Speech."

28. *Burdick v. Takushi*, 504 US 428, 445 (1992); see also *Timmons v. Twin Cities Area New Party*, 117 S. Ct. 1364, 1377 (1997) (Stevens, J., joined by Ginsburg and Souter, JJ., dissenting), where the dissent attributes this view to the majority.

29. Samuel L. Popkin, *The Reasoning Voter: Communication and Persuasion in Presidential Campaigns*; Arthur Lupia and Matthew McCubbins, *The Democratic Dilemma: Can Citizens Learn What They Need to Know?*

30. 470 US 480, 497.

31. *Buckley v. Valeo*, 424 US 1, 48–49 (1976).

32. *First National Bank v. Bellotti*, 435 US 765, 767 (1978).

33. Ibid. at 777.

34. Mill, *On Liberty*, chap. 2, paragraph 1.

35. As I noted earlier, *Nixon v. Shrink* may signal a change of direction on this essential point.

36. *Austin v. Michigan Chamber of Commerce*, 494 US 652 (1990).

37. *Citizens Against Rent Control v. City of Berkeley*, 454 US 290 (1981).

38. *Colorado Republican Federal Campaign Committee v. FEC*.

39. *FEC v. NCPAC*, 470 US 480 (1985) (overturning limits on independent expenditures on behalf of Presidential candidates who have accepted public funding).

40. *Day v. Holahan*, 34 F.3d 1356 (8th Cir. 1994), cert. denied, 513 US 1127 (1995).

41. *Rosensteil v. Rodriguez*, 101 F.3d 1544 (8th Cir. 1996), cert. denied, 520 US 1229 (1997). Also, *Gable v. Patton*, 142 F.3d 940 (6th Cir. 1998).

42. *Daggett v. Webster*.

43. *Writing Reform: A Guide to Drafting State and Local Campaign Finance Laws*, Deborah Goldberg (ed.), 1–7. The only evidence cited for the proposition quoted in the text is the infamous line in *Buckley* about the impermissibility of "restricting the speech of some elements of our society in order to enhance the relative voice of others." But the passage is specifically about restricting speech, not about the legitimacy of the interest in ensuring equal opportunity for political influence.

44. Bruce Ackerman's voucher scheme is so accompanied: it excludes real money, and permits only voucher-based expenditures. See Bruce Ackerman, "The Patriot Option."

45. See Zach Polett, "Empower Citizens," and Bruce Ackerman, "The Patriot Option."

46. This paragraph and the next two draw on Rawls's discussion of the three conditions that an acceptable regulation must meet. See *Political Liberalism*, pp. 357–358.

47. *Going Negative* (New York: Free Press, 1995).

48. *Buckley v. Valeo*, 424 US 1, 57 (1976).

49. "Political Money," p. 671.

50. Slip op., at 17.

51. For a parallel discussion, see Ronald Dworkin, "The Curse of American Politics." Dworkin emphasizes the dual role of citizens, as judges of electoral contests and as participants in those contests.

52. See Samuel Popkin's *The Reasoning Voter*, on the acquisition of information through informal discussion.

53. See my discussion of the deliberative and expressive interests, in "Freedom of Expression," pp. 224–229.

54. Ibid., pp. 224–226.

55. Bowman v. United Kingdom, *European Court of Human Rights*, 19 February 1998, slip op.

56. I should add that it is very much consonant with the view suggested in the concurrence by Justice Breyer in *Nixon v. Shrink*, which states that contribution limits are based on the "need for democratization," and not simply on concerns about quid pro quo corruption. Slip op., at 10.

57. This paper started as a talk to a meeting of the Northeast Citizen Action Resource Center. I have presented subsequent and expanded versions to the MIT Club in Washington, D.C., the Tufts University philosophy colloquium, McGill University departments of philosophy and political science, and a Brown University Conference on political equality. I also presented a draft at a meeting of the September Group, and earlier versions of the main ideas to political philosophy seminars (in fall 1995 and spring 1998). I am grateful for the comments I received, and wish particularly to thank Philippe van Parijs, Erik Olin Wright, and David Estlund for suggestions. I am indebted to Stephen Ansolabehere and James Snyder for discussions of the current system of election finance, and to Leonardo Avritzer for discussions of the persisting importance of the Schumpeterian view of democracy in contemporary democratic thought. As always, my debt to John Rawls runs throughout.

References

Ackerman, Bruce. "The Patriot Option," in Joshua Cohen and Joel Rogers (eds.), *Money and Politics: Financing Elections Democratically*, foreword by Gore Vidal (Boston: Beacon Press, 1999).

Ansolabehere, Stephen and Snyder, James M. "Money and Office," in David Brady and John Cogan (eds.), *Continuity and Change in Congressional Elections* (Stanford: Stanford University Press, forthcoming).

———. "Money and Institutional Power," *Texas Law Review*, 77, 7 (June 1999) pp. 1673–1704.

———. "Money, Elections, and Candidate Quality," unpublished.

———. "Money and Office," in David Brady and John Cogan (eds.), *Continuity and Change in Congressional Elections* (Stanford: Stanford University Press, forthcoming).

Ansolabehere, Stephen and Iyengar, Shanto. *Going Negative* (New York: Free Press, 1995).

Baker, C. Edwin. "Campaign Expenditures and Free Speech," *Harvard Civil Rights-Civil Liberties Law Review* 33, 1 (winter 1998): 1–55.

Beitz, Charles. *Political Equality* (Princeton, N.J.: Princeton University Press, 1989).

Blasi, Vincent. "Free Speech and the Widening Gyre of Fund-Raising: Why Campaign Spending Limits May Not Violate the First Amendment After All," 94 *Columbia Law Review* 1281 (1994).

Brady, David, and Cogan, John, eds. *Continuity and Change in Congressional Elections* (Stanford: Stanford University Press, forthcoming).

Cain, Bruce, and Sullivan, Kathleen. "Moralism and Realism in Campaign Finance Reform," *University of Chicago Legal Forum* (1995).

Center for Responsive Politics.
http://www.opensecrets.org/pubs/bigpicture/overview/bpoverview.htm.

Cohen, Joshua. "Freedom of Expression," *Philosophy and Public Affairs* 22, no. 3 (summer 1993): 207–263.

———. "The Natural Goodness of Humanity," in Christine Korsgaard, Barbara Herman, and Andrews Reath (eds.), *Learning from the History of Ethics* (Cambridge: Cambridge University Press, 1996).

Dahl, Robert. *Democracy and Its Critics* (New Haven: Yale University Press, 1989).

Dworkin, Ronald. "What Is Equality? Part 4: Political Equality," *University of San Francisco Law Review* (fall 1987).

———. "The Curse of American Politics," *New York Review of Books* 17, October 1996: 19–24.

Estlund, David. "Political Quality," *Social Philosophy and Policy* (forthcoming).

Goldberg, Deborah, ed. *Writing Reform: A Guide to Drafting State and Local Campaign Finance Laws* (New York: Brennan Center for Justice, 1998).

Guinier, Lani. *The Tyranny of the Majority: Fundamental Fairness in Representative Democracy* (New York: Free Press, 1994).

Habermas, Jürgen. *Between Facts and Norms*, trans. William Rehg (Cambridge, MA: MIT Press, 1996).

Jacobson, Gary. *Money in Congressional Elections* (New Haven: Yale University Press, 1980).

Krasno, Jonathan and Green, Donald P. "Preempting Quality Challengers in House Elections," *Journal of Politics* 50 (1988): 920–936.

Lupia, Arthur and McCubbins, Matthew. *The Democratic Dilemma: Can Citizens Learn What They Need to Know?* (Cambridge: Cambridge University Press, 1998).

Miller, Ellen, Donnelly, David, and Fine, Janice. "Going Public," *Boston Review* 22, 2 (April/May 1997). Reprinted in Joshua Cohen and Joel Rogers (eds.), *Money and Politics: Financing Elections Democratically*, foreword by Gore Vidal (Boston: Beacon Press, 1999).

Morris, Dick. *Behind the Oval Office*, second ed. (Washington, DC: Renaissance Books, 1998).

Note. "Soft Money: The Current Rules and the Case for Reform," *Harvard Law Review* 111 (1998).

Polett, Zach. "Empower Citizens," in Joshua Cohen and Joel Rogers (eds.), *Money and Politics: Financing Elections Democratically*, foreword by Gore Vidal (Boston: Beacon Press, 1999).

Popkin, Samuel L. *The Reasoning Voter: Communication and Persuasion in Presidential Campaigns* (Chicago: University of Chicago Press, 1991).

Rawls, John. *Political Liberalism* (New York: Columbia University Press, 1996 [1993]).

———. *A Theory of Justice*, rev. ed. (Cambridge, Mass.: Harvard University Press, 1999).

Schumpeter, Joseph Alois. *Capitalism, Socialism, and Democracy* (New York: Harper and Row, 1942).

Sullivan, Kathleen M. "Political Money and Freedom of Speech," *University of California, Davis Law Review* 30 (1997).

Verba, Sidney, Schlozman, Kay, Lehman, and Brady, Henry E. *Voice and Equality* (Cambridge, Mass.: Harvard University Press, 1995).

Chapter 4

Fiddling Second: Reflections on "A Defense of Abortion"

N. Ann Davis

"A Defense of Abortion" was initially published in the inaugural issue of *Philosophy & Public Affairs* in the fall of 1971. It had an immediate impact on philosophers' discussions of abortion. And, after more than a quarter of a century, it continues to play a pivotal role in the thinking and writing of both philosophers and nonphilosophers. When one reads "A Defense of Abortion" (ADA) in conjunction with Judith Jarvis Thomson's works that discuss killing more generally—especially those that address the question of what it is that makes something a killing, and how much normative force attaches to describing it as such—or with her theoretical work on rights,[1] one gains an even richer appreciation of the depth and importance of that essay. Whether or not one shares Thomson's views about abortion or is persuaded by the arguments and examples she presents in ADA, it must be acknowledged that ADA has had a lasting influence on the way philosophers think about abortion and other normative issues, and on how they view moral theory. The essay has also sparked serious reflection on questions about philosophical methodology. Often it has been the examination of the use of examples in moral argument, and the force of appeals to moral intuitions—in the form of reflection on Thomson's use of the (notorious) famous violinist example—that has provided the connection between matters of substance and issues of methodology.

In many respects, I think "A Defense of Abortion" embodies the shape of Thomson's powerful influence on contemporary moral philosophy. Using it sometimes as a focus and sometimes as a springboard, I want to reflect on some of the ways that Thomson's work has affected how a generation of philosophers have come to view, and to do, philosophy. I want in particular to engage with the question of how philosophers deploy examples, and with what they take the function of examples to be in moral argument. My intention is not to trace the causal reach of ADA (or that of the violinist example) through the voluminous literature that has emerged in response to it, or to render a verdict on its success as a defense of abortion.[2] What I want to do is step a bit further back, in the hope that doing so will help us gain perspective both on the impact of ADA and on Thomson's approach to doing philosophy. It is my hope that this will deepen our understanding of how Thomson's work has influenced the character of contemporary moral philosophy, and the sensibilities of those who have chosen to engage in it.

In section 1, I will discuss the (familiar and widely accepted) view that ADA was instrumental in changing people's perception of the abortion debate, and make some comments on the larger implications of effecting that change. In section 2, I will focus on the use of examples—notably, though not solely, Thomson's violinist example.

1 Changing People's Perceptions of the Abortion Debate

"A Defense of Abortion" was pivotal in changing people's perceptions of the nature and significance of their disagreements about abortion. Two of the ways in which it did so are especially salient.

First, prior to the publication of ADA, the prevailing view (both inside and outside of the academy) was that the issue of fetal personhood was fundamental to, and perhaps determinative of, one's position on the moral permissibility of abortion. Thomson elegantly and decisively dispatched this view. By supposing for the sake of argument that the fetus was a person, and persuading readers to agree that there were, nevertheless, cases in which they would grant that abortion might be permissible, Thomson showed that the presumption that the permissibility of abortion turned simply and straightforwardly on the denial of fetal personhood was unfounded. Disagreements about abortion could not be reduced to, or gainfully recast as, disagreements about fetal personhood, or the criteria upon which it was to be asserted or withheld. There were other issues of substance that had to be addressed before one could hope to be able to present a compelling case for adopting a restrictive view of abortion.

Second—or obversely—in inviting readers to consider a variety of cases involving choices between lives that did not involve decisions about abortion (yet could be extrapolated to abortion contexts), Thomson undercut the widely shared and largely unexamined belief that one could resolve abortion issues simply by addressing questions about whether the fetus possessed a right to life. By supplying us with cases in which it seems permissible to kill an innocent person,[3] Thomson posed a challenge to another widely accepted, but dubious, view: the view that the possession of rights to life provided persons

with an unassailable moral defense against being (permissibly or justifiably) killed.

Though appreciation of the force of Thomson's arguments did not
dawn with the rapidity that it seems—in hindsight—it should have
done, their collective force was staggering. It was not merely that one
could not defend restrictive (or: permissive) views about abortion
simply by asserting (or: denying) that the fetus was a person, or by
asserting (or: denying) that the fetus, as a person, possessed rights to
life. What Thomson showed was that those who sought to advance a
view about the permissibility or impermissibility of abortion had to
address a host of larger questions about the structure, scope, and force
of the protections that rights were thought to confer upon an individual, and about when (and why) it was that the possession of a right to
life should be thought to confer protection against being killed. Those
who hoped to take a stand on the morality of abortion thus needed to
address a much broader range of cases in order to defend, or even
explicate, their view. They needed, first of all, to consider how cases of
abortion were (and were not) different from other cases involving conflicts of rights between persons. To do this effectively, they needed both
to address cases in which one was faced with the need to choose
between the life of one person (the woman) and the life of another (the
fetus), as well as those—like the case of the unconscious violinist—in
which one had to choose between preserving one person's life and
serving another's Good, or fulfilling other obligations. To defend—
perhaps even to articulate—a view about abortion, one would thus
have to do much more to delineate the scope of rights, and calibrate
their force. And one would also have to situate rights more precisely
within their larger normative and theoretical domains: to explain what
was involved in violating a right, and whether (and why, and when) it
was morally wrong to do so.

Such issues are neither narrow nor tractable; nor is the path toward
their resolution simple or straightforward. Indeed, the issues that
Thomson uncovered behind the velvet curtain of abortion adversaries'
talk of persons' rights to life were ones that extended throughout the
body, and flowed from the very heart of, moral theory. Those who
would engage with Thomson's arguments in ADA must undertake a
serious excursion into the domain of moral theory. Some may never
fully recover from the trip.

"A Defense of Abortion" was revolutionary in other ways as well.
Though prior to the essay's publication, most of those who wrote
about abortion seemed to share the view that the issue of fetal personhood was normatively decisive, there was little agreement on how

one was to determine whether the fetus was a person. Questions about personhood were viewed largely as metaphysical (or religious) matters. And that was enough, by many philosophers' lights, to support the view that they were philosophical "nonquestions." By the time ADA was published, many Anglo-American philosophers had become uncomfortable with tidy positivist dismissals of entire areas of philosophy as worthless (because of their unverifiability, and hence their supposedly unscientific nature). And both the influence of Wittgenstein and the methodology of ordinary language philosophy allowed philosophers to embrace a more inclusive—or less dismissive—view of questions that would previously have been banished outright by positivist decree. When ADA was published, there may not have been many philosophers who would wholeheartedly accept the tenets of positivism, or dismiss ethics as devoid of philosophical content. But the influence of positivism lingered nonetheless, and the choice to study ethics was still viewed as a retreat from "real" philosophy. Those who chose to study ethics were often thought to do so simply because they were intimidated by the "hard stuff," or were not bright enough to do it.[4] Abortion issues, and issues about personhood, thus bore the double stigma of being viewed as metaphysical and moral ones.

Even on purely intellectual grounds, this was intolerable. And it is hard to understand how philosophers can have embraced a view of their discipline that was so deeply engaged with the world in some respects (i.e., with the world of science) and so radically disengaged in others. Why should philosophy be deemed interesting or legitimate only if it functioned as the helpmeet (if not the handmaid) of science? And, faced with the abuses and manipulations wrought in the name of science in the 1930s and '40s, how could anyone suppose that science could (or would, or should) credibly pose as value-free? Those who were teachers or students of philosophy in the 1960s had even more reason to reject the positivist, passivist dogma, for they were reading, writing, and teaching in the shadow—if not the glare—of massive moral and political upheaval: the civil rights movement, the resurgence of feminism, and the growing public horror at the nature of the United States' involvement in Vietnam. The view that, *qua* philosophers, philosophers could offer nothing to discussions of the moral and social issues of the day beyond providing definitions, analyses of central concepts, and revelations of inconsistencies in other people's views, was a view that was profoundly at odds with many individual philosophers' picture of themselves as morally serious people. Being a philosopher and being concerned about the state of the real world—race relations, the role of women in society, the defensibility of the United States' involvement in southeast Asia, for example—did not seem to be only anecdotally or coincidentally related.

"A Defense of Abortion" provided compelling evidence that social solipsism was neither philosophically necessary nor morally sustainable, and compelling reason to believe that philosophical work could help illuminate socially important, historically difficult—even ostensibly intractable—debates. ADA was thus fulcral in changing people's view of philosophy, and of the nature of many people's commitment to it. More philosophers came to recognize that the discipline possessed rich substantive and methodological resources that they could use to engage with social problems. No longer were philosophers obliged, as philosophers, to effect (or affect) social nonengagement, and then struggle to rationalize it, or to view their moral and political engagement as merely idiosyncratic and autobiographical. The article was revelatory, and redemptive.

The dramatic effects of ADA were not merely a response to its substance. Its style, too, was revolutionary. By effectively neutralizing the debate about fetal personhood, Thomson showed that disagreements about the morality of abortion could be extracted from the realm of speculative metaphysics, an area of philosophy that—despite the waning of positivism—still seemed disreputable. By casting her central example—the notorious, unconscious violinist—in the second person, Thomson showed philosophers that there was a viable alternative to the disengaged stance of the philosophical analyst, one that helped strengthen individual philosophers' convictions that they could—and should—be involved in social issues as committed participants, not merely as neutral observers or analysts. By making it clear that issues like abortion—ones that were normative, contentious, and (in a clear sense) both woman-centered and feminist—were deeply connected with issues that lay at the core of moral, political, and legal theory, Thomson helped liberate philosophers from the oppressive belief that they needed either to (try to) put aside their convictions when they did philosophy, or to view their moral, social, and political concerns as impediments to their doing good philosophical work, rather than as (sometimes) stimulants or objects of it.

The philosophy and public affairs movement did not begin with the publication of ADA. It already had roots, sources, and sustainers. But the publication of ADA helped expand its base. The reception of Thomson's article was no doubt affected by the recent publication of John Rawls's *A Theory of Justice*, which gave philosophers with interests in social and moral issues both the incentive to undertake serious work in moral and political theory, and an inspiring model of how work in that portion of philosophy could be both theoretically powerful and normatively rich. Nevertheless, it was the publication of ADA that provided the true catalyst in many cases: the spark that fused students' passionate interest in philosophy with the belief that the discipline might have a place for them, and the conviction that they might have something important to contribute to it. This was especially true, I think, for students of philosophy who were women.[5] Thomson's work helped sustain both their self-esteem and their commitment through even the most difficult phases of graduate study.

Thomson did not purport to produce a definitive positive answer to the normative question of when abortion was (and was not) defensible in "A Defense of Abortion" or to provide a casuistry or metric to be used to ascertain whether a given abortion decision was a morally defensible one.[6] But ADA inspired readers both to reflect on the desirability of reframing their approach to abortion issues, and to explore the possibility of making more global changes in their strategic and methodological approaches to other problems in philosophy.

2 Examples

No brief discussion of Thomson's use of examples—in "A Defense of Abortion," or in her other work—can convey the liveliness of her philosophical imagination or the subtlety of the argumentation in which her examples are employed. Nor can it do justice to the complexity of larger questions about the role of examples in philosophy, or the distinctive features of the use of examples in moral theory. The remarks I make in this section will thus be programmatic and suggestive.

Attempts to explain how examples are (and are not) used effectively invoke both larger methodological issues and substantive matters. Questions about the force of a specific example—about the force of the violinist example, for instance—blend into questions about the relations between persuasion and argumentation, and into more global concerns about what examples actually do, and how philosophers should employ them. The challenge to articulate the relationship between examples' psychological efficacy and their probative force is especially great in moral philosophy. Though it may require skillful pedagogical badgering both to elicit students' intuitions about pure theoretical issues like, for example, the nature of numbers, and inspire their passionate concern to articulate their views about such questions, the pedagogical challenge for philosophers who are discussing normative moral issues is generally far less onerous. To say this is not to say that moral intuitions are more privileged than mathematical ones, or that they are more important, but rather to issue the reminder that moral intuitions are generally things that people both have, and are aware of having. The more salient aspects of our moral intuitions may seem to be more readily accessible to us, and more compelling, than our views about the ontology of numbers. At the same time—unlike our views about the nature of numbers—our initial responses to normative moral questions are more often catechized, and uncritical. The challenges for the teacher of normative ethics are thus different, and in some respects more strenuous, than those that face teachers of metaphysics and the philosophy of mathematics. For students of normative ethics must be taught both to honor their moral intuitions and to criticize them: to approach them with a stance that is at once personally authentic, dispassionately analytical, and powerfully self-critical. That is a tall order. (I shall return to this.)

When we think about how to assess our response to a philosopher's example, or about what sort of example to adduce to strengthen our own argument, we become inextricably involved with issues of personal authenticity, and questions about philosophical pedagogy: questions about the relationship between being a philosopher, and the business of doing and teaching philosophy. Such concerns have been lively ones for philosophers since at least the time of Socrates, but they do not seem to have sparked much interest in the philosophers who were writing in the middle portion of the twentieth century. Nor is it hard to form conjectures as to why this might have been the case. If the prevailing orthodoxy is that philosophy (or "real" philosophy) is a narrow technical discipline, or the gnostic elaboration of the history of ideas, then neither questions about authenticity nor questions about proper pedagogy are likely to come to the fore. The power of "A Defense of Abortion" thus lay not merely in the success of its attack on restrictive views of abortion, nor in the subtlety and persuasiveness of its examples, but also in its embodiment of an approach to doing philosophy that made the reader a participant rather than merely an analyst or observer. In casting both the teacher and the student in the role of participants, it helped turn the teaching of philosophy into a form of (more) democratic collaboration, one that engaged the student and the teacher both with the material and with each other. The style of ADA made it pedagogically valuable at many different levels.

ADA's accessibility was also magnified by the cleverness of Thomson's examples, and by the brilliant decision to cast her central example in the second person. This was instrumental both in expanding the reach of Thomson's argument, and in deepening the nature of philosophers' engagement with the topic of abortion, a topic that had been tainted by people's (generally unvoiced) moralistic assumptions about sex and sexuality, and by their dismissive characterization of it as a "woman's problem."[7,8] ADA thus raised issues, questions, and concerns that were neither articulated in, nor exhausted by, the substance of the examples, or even the body of the argument, ones that involved far larger concerns about the methodology of doing philosophy and teaching it. That ADA continues to be so widely read is thus as much a function of its ability to engage us as of its subtlety and depth. It is not merely readable and rewarding to teach, but also continually challenging: it presents both teachers and students with the opportunity—if not the demand—to engage in critical self-reflection at the same time as they hone their analytical skills, and get pleasure in exercising them. "A Defense of Abortion" challenges readers not only to articulate their views about the (basis of the) permissibility of abortion—which is a massive challenge in itself—but also to reflect on how they go about discovering, and assessing, their own beliefs and assumptions. Few essays can lay claim to be so rewarding, or so rich.

From reflecting on Thomson's use of examples we can learn valuable things about how to write and teach philosophy: how better to articulate the points we are trying to make, how to invoke examples, and how to construct arguments, and present them more effectively. In some circumstances, we discover, the substantive content of the example does not matter much; the example may be effective even if the scenario it invokes is thin, frivolous, fanciful, or far-fetched. Consider, for instance, the Gettier-style examples involving speculations about the sort of automobiles to be found in colleagues' offices. Neither the implausibility of finding a car (any car) in a colleague's office nor the silliness of speculating about the historical details of its arrival there undermines the examples' efficacy. The Gettier-style cases are meant to function as counterexamples to a logical thesis or definition: the claim that knowledge merely is justified true belief. Neither the factual implausibility of the cases nor the inanity of their subject matter provides any impediment to judging them to be successful in achieving their desired result, the defeat of the claim that the possession of justified true belief constitutes the possession of knowledge. On the other hand, when a philosopher's aim is explicitly to embrace the mundane—to show that the process of Cartesian doubt is not an invention, or an invocation of philosophical arcana, but something that can emerge even in the most banal, ostensibly nonphilosophical circumstances—then reminders like the one issued by H. H. Price, that (even) when we look at a tomato "there is much that we can doubt" will do the job.

But there are cases in which there are more stringent constraints on the choice of an example's substantive content. Most notable, perhaps, are those in which a writer seeks to elicit readers' response to an imagined or postulated phenomenon. In such circumstances, the substantive content of the example must be more sensitively chosen. Consider the example that figured prominently in midcentury debates about whether personal identity consisted in the continuity of memory (or more broadly, the persistence of psychological traits) or in the spatiotemporal continuity of an individual's body, the Guy Fawkes Example (or GFE). The GFE seems to provide us with conclusive grounds for rejecting the memory criterion, or any of its psychologically related cousins. If it is conceivable that you could awake with the memories, etc., of Guy Fawkes, then it seems conceivable that the same thing could happen to me, at the same time. But if this would give us both equal claim to be (thought to be) personally identical to Guy Fawkes, then something has gone awry: it would appear either to commit us to saying that one person may be present where there are two human bodies, or to challenge our belief in the transitivity of '(person) x is identical with (person) y', since both you and I are (allegedly) each personally identical with Guy Fawkes, but distinct from one another.

But the example fails to establish its intended point. This is not merely because it begs the question at issue (if memory were sufficient for personal identity, then it would not in fact be logically problematical to suppose that—however briefly—one person might be present where there were two bodies). It is also because the GFE—or our reliance on our intuitive response to it—may function as an impediment to our taking a more comprehensive view of the problem of personal identity, one that would potentially afford us a response to the (supposed) problem, a more perspicuous view of the issues, and a livelier appreciation of the constraints on their resolution. Perhaps, if both you and I awoke with memories that fit (what is known of) Guy Fawkes's life, then each of us could coherently and justly claim to be personally identical with Guy Fawkes (and remain silent on the question of whether we are personally identical with one another. If—as seems plausible—we continue to live our lives at a distance from each other, and to acquire different memories and experiences, it is doubtful that we would ever again be confronted with the question). It is easy enough to articulate the circumstances we are supposed to be imagining—on a clear morning in November, a woman in California and a man in Massachusetts awake with the memories, etc., of Guy Fawkes. But it is not clear that they are circumstances that it is easy—or even possible—to imagine. If, as a number of philosophers believe, there are good reasons to suppose that our notion of self is not world-independent, there may be good reasons to suppose that personal identity is more fragile than the GFE presumes (and thus good reasons to reject the possibility that my autobiography could include reports of a stint as Guy Fawkes, to say nothing of a spider or a bat). The GFE may thus fail in another way as well: the scenario that it asks us to imagine may be one that is simply not coherent.

Other examples that have figured in philosophers' discussions of personal identity as putative counterexamples—cases of teleportation, and of physical destruction and reconstitution—seem both imaginable and intelligible. But here, too, there are grounds for hesitation in relying on our responses to such cases. It is reasonable for us to be suspicious of intuitive responses that are elicited by scenarios that we currently do not have grounds for supposing to be possible. This is not because envisaging such scenarios may involve positing things that are in fact not possible, but because some of the things thus envisaged are truly alien to us. It is not the prospect of impossibility that should impede our reliance upon our intuitions about such cases, but rather the need to acknowledge that there is a depth of mystery surrounding our alleged imaginings that clouds our attempts at imaginative projection. A world in which fantastic things (like teleportation) could happen would be a world that was profoundly different from this one in a myriad of ways. It seems a plausible conjecture that, in such a world, human understanding, conceptualization, and evaluation might be profoundly different too.

There are other reasons for thinking that philosophers' claims about the force of their examples may be hyperbolic. Consider, for example, the line of criticism that has been frequently directed at utilitarianism (and often, consequentialism more generally), the charge of normative unacceptability. In various forms, the charge of normative unacceptability has been a mainstay of anticonsequentialist arguments since the 1950s, when critics sought to attack utilitarianism by claiming that it would license behavior that is morally objectionable: defaulting on a promise to a friend, clandestinely arranging for the framing and execution of an innocent person, killing one healthy person in order to distribute his or her organs to five individuals who each need an organ transplant to survive. In all of these cases, the example is supposed to inspire the rejection of utilitarianism as normatively unacceptable. The charge of normative unacceptability thus tacitly involves three claims: first, that utilitarian reasoning would, in fact, permit us or require us to do the repugnant deed (break the promise, frame the innocent person, kill the healthy person and redistribute his or her organs); second, that our (allegedly counterutilitarian) intuitions that it is wrong to break the promise, frame the innocent person, or cut up the healthy person are sound ones; and third, that they are intuitions whose content, form, and scope can be specified with reasonable precision.

As numerous commentators have pointed out, the first claim is problematic: it is not obvious that utilitarianism would, indeed, license the doing of the untoward deeds. If one thinks carefully about the larger consequences of our doing those "wrongful" things, or the larger implications of our implementing the intuitively repellant practices, it is far from clear that such behavior would be recommended, or even tolerated, by an appeal to a utilitarian view.[9] Moreover, even in those cases in which it would be plausible to suppose that utilitarian reasoning licensed or enjoined the behavior that we find intuitively repellant, there is reason to question both the second claim and the third: reason to question whether the counterutilitarian intuitions can generate, explain, or even provide us with the details of the competing nonutilitarian view that is tacitly being invoked.

Things rapidly get complicated here. On the one hand, there is the possibility that, though the thought of doing x horrifies, disgusts, or offends us, it would still be better (and right?) for us to do x rather than refrain. The deep and inescapable facts of acculturation render the practice of uncritical reliance on our feelings of repugnance problematic. We know that different cultures (and subcultures) characterize different things as being "beyond the pale." And we also know that it is often difficult for us to distinguish our (reason-based) moral repugnance from more visceral, less obviously morally compelling responses. Compare the following range of cases:

> A. I suggest that we dine at a restaurant whose specialty is pickled octopus.
> B. I suggest that we dine at a restaurant whose specialty is curried dog.
> C. A farm child learns that the pork chops she has just eaten came from Frankie, the pig she bred and raised.
> D. You discover that the meat from the hamburger you are eating came from a processing plant that has recently been the source of tainted food.
> E. You learn that the chicken that is available in your local supermarket come from animals that are (while living) heavily dosed with antibiotics, and (when dead) heavily treated with preservatives.
> F. You learn that the chicken that is available in your local supermarket comes from factory farms, where animals are raised in extremely inhumane conditions.
> G. An ethical vegetarian discovers, midmeal, that she has been served an entrée that has (free-range) chicken in it, rather than the tofu dish she ordered.

H. You discover that the meat you are eating was procured from an animal who was (gratuitously) tortured before being put to death.

What I take this range of cases to remind us is that it is not the mere fact that something is repugnant to us that constitutes a morally solid reason for thinking that it is something we must not (or even may not) do. As it presents itself phenomenologically, repugnance is difficult to sort into the kind of feeling that constitutes the ground of moral dismay; the kind that constitutes proof of one's deep subscription to moral principles that one has subjected to deep and systematic scrutiny; the kind that constitutes a merely visceral response; and the kind whose visceral response derives (merely) from the prospect of our departing from our standard practices.

But even if we were able both to subject our feelings of repugnance to critical scrutiny, and to determine when they are indeed moral rather than merely visceral, we would not be justified in claiming that doing the repugnant thing is wrong (or for claiming that because utilitarianism supports our doing it, utilitarianism must be untenable). Until we can articulate a theory (or a set of principles) that enjoins our acting in the nonrepugnant way—the way *we* think we should act rather than the way we think utilitarianism bids us act—and subject the theory (or set of principles) to rigorous critical scrutiny, our argument is, at best, incomplete. For there is always the possibility that, although our theory avoids the counterintuitive results that utilitarianism would generate under conditions c, it also enjoins us to act in ways that are repugnant in other cases, where conditions c' obtain. And if, in addition, utilitarianism seems to give us better advice than its rivals in conditions c', then what we have is, at best, a stalemate.

The point here is simpler than its exposition. Examples that are purely normative—ones that appeal merely and directly to our intuitions about what we may or may not do—are not in and of themselves effective counterexamples to proposed principles or theories. To show that they have probative force, we must articulate the alternative principle(s) or theory that generates the results we find more palatable, and show that it does not yield more worrying results than its rivals do.

These remarks may seem to contain the seeds of criticism of Thomson's use of the violinist example, especially when they are conjoined with my skeptical worries about our relying upon intuitions in circumstances that involve our positing scenarios that (may) transcend the possible, or the intelligible. After all, Thomson's example appears to work merely by appealing to our gut response that it would be outrageous to be forced into nine months of servitude to the violinist, or our intuition that it would not be wrong for us to disconnect ourselves (or have ourselves disconnected) if we were so inclined.

But I think this interpretation of my remarks misconstrues Thomson's use of the example, and (perhaps) the rest of ADA. For Thomson's negative argument to work, the violinist example needs only to be seen as a counterexample à la Gettier: as presenting a somewhat outré (but intelligible) set of circumstances, and eliciting the concession that one would not think it wrong to take actions that would terminate the violinist's life. If we make that concession, then we have granted Thomson the point(s) she seeks to establish against the defender of a conservative (or restrictive) view of abortion: that it is not necessarily wrong to kill an innocent person, or that permissible killing does not always involve the violation of a right to life. For Thomson's violinist example to succeed as a counterexample, we must grant only minimal assumptions: that the violinist is a person, that he is innocent, and that—under at least some circumstances (perhaps only the more dramatic ones but under *some* circumstances)—it is not the case that killing him would be wrong. And that—like Smith's Ford in Jones's office (or was it the other way around?)—is that. Knowledge is not de facto justified true belief, though some cases of knowing may be characterized that way. And abortion does not de facto involve the violation of a person's right to life, though some abortions may be thought to do so.

Thomson also attempts to persuade us to accept her view of abortion's defensibility, her specific reasons for supposing that it may sometimes be permissible (and sometimes not) for a pregnant woman to have an abortion and to seek necessary assistance in doing so. But Thomson's (qualified, or moderate) defense of abortion is clearly less successful than her attack on the restrictive view of abortion. Its success depends on far more than our granting that the case of the violinist constitutes a counterexample to sweeping claims about the normative force of personhood, the wrongness of killing, and the scope of rights to life.

For Thomson's positive account to succeed, we would have to accept her view of abortion as essentially a form of pregnancy termination that involves fetal detachment, rather than as the deliberate termination of the life of the fetus. (Thomson professes to support only weak reproductive rights, not strong ones.) And we would have to agree that the strenuousness (and reasonableness) of a woman's attempts to avoid pregnancy were relevant to (if not determinative of) the answer to the question of whether the decision to cease to provide fetal life-support—to have an abortion, and thus kill the fetus—was just, and thus not a violation of the fetus' right to life. We would also have to grant that it is only grounds of justice, or only appeals to rights, that should be the basis for opposing abortion, or asserting that women may be more often obliged to continue with their pregnancies. Finally, since Thomson believes that not all abortions are permissible—there are cases in which it would be "indecent," and thus presumably wrong, for the woman to seek an abortion (or for us to accede to her request)— the plausibility of her defense of abortion depends both on our being able to distinguish the "indecent" cases from those in which abortion would not be "indecent," and our sharing Thomson's views about how the cases are to be distinguished.

I do not think that Thomson's defense of abortion succeeds. But the success of the violinist example and the success of Thomson's positive (and qualified) defense of abortion are quite independent of each other. One can grant that the violinist example provides a counterexample to the claim that it is always wrong to kill an innocent person, or that such killings always violate rights to life, and remain unpersuaded by the arguments and examples she employs to establish her positive view. And one can reject the moderate view that Thomson articulates—one that is not an unqualified defense of abortion, but only a defense of pregnancy discontinuation (fetal removal), and a defense of fetal removal only when the refusal to allow it would be unjust—without thereby having to take exception to the violinist example, or take issue with the intuitions that it (supposedly) invokes.[10]

Here, I have not taken issue with Thomson's (positive) defense of abortion. Nor have I discussed the tenability of some of the article's central theoretical claims (which emerge more fully in other essays), notably the claim that the violation of a right to life involves the unjust termination of a person's life, or the conviction that it is rights in general—and rights of ownership or self-determination in particular— that should be viewed as outweighing whatever claim a fetus may have to continued life. Nor have I been able to examine closely the view of moral theorizing, or of doing philosophy, that underlies, or emerges from, Thomson's work. As I hope is clear from my earlier discussion, I do not share Thomson's confidence in appeals to intuition. Nor do I share the theoretical commitments and moral presuppositions I take to underlie some of Thomson's own intuitions, most notably her conviction that appeals to rights play such a central normative and theoretical role in our moral thinking.

But these are views that I have reached only by engaging deeply with "A Defense of Abortion," and with Thomson's other work that fleshes out the theoretical claims and normative intuitions it draws upon. In thinking about which of Thomson's examples work, and how, and which do not, and why, I have had to think a lot about what I suppose the purpose of moral theorizing is, and about what sorts of constraints and demands attend the undertaking of the enterprise.

I do not imagine that my situation is unique. My hope is that, in spelling out some of the ways "A Defense of Abortion" both invited and rewarded my deep engagement with Thomson's work, I am speaking for the generation of philosophers who learned from Judith Jarvis Thomson (and relearned, and learned again) that the call of moral theory is haunting, and that the life of a moral theorist can be a profoundly rewarding one, both philosophically and personally.[11]

Notes

1. What I have in mind in the first instance is principally, but not solely, *Acts and Other Events* and the essays reprinted in *Rights, Restitution, and Risk*, and in the second instance, *The Realm of Rights* and some of the more technical material in legal philosophy.

2. I have undertaken large parts of this task elsewhere. See, e.g., "Abortion and Self-Defense," *Philosophy & Public Affairs* 13 (1984), pp. 175–207 (reprinted in Jay Garfield and Patricia Hennessey, eds., *Abortion: Legal and Moral Perspectives* [University of Massachusetts Press, 1984], pp. 186–210); "Rights, Permission, and Compensation," *Philosophy & Public Affairs* 14 (1985), pp. 374–384; "Rights and Moral Theory: A Critical Review of Judith Thomson's *Rights, Restitution, and Risk*," *Ethics* 98 (1988), pp. 806–826; "The Abortion Debate: The Search for Common Ground" parts 1 and 2, *Ethics* 103 (April 1993), pp. 516–539, and *Ethics* 103 (July 1993), pp. 731–778; and "Not Drowning But Waving: Reflections on Swimming Through the Shark-Infested Waters of the Abortion Debate," in Rem B. Edwards (ed.), *New Essays on Abortion and Bioethics*, volume 2, (JAI Press, 1997), pp. 227–265.

3. I am here ignoring the various complications and qualifications surrounding the description of someone as "innocent"; though—of course—much of Thomson's work involves the attempt to explain the nuances of our views about "technical" and "moral" innocence.

4. To those who did not attempt to do ethics at this time, it is hard convey how deep, or how toxic, the effects of residual positivism were. In my second year of graduate school, it was rumored that the professor advising incoming graduate students had told them not to "waste their time" with ethics. What they should do instead (this advisor was said to have opined) was the real stuff, the hard stuff. If they later came to need to know something about the field (so that they could teach it) they would have no problem just "picking it up." I mention this here to convey how strong the prejudice against ethics remained, even after the (semi-official) demise of positivism, and out of respect for the memory of V.K.R., who would not want the story to die with her.

5. Within two weeks of the article's arrival in the library, every one of the female graduate students in philosophy had read it.

6. Interestingly, some readers apparently read it as doing, or intending to do, just that. Justice Sandra Day O'Connor's rhetoric about "not unduly burden(ing) a woman's choice" certainly seems redolent with Thomsonian overtones.

7. The combination was especially deadly (or dismissive): the tacit assumption was that it was primarily women who were unmarried, promiscuous, and/or stupid who

would concern themselves with the permissibility (and availability) of elective (as opposed to therapeutic) abortion.

8. I cannot do justice to the wit, irony, or power of Thomson's choice of examples here. But it is worth noting that, prior to the publication of ADA, women made only infrequent appearances in philosophers' examples (and then it was generally in their capacity as wives of the authors). Women were not, of course, excluded from examples used in discussions of abortion. Thomson's creation of an example that both sought to model the intense physicality and overwhelmingness of pregnancy (rather than presenting it as a mere inconvenience, or viewing the prospect of enduring it as one might view the prospect of having a twenty-five-pound backpack strapped around one's middle) and involved men as major players—I am assuming that most professional philosophers in the early 1970s were male, and that Thomson knew that was the case—was, I think, brilliant.

9. The same is true, I think, of many other versions of normative unacceptability claims: as Hare, Singer, Sen, Glover, and others have shown, consequentialist theories are far more plastic, and (perhaps) far less drastic, than many philosophers have supposed.

10. Indeed, there are many who do. Some reject Thomson's view as too permissive on the ground that the violinist example applies unproblematically only to a range of cases that is more limited than the one that she supposes. (Such a case is sustainable, I think, only if one ignores the rest of Thomson's examples, or takes issue with them.) Others reject it as too restrictive, either on the grounds that it (implausibly) disavows strong reproductive rights—the right not to have a child that is my child—or on the grounds that in placing weight on the distinction between pregnancy termination (fetal removal) and termination of fetal life (abortion in order to prevent there being a child who is my child) it places weight on the distinction between intention and mere foresight, and thus ostensibly inherits the many problems that attend the doctrine of double effect. Still others reject her view because they reject its foundations or presuppositions: e.g., her (alleged) assumption that the distinction between consensual sex and nonconsensual sex is both meaningful and relevant to questions of the defensibility of abortion.

11. I wish to thank Holly Beckner, Hilary Bok, John Deigh, Barbara Herman, Holly Smith, Raphael Susnowitz, and (of course) Judy Thomson for their remarks on issues that I have touched upon here. None has read (or could reasonably be supposed to agree with) the details of this essay.

Chapter 5

Word Giving, Word Taking

Catherine Z. Elgin

We live, sociologists tell us, in an information age. People continually impart information, purporting to speak with authority. "Take my word for it," they urge. "You can rely on me." Nevertheless, it is not altogether clear what it is to take someone's word or when it is reasonable to do so. In investigating such matters, a good place to start is *The Realm of Rights*, where Judith Jarvis Thomson provides an insightful discussion of word giving. She advocates accepting

> The Assertion Thesis: Y gives X his or her word that a proposition is true if and only if Y asserts that proposition to X, and
> (i) in so doing Y is inviting X to rely on its truth, and
> (ii) X receives and accepts the invitation (there is uptake).[1]

If the Assertion Thesis is correct, word giving requires two parties: a word giver and a word taker. The word giver issues an invitation; the word taker accepts it, thereby acquiring a right. In particular, she acquires a claim against the word giver, a claim that is infringed if the proposition in question is not true.

Thomson focuses on promising, where the moral dimension of word giving is particularly salient. But she recognizes that there are other modes of word giving as well. In what follows, I use her account as a springboard for investigating a different species of word giving, the one that epistemologists (perhaps misleadingly) label testimony. I do not want to endorse everything Thomson says about word giving. But appreciating the virtues of theft over honest toil, I propose to steal what I can use from her analysis. With her unwitting help, I hope to shed some light on the epistemology of testimony.

Testimony is a mechanism for information transfer. Here are some examples: The guide says, "The cave paintings at Les Eyzies are 14,000 years old." The reporter announces, "The Dow lost twenty-three points today on heavy trading." The physician warns, "Obesity increases the risk of heart attack." The passerby obliges with directions, "The museum is two blocks down, on the left." In each case, the speaker represents herself as in a position to speak with authority. Although she intimates that her assertion is backed by epistemically adequate reasons, she does not supply them. Testimony, then, conveys information without supplying arguments or evidence to back it up.[2] To be sure, an idle assertive aside could do that. But because testimony is a mode of word giving, it does more. The testifier invites her word receiver to believe on the basis of her say-so. She assures him that her testimony is true. Should her testimony turn out to be false, she will have done him a wrong.

If we understand the nature of that wrong, we get a handle on what the good of testimony is, what benefits it provides. Here the contrast with promising is helpful. Promising provides a framework for voluntarily restricting one's freedom. It facilitates planning and fosters cooperation. Thomson identifies several characteristics of the type of word giving that constitutes promising. (1) Promising is future directed. The propositions whose truth a promisor commits herself to are in the future tense. I can promise that I will eat my spinach. But if I give my word that I am now eating my spinach or that I ate my spinach yesterday, my word giving is not a case of promising. (2) Promising has the promisor as its subject. I can promise that I will eat my spinach. I can promise that I will do my best to get Sam to eat his spinach. But I cannot promise that he will eat his spinach. The reason, evidently, is that no act or omission of mine can ensure his compliance. Promising, then, is essentially first personal. (3) Only a limited range of acts or refrainings or states of affairs fall within the scope of promising. I cannot promise that I will live to be 150, for I lack the capacity to bring that about.[3] Taken together, these features show that promising is restricted to future contingents that are within the agent's power. To the extent that it is indeterminate which states of affairs are contingent in the relevant sense, and which of those are within an agent's power, the scope of promising is indeterminate as well.

Testimony consists of statements of (purportedly) established fact. It has no restrictions as to tense or person. I can testify that Woodrow Wilson was president of Princeton University, that $E = mc^2$, that I am a resident of Massachusetts. I can't testify that I will eat my spinach, though, for despite my best intentions, I might not. Future contingents then lie outside the scope of testimony. But not all statements about the future are excluded. If a prediction is so grounded in established facts and laws that its truth is not up for grabs, it can be the content of testimony. A scientist can testify that a sample of plutonium will continue to emit radiation for hundreds of thousands of years, since established physical facts and laws ensure that the prediction is true. There may, of course, be some question as to what facts and laws are capable of underwriting testimony about the future. So whether a particular prediction qualifies as testimony may be controversial. But a statement's being in the future tense does not automatically rule it out.

Talk of future contingents and freedom to act is apt to induce flutters of metaphysical anxiety. Is the future genuinely open? Is it open in the ways that we think it is? Do we even have a clear conception of what it means to say that it is? Are human beings genuinely free to choose and able to act as they choose? Are we free and able in the ways that we think we are? Do we have a clear conception of what that means? These are legitimate questions whose answers are by no means obvious. If we have to answer them correctly in order to explicate word giving, our prospects are bleak. Luckily, I think we need not do anything so ambitious. Promising, testimony, and other modes of word giving are human practices. They depend for their utility not on what is *really* the case with regard to contingency or human freedom but on shared assumptions about these matters. Even if human beings can, through a sheer act of will, live to be a hundred and fifty years old, no one believes that we can do this. So we are unwilling either to make or to accept a promise to live that long. Even if a psychologist's predictions about infants' eventual career choices have as high an objective probability as physicists' predictions about radioactive decay, we do not believe that psychological predictions are anywhere near that good. So a responsible psychologist would not proffer, nor would we accept, such a prediction as testimony. Promising, testimony, and other modes of word giving are circumscribed by shared, commonsensical assumptions about metaphysical matters. Many of these assumptions are vague and inarticulate. Some, no doubt, are false. But because they are shared, they supply the mutual understanding that we need for the issuing and accepting of invitations to rely on a statement's truth.

To explicate testimony and promising, we need to recognize the shared metaphysical assumptions that underwrite them. We understand a good deal about practices when we see how those assumptions function. If everyone agrees that people have the ability to return books that they borrow, we permit one another to promise to return books and hold them responsible for their failures to do so. If everyone agrees that some people are cognitively competent to calculate the rate of radioactive decay and to report the results of their calculations accurately, we count suitable assertions about such matters as testimony and consider testifiers blameworthy if their reports are wrong. By reference to the presuppositions in effect, then, we can make sense of the actions, motivations, and assessments they give rise to.

'Ought' implies 'can'. If a person cannot do p, he is under no obligation to do p, and cannot rightly be faulted for failing to do p. Appeal to shared presuppositions explains why we hold people responsible when we do. But if the presuppositions are wildly off the mark, we may be holding people responsible when in fact they are not. Doubtless we sometimes hold people responsible for things they could not avoid. Probably some of our mistakes are due to our faulty views about matters like freedom, agency, and contingency. Still, our word-giving practices are remarkably successful. People frequently behave in the ways they promised they would. Experts often convey information that later events bear out. This suggests that however inaccurate the underlying assumptions are, they are not so far off that they discredit our word-giving practices entirely. I suggest, then, that we bracket concerns about metaphysical underpinnings and proceed on the assumption that our word-giving practices are reasonably well founded and do pretty much what we take them to do.

If I promise you that I will eat my spinach, I give you my word that 'I will eat my spinach' is true. I give you a right to expect that I will eat my spinach. Of course, you already had *a* right to expect that. Freedom of thought ensures that you have the right to expect anything you like. You want to expect that I will eat my spinach? Who's going to stop you? But if an expectation grounded in nothing but freedom of thought is unfulfilled, no one is to blame. When I make a promise, the situation is different. I give you a claim against me. Ceteris paribus, if despite my promise, your expectation is unfulfilled, I am at fault. I gave you a reason to expect that I would eat my spinach, a reason that you otherwise would not have had. In giving you that reason, I increased your warrant for the belief that I will eat my spinach. You have a claim against me, then, because I altered your epistemic circumstances. This epistemic element to promising is, I suggest, what converts the bare right into a claim.

A claim, Thomson argues, is a behavioral constraint. In giving you a claim against me, I agree to keep my behavior within particular bounds.[4] In promising to eat my spinach, I agree to constrain my future behavior so as to include spinach consumption in it. The burden I shoulder is to make 'I will eat my spinach' true. Plainly, I am up to the task. But I can testify to all sorts of things that I am utterly powerless to effect. I might, for example, testify that the cave paintings in Les Eyzies are 14,000 years old. Clearly, there is no way that I can make that statement true. The question arises: In so testifying, what claim do I give? How is my behavior constrained? If I don't eat my spinach when I promised that I would, I am subject to censure for failure to eat my spinach. But if the cave paintings are not 14,000 years old, it's hardly my fault. There is no way I can bring it about that the paintings are as old as I say they are. 'Ought' implies 'can'. If I cannot make it the case that the paintings are 14,000 years old, I am under no obligation to do so, and should not be faulted for failing to do so.

Nonetheless, I can be faulted. Why? Perhaps the most obvious answer is causal. My testimony that p caused you to believe that p. So, it might seem that I am to blame for your harboring a false belief. But I can cause you to believe that p in any number of innocent ways. You might, for example, overhear me rehearsing my lines for a play, mistake my utterance for an assertion, and so come to believe what you take me to assert. Although my utterance of p caused your belief, the mistake is surely yours. I am not responsible for your misconstruing my speech act and acquiring a false belief as a result. Maybe a more complicated causal story is needed. Perhaps I am to blame for your falsely believing that p if you come to believe that p because you rightly believe that I believe that p. This is more plausible, but it still won't do. Suppose you overhear me sincerely asserting that p, and rightly conclude that I believe that p. You therefore form the belief that p, on the basis of my assertion. What you don't realize, though, is that I am speaking to my therapist, and that my assertion is (and indeed, I recognize that it is) one of the baseless beliefs that I am in therapy to overcome. Although I have plenty of evidence that $\sim p$, I cannot disabuse myself of the belief that p, having been taught that p at a particularly impressionable age. Again, it seems that I am not at fault for your mistake. It is not enough that I cause you to believe that p or even that I cause you to believe that p by causing you to recognize that I believe that p. I am responsible for your error, not when I cause you to believe that p, but when I entitle you to believe that p. I convey to you not just a belief, but a right to believe. As in promising, you already have *a* right—a moral right—to believe whatever you like. But neither that right alone nor that right in conjunction with a causal story of how you came to believe gives you a claim against me. You have a claim against me because I invite you to take my word. I volunteer to shoulder the epistemic burden. Testimony, like promising, is a liability-shouldering device.[5]

In testifying that p, I implicate that you can rely on me. For what? Let's look again at promising. When I break my promise, it is not because I failed to eat my spinach simpliciter that I am to blame. People are, in general, under no obligation to eat their spinach. I am to blame because I failed to eat my spinach *having given my word that I would*. Similarly, I am not to blame for the fact that the cave paintings are not

14,000 years old, but for the fact that they are not 14,000 years old *when I gave my word that they are*. In both cases, it seems, what is at issue is a conjunction of the form:

p & Y gives her word to X that p.

The promisor can affect the truth value of each conjunct. She can either bring it about that p or she can refrain from giving her word that p. The testifier can affect only the second. So the locus of blame may be different.[6] The promise breaker is subject to reproach for failing to keep her word. In the case of testimony, there is no question of keeping one's word. Rather, the locus of responsibility lies in the word giving itself. When I promise you that p, the claim I give you constrains my future behavior. I commit myself to behaving in the future so as to ensure the truth of p. When I testify to you that p, the claim I give you manifests a constraint on my current behavior. I present myself as having the resources to underwrite your reliance on p. If p turns out to be false, I am to blame, since I invited you to rely on the truth of p, and I implicated that I was in a position to issue such reliance. The false testifier is blameworthy for having given her word in the first place, for having invited the word taker to rely on it. The proper reproach then is something like: "You shouldn't have said it if you weren't sure." False testimony is morally wrong because it is epistemically wrong.

It is irresponsible to invite someone to rely on your word when your word is not reliable. But when is that? One might think that a person's word is reliable whenever what she says is true, and is unreliable whenever what she says is false. In that case, my promise is reliable whenever I do what I promise to, and unreliable whenever I do not. It is not clear that we should say this, though. Suppose I promised to meet you at the railroad station at 5 P.M., but I had no intention of keeping my promise. Or suppose that although I intended to keep my word, I was obviously unlikely to be able to do so. (In the last five years, the noon train from New York has almost never been on time, as it would have to be for me to arrive in time to keep my promise.) As it turned out, though, my train was early, so I encountered you in the station at five o'clock. Thomson contends that I infringed no claim of yours, since I kept my word. She takes it that the claim my promise gives you lies in the truth of p, and thus is not infringed so long as p turns out to be true.[7] This may be so.[8] But it seems plain that you ought not to have counted on me. It was too nearly a coincidence that we met at the appointed time and place. My word was unreliable. Similarly, if I testified on inadequate grounds that the prehistoric cave paintings served a religious purpose, even if it turns out that my assertion is true, my word was unreliable. You ought not to have relied on it.

Should we say, nevertheless, that my testimony did not infringe your claim? Even if Thomson is right about promising, I do not think that we should. To see why, we need to consider the point of each practice. Promising is future directed and action oriented. Because we in fact met at the station at five o'clock, I did what you were counting on me to do. Hence I did not cause your plans to go awry. Whether or not I ought to have given my word as I did, I arguably infringed no claim, for I (*per accidens*, to be sure) kept my word. Testimony's epistemological function is more central, since testimony serves as a conduit of epistemic entitlement. A speaker cannot convey epistemic entitlement if she has none. And the mere fact that her statement is true is not enough to epistemically entitle her to it. It could just be a lucky guess. If, purely on a hunch, I testify that the cave paintings served a religious purpose, I am not epistemically entitled to say what I do; hence I have no epistemic entitlement to convey to you. This suggests that a testifier infringes a word taker's claim when she testifies to something for which she lacks sufficient grounds.

Let's look at it from the word taker's perspective. If I believe someone's testimony, it is because I believe she speaks with authority, and if it is reasonable for me to believe her testimony, it is reasonable for me to believe that she speaks with authority. In believing she speaks with authority, I don't believe merely that she believes what she says. Nor do I believe merely that she has what she takes to be adequate grounds for her remarks. Rather, to take her word for something involves believing that she has what are in fact adequate grounds. The question then is what constitutes adequate grounds? A seemingly obvious answer is that adequate grounds consist of evidence or reasons that are in fact sufficient to support the assertions that constitute the testimony. But this is not enough. Unless there is good reason to think that the evidence or reasons are adequate, we should not take her word. Suppose a blood test reveals the presence of antibodies that are in fact antibodies to a newly discovered virus. Skeptical worries aside, the antibodies are sufficient evidence of the virus. Dr. No testifies on the basis of the blood test that Zeb has the virus. Unless there is consensus in the medical community that the antibodies in question are the antibodies to that particular virus, Dr. No, although speaking the truth and having what is in fact adequate evidence, does not speak with authority. Until the connection between the antibodies and the virus is established to the satisfaction of the medical community, we ought not take her word.

Should we take someone's word if the evidence she relies on satisfies the standards of the relevant epistemically reputable community, even if the evidence turns out to be misleading? Suppose Professor

Cro testifies on the basis of the best available evidence—evidence that satisfies the paleoanthropological community—that the cave paintings are 14,000 years old. The best currently available evidence is circumstantial. There is, to be sure, a margin of error in the dates paleontologists assign. But the experts are confident that 14,000 years old is about the right age, and they have good reason for their confidence. Suppose, though, that they are wrong. If the paintings are in fact 15,000 years old (an age that lies outside the acknowledged margin of error), should we consider Professor Cro epistemically blameworthy for having testified as she did? Does her testimony infringe a claim?

We can and should hold people blameworthy for testifying on the basis of insufficient evidence. If purely on the basis of anecdotal evidence or an experiment run on just twelve subjects, a scientist were to testify that drinking green tea cures poison ivy, we would consider him epistemically remiss. But arguably, the case we are considering is different, for Professor Cro had what everyone concedes was excellent evidence. We might, of course, take a hard-line. You have a right to remain silent, so anything you say can be held against you. Despite the best efforts of the community of paleontologists, which were in fact quite good, Professor Cro testified falsely, and thereby misled scholars who took her word. Hard-liners insist that responsible testimony, like knowledge, requires truth. If so, she should not have testified as she did.

If we take the hard-line, false testimony violates a right, even if at the time of the testimony there was no reason to believe it false and overwhelming reason to believe it true. Perhaps the counterexample to a highly confirmed universal generalization had not yet even arisen. Perhaps the methods required to discredit it had not yet been developed. Nevertheless, if I give you my word that p, and in fact $\sim p$, I infringe your claim. Such a hard-line might seem to violate the maxim 'Ought implies can'. If I genuinely could not have known that p is false, and/or that the evidence for p is misleading, then I was under no obligation to deny that p. Hence, it may seem, I ought not be faulted for testifying that p. But things are not so simple. For I need not have testified at all. Perhaps I could not have known that p is false. But I surely could have known—indeed, surely did know—that p might be false. I could simply have held my tongue. 'Ought implies can' then does not directly discredit the hard-line.

We can avoid imparting falsehoods by exercising our epistemic Miranda rights. In scholarly circles, testimony cannot be compelled. But withholding testimony has a price. In hoarding information, we lose opportunities to advance understanding through education, collaboration, testing and building on other people's findings. It is irresponsible to testify without adequate evidence. It may be equally irresponsible to be excessively demanding in matters of evidence. There is a familiar tension between the desire for well-grounded information and the requirement that the information consist entirely of truths. Reasonable levels of evidence tend to be satisfied by falsehoods as well as truths. If we raise our standards enough to eliminate the falsehoods, cognitively valuable truths are excluded as well. The parallel to arguments that push us toward skepticism is plain. We can avoid judging falsely by refraining from judging at all. We can avoid testifying falsely by refraining from testifying at all. But refusing to believe and refusing to testify are cognitively costly. The risk of error is sometimes worth taking. Nevertheless, if the hard-line is correct, I put myself morally and epistemically at risk every time I testify. That gives me an incentive to increase the level of evidence I demand. To protect myself from inadvertent wrongdoing, I don't just want adequate grounds. I want grounds that I am sure are adequate. That is a more demanding standard. It may be an unsatisfiable one. If Dr. Cro was blameworthy, despite the fact that the test needed to discredit her report had not even been invented at the time she testified, I should hardly be complacent merely because my remarks satisfy contemporary standards. The worry is that the hard-line, by supplying a disincentive to testify, stifles information transfer at the cutting edge of inquiry.

A similar worry can be raised about promising. If my failure to keep my promise, for whatever reason, puts me morally in the wrong, I should be extremely circumspect about making promises. Before I give my word I should be absolutely sure I can deliver. Unfortunately, I cannot be absolutely sure. Neither can anyone else. Should we stop making promises? Given the utility of the practice, that seems a high price to pay. Luckily, we don't have to pay it. Granted, we shouldn't give our word cavalierly, but obsessive caution is not required. When I make you a promise, we both recognize that I *might* not be able to keep it. Unforeseen circumstances might interfere. Even if I am scrupulous about my moral character, that recognition should not prevent me from giving my word. For part of the institution of promising is that there are forgivable lapses and acceptable excuses. If I failed to keep my promise to meet you to go comparison shopping for grass seed, I infringed the claim I gave you. But if the reason for my absence was that I was negotiating with a deranged student who was holding the dean hostage, my failure to keep my word is excusable. Perhaps I owe you an explanation, but it is not clear that I owe you an apology, since we agree, and know that we agree, that that sort of demand on one's time takes precedence.

We might want to say the same about testimony. Although truth is required and falsehood infringes the word taker's claim, there are forgivable lapses and acceptable excuses. You exonerate me for breaking my promise, saying, "You couldn't have known." My lapse is excusable, for there was no way I could have foreseen the hostage situation that prevented me from keeping my word. The message is this: Had you known that q when you said what you did, you would have been seriously remiss. But since you couldn't have known, you are morally off the hook. We might want to make the same sort of move in the case of false but well-grounded testimony. Had Professor Cro known that the cave paintings were 15,000 years old, or had more accurate dating methods been available, she would have been seriously remiss when she testified that they are 14,000 years old. But since she couldn't have known—since the requisite ferrous oxide dating test will not be developed for another fifty years—her lapse is excusable. We can then retain the hard-line requirement that the content of testimony must be true, while weakening the disincentive to testify by conceding that some false testimony is excusable.

Still, one might wonder whether the truth requirement is an idle wheel. In deciding whether it is reasonable to give or accept testimony that p, we consider whether the assertion that p is well grounded. Even though we recognize that well-groundedness is no assurance of truth, we don't and can't go on to ask the further question: Besides being well grounded, is p also true? For our best hope of discovering whether p is true lies in discovering whether p is well grounded. Current standards of acceptability are the best standards we have for deciding that. It makes no sense, then, to construe the truth requirement as an additional factor that figures in the decision whether to give or to accept testimony that p. Nevertheless, it does not follow that the truth requirement is idle. It may play a different role. Testimony is responsibly proffered and accepted when it satisfies the current standards of the relevant epistemically reputable community of inquiry. Subsequently, new evidence, improved techniques, or refined standards may lead us to conclude that previously accepted testimony is false. If its being false is a sufficient reason to reject it as error, we have the resources to construe revisions in beliefs, methods, and standards as improvements rather than mere changes in our understanding. If the best we can say is that p satisfied the standards accepted at one time but not those accepted at a later time, we do not have such resources. For in that case changes in what it is reasonable to believe or to testify are like changes in fashion. Sometimes one standard or skirt length is in style, sometimes another. A truth requirement is not the only requirement that could play this role, nor is it clearly the best choice.[9] But some such requirement is needed to distinguish advancing understanding from changing intellectual fashions.

Word giving, according to Thomson, requires uptake. The invitee, she says, needs to receive and accept the invitation to rely on the truth of p. But, it seems, we are inundated with testimony we have no use for. Textbooks, news reports, lectures, and gossip supply vast amounts of seemingly useless information. Does this discredit Thomson's account? To decide, we need to consider what accepting an invitation involves. To accept my invitation to dinner on Sunday at seven requires appearing for dinner on the appointed day at roughly the appointed time. To accept my invitation to call on me if you need help is different. You accept my invitation if you henceforth consider yourself free to call—if, that is, you adjust your attitudes so that asking me for help is now a live option. You may turn out not to need my help. But even if no call is made, the invitation is accepted. Testifiers issue invitations of both kinds. My testimony may provide you with the specific information you need for a particular purpose. I inform you that in the 1760s Hume was a diplomat in Paris. Relying on my expertise, you incorporate that information into your history of Scottish thought. But not all information transfer is on a need-to-know basis. I make the same remark in an introductory philosophy lecture. I invite my students to rely on its truth, just as I invited you. Most of them will do nothing with it. They have nothing to rely on it for. In my lecture I, as it were, issue an open invitation. I invite my students to rely on the truth of my assertion when and if they need to. If they are prepared to do so, they accept my invitation. Both of these sorts of reliance fit Thomson's model easily. The argument that we receive vast amounts of useless information does not discredit her analysis.

What should we say about proffered testimony that is flatly disbelieved? The invitation to rely is issued, received, and refused. Should we say that such testimony is abortive? If so, there is no word giving without word taking. This seems wrong. The suspect's mother asserts under oath that he was home watching television at the time the crime was committed. No one believes her. Still, it seems, she testifies that he was home. (She couldn't be charged with perjury if she didn't testify.) But simply to jettison the uptake requirement also seems wrong. If my students sleep through the lecture where I assert that Hume was a diplomat, or I make that assertion in a language they don't understand, we would be reluctant to say that I gave them my word that Hume was a diplomat. They can't take my word for it, since they have no idea what my word is. I recommend, then, that the uptake requirement be modified. Testimony is abortive, I suggest, unless the invitation is received. But the invitation need not be accepted. Receiving an invitation to rely on the truth of an assertion is not just having one's sense organs stimulated by the assertion. To receive such an invitation requires understanding the content of the assertion, recognizing it as an assertion, and acknowledging that one has been invited to rely on its truth. This in turn involves recognizing that it has been put forth as having appropriate epistemic backing. I suggest that testimony occurs when a statement of purportedly established fact is offered as someone's word and the offer is understood, recognized, and acknowledged, whether or not it is believed.

When I testify that p, what do I invite you to take my word for? The obvious answer is that I invite you to take my word that the sentence I utter—the sentence that replaces the schematic letter p—is true. This can't be right, though. For I can give you my word that the cave paintings are 14,000 years old by uttering any of a variety of syntactically and semantically divergent sentences, as well as via contextually appropriate nods, gestures, and inarticulate grunts. I might, for example,

(1) assert, "The cave paintings at Les Eyzies are 14,000 years old."
(2) assert, "At Les Eyzies, the cave paintings are 14,000 years old."
(3) assert, "14K years ago the cave paintings at Les Eyzies were painted."
(4) respond to the question, "How old are they?" by saying, "14,000 years old."
(5) nod when asked, "Are you testifying that they are 14,000 years old?"

As testimony, (1)–(5) amount to the same thing. I issue the same invitation, I shoulder the same epistemic burden, regardless of which of the five I use. The common denominator, Thomson believes, is the proposition they all express. According to Thomson, I invite you to take my word, not for the sentence, if any, that I utter, but for the proposition that I assert.[10] Like Goodman and Quine, I have doubts about the existence of propositions. So I am disinclined to accept this part of Thomson's analysis. But even if we eschew propositions, we are not forced to conclude that every difference between sentences uttered constitutes a difference in the content they convey. Sameness of proposition is not the only criterion of semantic equivalence for sentences. Other, more flexible criteria are available. We might follow Goodman and Scheffler and explicate the equivalence of (1)–(5) in terms of secondary extensions.[11] Then (1)–(5) amount to the same thing because they are all that-the-caves-paintings-at-Les-Eyzies-are-14,000-years-old-assertions. Or we might follow Sellars and explicate the equivalence in terms of dot quotes.[12] Other alternatives are also available. We need not decide among them here. Various symbols amount to the same thing in the sense that concerns us just in case a testifier shoulders the same epistemic burden regardless of which of them she uses in giving her word. Let us say that all such symbols *convey the same message*. Doubtless this is imprecise, but further precision is unnecessary for our purposes. Thomson is surely right to recognize that what I invite you to rely on when I give you my word that p, is not, or not only, the truth of the particular sentence that I utter. In fact, I would go further and say that it is not, or not only, the truth of the sentence or proposition (if such there be) that I assert.

If I testify that p, I give you my word that p is true. But if I testify that the cave paintings are 14,000 years old, I do not commit myself to the truth of the sentence 'The cave paintings are 14,000 years old'. I would be astounded if they were exactly 14,000 years old. I would consider myself, and be considered by others, to be right, if I was off by no more than a few hundred years. Indeed, in the absence of new evidence, I am apt to utter the very same sentence in my lectures year after year. If I thought the paintings were exactly 14,000 years old this year, I should update my notes and say that they are 14,001 years old next year. Evidently, I use a seemingly precise sentence to convey a considerably vaguer message. It is the truth of the vague message, not the truth of the precise sentence, that my testimony commits me to. There is nothing disingenuous about this. I am not pretending to provide more precision than I do. It is tacitly acknowledged on all sides that the age I ascribe has a fairly generous margin of error. If the actual age of the painting falls within the margin, my testimony counts as true.

Contextual factors also create a discrepancy between medium and message. When in my lecture on prehistoric Europe, I say, "There are no cave paintings of women," my testimony is not falsified by the recent work of a graffiti artist in a cavern in Kentucky, for the scope of my quantifier is tacitly restricted. The message my testimony conveys is that none of the paintings in a contextually circumscribed range (which excludes graffiti in Kentucky) portrays a woman. A testimony's message may diverge considerably from the medium that conveys it—the contents of the conveying sentences, strictly construed.

How then is it that the message conveyed is the message received? What prevents my audience from concluding that my testimony reports the exact date the paintings were produced, or from ascribing to it a significantly different penumbra of vagueness? If all parties to an exchange share the relevant assumptions, there is no mystery. In that case, everyone imposes the same constraints on the interpretation of my words. But why should we think this? If the assumptions have not been expressly agreed to, why should we think that they are shared? Background assumptions plainly vary from one linguistic context to the next. Moreover, they are continually revised and updated as discourse proceeds. But they are neither random nor idiosyncratic. Grice's account explains why. Linguistic communication, he contends, is governed by general principles that focus discussion and coordinate presuppositions. Communication has a variety of functions. Consoling someone may require different principles than informing him does. Grice articulates the maxims that he takes to underlie communication for the purpose of information transfer. I am not confident that the scope of the maxims is as wide as he believes. Producing a sound argument may require stating the obvious, thus violating a maxim of quantity. Nevertheless, I believe the Gricean maxims, or maxims very close to them,[13] apply to testimony, and explain how testimony conveys information when medium and message diverge.

Grice's basic insight is that communication is genuinely interpersonal. Although this does not sound particularly momentous, Grice shows that it is a deep and deeply important point. The informant is not just a spouter of truths; nor is the receiver an empty vessel into which data are poured. Because every interchange involves presuppositions, speaker and hearer must understand each other. This is not just a matter of grasping the words that constitute an utterance or inscription. It involves appreciating why, to what end, and against what background those particular words are uttered or inscribed. To understand an utterance requires understanding its utterer, for communication is a matter of mutual attunement. This is why Grice contends that communication depends on cooperation. Informative exchanges are, he maintains, governed by the Cooperative Principle: "Make your conversational contribution such as is required at the stage at which it occurs, by the accepted purpose or direction of the talk exchange in which you are engaged."[14] To satisfy this principle, he argues, involves satisfying subsidiary maxims. Among these are

(a) the maxims of quantity:
1. Make your contribution as informative as is required (for the current purposes of the exchange);
2. Do not make your contribution more informative than is required.

(b) a supermaxim of quality:
Try to make your contribution one that is true.

as well as two submaxims:
1. Do not say what you believe to be false.
2. Do not say that for which you lack adequate evidence.

and:

(c) a relevance requirement.[15]

Although the cooperative principle and the maxims are cast as instructions to the speaker, they supply rules for the hearer as well. Ceteris paribus, in order to interpret an informative utterance or inscription correctly, we must construe it as one that satisfies (or at least purports to satisfy) the Gricean rules. In a communicative exchange, not only does each party conform her contributions to the maxims, she also takes it that the other parties are doing so. Interpreting, then, is not a matter of rote application of the homophonic rule or of some regimented principle of interlinguistic translation. It involves consideration of what interpretation of the speaker's remarks would be one that the speaker could have, or at least believe herself to have, adequate evidence for, what interpretation would yield a statement that the speaker would consider informative, relevant, and so on. You don't take me to have testified that the cave paintings are *exactly* 14,000 years old, because you don't think it remotely likely that I have evidence that could support such a precise statement, nor do you think that such precision is required, or even desirable, in the context in which we are speaking. You take me to have testified that the paintings are in the neighborhood of 14,000 years old, since that is an informative, contextually relevant contention that you think I could have adequate evidence for. You also deploy the maxims in assigning the neighborhood a size. What is conceded on all sides goes without saying, for if all parties agree that p, 'p' is uninformative. Therefore, you take me to be saying something more specific than what everyone in the audience already knows anyway. Considerations of relevance provide further constraints. If the discussion requires that the date be specified within 500 years, I am uncooperative if my remark is not that specific. Since you take me to be cooperative, you therefore interpret my remark as saying that the paintings are within 500 years of being 14,000 years old. If we only need a date within 500 years of the right one, it would be uncooperative of me to be much more precise than that. So you have reason to refrain from taking my statement to be overly specific.

Gricean considerations show how complex and context-sensitive uptake is. To properly interpret a speaker's testimony involves an awareness of the course and point of the discussion, as well as an appreciation both of what has already been established and of what goes without saying. It also involves epistemic sensitivity. The speaker purports to be satisfying the maxim of quality. So we need to construe her as saying something she has, or takes herself to have, or purports to have adequate evidence for. To do that, we need to be sensitive to the relevant epistemic norms. We need, that is, to understand what sort of and how much evidence is required. To decide among the available interpretations of a speaker's words requires recognizing which of them she can purport to have adequate evidence for, hence what evidence she might have and what evidence would be adequate. Evidential standards vary. A measurement that would be acceptable in the kitchen is apt to be too rough to accept in the lab. Finally, we need interpersonal awareness. It is not enough to know what has actually transpired in the course of the discussion and what is actually required by way of evidence. We also need to understand what each party takes to have transpired and what each takes to be required.

To understand someone's testimony is to construe it as a statement of fact (or a collection of statements of fact) for which the testifier purports to have adequate grounds. People sometimes testify without adequate grounds, being either misleading or misled about the strength of their evidence. In taking someone's word, we assume that she is neither. We take it that she has the adequate grounds that she purports to have. This might be doubted. Suppose Pat says, for no good reason, that p. Although she realizes that Pat has no justification for her remark, Sarah has very good reasons for believing that p, reasons she never brought to bear on the issue prior to hearing Pat's totally unfounded utterance. Sarah is now justified in relying on the truth of p, and came to be justified via Pat's testimony. Still, one wants to say, Sarah does not take Pat's word that p. Pat's statement was a catalyst, but conveyed no epistemic entitlement. Sarah did not accept Pat's invitation to rely on her word, but took the occasion to marshal her own evidence. Sarah did not take Pat's word. There is a harder case, though. Suppose Sasha testifies, on relatively weak grounds, that q. Sasha's grounds are inadequate. But they're not *nothing*. They afford some reason to believe that q. Jenny has additional grounds, which are also insufficient if taken alone. But combined with Sasha's grounds, they yield sufficient evidence for q. Jenny relies partly, but not wholly, on Sasha's testimony. I suggest that the strength of Jenny's reliance on Sasha's testimony is determined by the strength of the backing Jenny takes Sasha's testimony to have. Word taking, then, can be a matter of degree. We may partly rely on the word of someone whose evidence we consider weak.

We are justified in taking someone's word only to the extent that we are justified in thinking her grounds are adequate. But we can take a speaker's word and be justified in doing so without knowing what her grounds are. In some cases, a speaker's behavior might afford ample evidence that she is satisfying the cooperative principle, hence satisfying the second maxim of quality. Sometimes, for example, in reporting one's zip code, that is enough, since this is the sort of thing a normal speaker knows. In cases where evidence of cooperation is not enough, we may know the particular speaker to be morally and epistemically trustworthy. Then even though we lack access to her grounds, we know that she would not be testifying if they were inadequate. In yet other cases, testimony may be given in a context where there are sufficient institutional safeguards to block epistemically irresponsible testimony. The fact that the experts in the field raise no objection indicates that the evidence, whatever it is, satisfies the relevant standards. If the field is epistemically estimable, institutional safeguards are safeguards enough.

Testimony, then, conveys more than the facts that constitute its message. It also conveys that those facts have been established to the satisfaction of the relevant community of inquiry and that the testifier is in a position to epistemically entitle her audience to believe them. That being so, a speaker testifies responsibly only if she is in a position to shoulder the epistemic burden for everything her testimony conveys. It might seem that this does not add to the load. Perhaps a speaker is epistemically entitled to convey anything she is epistemically entitled to believe, and epistemically entitled to believe anything that satisfies the standards of the relevant community of inquiry. If so, the brute fact that she has adequate grounds suffices. She need not be aware that her grounds are adequate. She need not even be aware of what her grounds are.

This is in line with currently popular epistemological theories that hold that a subject can be fully warranted in believing that p, without being aware of what supplies the warrant. Such theories provide an attractive account of perceptual warrant. Seeing a rabbit twenty feet away in the center of his visual field wholly justifies a subject with good eyesight in believing that there is a rabbit in front of him. He need not have the conceptual resources to appreciate that his perception supplies him with grounds, much less know anything about the perceptual mechanisms that make seeing reliable. At least in some cases, then, there is reason to believe that it is the having of grounds, not the awareness that one has grounds, that is required for warrant. But even if this is so, and even if it holds for warranted belief generally, nothing directly follows about what is required to convey warrant.

Being in a position to convey warrant requires more than merely being warranted. A subject who has scattered evidence that warrants her belief that p, but has never put that evidence together, does not realize that she is warranted in believing that p. It does not seem that she can give her word that p, since she is not prepared to shoulder the epistemic burden for the truth of p. A subject whose evidence in fact warrants q might fail to realize that her belief that q is warranted because she thinks that stronger evidence is required. (Perhaps she thinks that Cartesian doubts have to be answered before one is epistemically entitled to believe an empirical theory. Or perhaps, having confused *The Philadelphia Inquirer* with *The National Enquirer*, she considers her source unreliable.) Again, it seems, she is unable to shoulder the epistemic burden, since she considers her grounds inadequate. These examples suggest that in order to testify responsibly, one must not only be justified in believing that p, one must also be justified in believing that one is justified in believing that p.

This sets an additional demand, but not an unsatisfiable one. It does not require ever more evidence for p. Rather, it requires reason to think that one's evidence or grounds for p are adequate. It therefore introduces second-order considerations about the adequacy of grounds. If Jenny is to be justified in believing that she is justified in believing that p, she needs to appreciate her grounds. This requires critical self-awareness. She needs self-awareness because she must be cognizant of the beliefs and perceptual states that supply her grounds. The self-awareness must be critical, for she must recognize that the considerations she adduces qualify as reasons to believe that p. The fox is warranted in believing that there is a rabbit in front of him, but is not justified in believing that his belief is warranted, for he has no idea why he trusts his senses or whether it is reasonable to do so. Jenny also needs some awareness of the relevant epistemic standards. She has to know what sort of evidence and how much evidence is required in a context like this to support a belief like the belief that p. She needs, moreover, to credit those standards. She must consider them reasonable, or at least not unreasonable. If she considered the accepted standards of evidence to be epistemically shoddy, she would have no reason to take their satisfaction to confer epistemic entitlement. Knowing that one's reasons satisfy the standards of the contemporary astrological community does not inspire confidence in the belief they are supposed to support. Finally, she needs to recognize that her grounds satisfy the relevant epistemic standards.

This is fine, one might say, if we are talking about the first link in the chain of epistemic entitlers. If a subject is attuned to the standards of the relevant community of inquiry, recognizes that they are reasonable standards, and realizes that her evidence satisfies those standards, she justifiably believes that she is justified in believing and in testifying that p. Often this is not the case. As an intermediate link in the chain, Mike has it on good authority that p, and undertakes to pass the information along. He read it in the newspaper, heard it in a lecture, learned it in school. But he is in no position to supply the backing for it. Nor does he have the expertise to recognize or endorse the standards of the community that underwrites his belief. Still, one wants to say that as an informed layman he can testify responsibly that the political situation in Rwanda is unstable, that electrons have negative charge, that Hume was a diplomat. The reason is that an informed layman is not just a gullible stooge. He believes and has good reason to believe that the authorities his judgment rests on are good. The source he relies on to back up his assertion is not only a reliable source; it is also a source he considers reliable and has good reason to consider reliable. Even intermediate links in the chain of epistemic entitlers, then, satisfy the demands of critical self-awareness.

Testimony turns out to be more complex than the idea of information transfer might initially suggest. Testifying that p is not just asserting p. Nor, of course, is testifying that p the same as testifying that one is warranted in testifying that p. But it would be unreasonable for you to take my word for it that p, if I was not warranted in testifying that p. When I testify to you that p, then, I do not merely impart the information that p is the case. I also give you reason to believe that p is warranted and that I am warranted in testifying that p. In addition, my testimony gives you moral and epistemic claims against me. If p is false (and no exonerating conditions obtain), then in testifying that p, I both impart false beliefs and do you a moral wrong. I mislead you about p's epistemic standing by assuring you that it is epistemically safe to rely on the truth of p, when in fact it is not. So the ground for the moral wrong is an epistemic wrong. In the realm of rights, epistemology and ethics overlap.

Notes

1. Judith Jarvis Thomson, *The Realm of Rights* (Cambridge, MA: Harvard University Press, 1990), p. 298.
2. There are matters of degree here. Sometimes a speaker supplies some reasons but relies on authority to provide the additional backing that her statements need.
3. Thomson, pp. 299–300.
4. Thomson, p. 64.
5. Thomson, pp. 94–95.
6. It may be, but it need not. We sometimes reproach promise breakers by saying, "You should not have promised what you weren't going to deliver."
7. Thomson, pp. 305–306.
8. I am not sure about this. Thomson may unduly downplay the epistemological factor in promising. My point, though, is that whatever we should say about promising, the epistemological dimension is crucial to the claims given through testimony.
9. See my *Considered Judgment* (Princeton, N.J.: Princeton University Press, 1997), chapters 3–4, for an alternative.

10. Thomson, p. 295.

11. Nelson Goodman, *Problems and Projects* (Indianapolis: Hackett Publishing, 1972), pp. 221–238; Israel Scheffler, *Inquiries* (Indianapolis: Hackett Publishing, 1986); see also Catherine Z. Elgin, *Between the Absolute and the Arbitrary* (Ithaca, N.Y.: Cornell University Press, 1997), pp. 110–130.

12. Wilfrid Sellars, *Science and Metaphysics* (London: Routledge and Kegan Paul, 1968), pp. 91–116.

13. I have suggested elsewhere that the first maxim of quality should be revised to 'Do not say what you believe to be misleading', rather than 'Do not say what you believe to be false'.

14. Paul Grice, "Logic and Conversation," *Studies in the Way of Words* (Cambridge, Mass.: Harvard University Press, 1989), p. 26.

15. Grice, pp. 26–27.

Chapter 6

Virtue Ethics without Character Traits

Gilbert Harman

Presumed Parts of Normative Moral Philosophy

Normative moral philosophy is often thought to be concerned with at least three questions. Using standard (misleading) terminology, these questions are: (1) What is it for something to be one's moral *duty*? (2) How are we to assess the relative *goodness* or *value* of situations? (3) What are the *moral virtues* and *vices*? So, normative moral philosophy is often supposed to have at least three parts: the theory of duty, the theory of value, and the theory of virtue.

Deontology, or the study of *moral duty*, is supposed to be concerned with what agents ought morally to do on various occasions, what they have to do or are morally required to do, what they may do or are morally permitted to do, and what it is morally right or wrong for them to do. The theory might also discuss what sorts of moral obligations people have and perhaps even what sorts of moral duties they have in some ordinary sense of "duty."

The theory of *value* is supposed to try to say what it is for a state of affairs to be good, all things considered, and for one situation to be better, all things considered, than another. More generally, such a theory might try to indicate what it is for a situation to be evaluated correctly as right or wrong, just or unjust, and so forth. There is a dis-agreement as to whether it makes sense to ask whether one state of affairs is simply better than another, all things considered, as opposed to being better in one or another way. Philippa Foot[1] and Judith Jarvis Thomson[2] have argued that this does not make sense. Others believe that it does make sense to ask what Foot and Thomson say does not make sense. One complication is that Thomson does allow that it makes sense to say that one situation is better than another for people in general. In any event, she has a theory of value in the sense of a theory of what it is for something to be good or bad in one or another way.

Finally, the theory of *moral virtue* is supposed to try to specify the moral virtues and vices. It would try to indicate what it is to act virtuously or viciously on a particular occasion and how that is related to what it is to have a good or bad moral character. It would try to specify which traits (of acts or character) are moral virtues, which are moral vices, and which are neither moral virtues nor moral vices.

It is controversial whether moral philosophy has these three parts or whether the relatively standard terminology I have used is the best. One might object to calling the first sort of theory a "theory of moral duty" on the grounds that the ordinary notion of "duty" is too narrow or that there is no such thing as "moral duty" in any strict sense. I have already mentioned that Foot and Thomson object to the idea that there is a single sort of goodness of situations relevant to morality. There are reasons to doubt the existence of the sorts of robust character traits that figure in standard accounts of virtue.[3] Many writers distinguish "the right" from "the good," where this might be the distinction between what I called the theory of duty and what I called the theory of value,[4] with or without a special theory of the goodness of situations. The theory of "the good" is sometimes taken to include the theory of virtue. Alternatively, the term "virtue" can be used to stand for any good-making characteristic whatsoever, so as to be able to talk, for example, about the virtues of aerobic exercise, in which case the theory of virtue is the same as the theory of value. Sometimes the right is taken to include the rightness of states of affairs and even the basic justice in a state,[5] which for many writers are issues that fall under what I am calling the theory of value rather than the theory of duty. So, there are various issues both of terminology and of substance. Nevertheless, many writers do accept something like the threefold distinction in notions that I am using here.

Treating One Notion or Theory as Basic

General normative moral theories sometimes take one of these notions to be more "basic" than the others. There are at least three ways to do this, deontological ethics, consequentialism, and virtue ethics.

Deontological ethics takes the theory of duty to be most basic. For example, a deontological theory might say that a situation is good to the extent that it involves a person's doing his or her duty or (in one sort of Kantian version) in a person's *trying* to do his or her duty. A virtuous character might be identified with a robust disposition to do one's duty. Different virtues and vices might be identified in terms of dispositions to perform different duties.

Utilitarianism or *consequentialism* takes the theory of value to be most basic and explains the rest of morality in terms of value. Moral duties might be explained as acts that make things better (or better for people generally), or that tend to do so, or that are instances of rules that would make things better if everyone followed them. Moral virtues might be identified with those character traits possession of which tends to make things generally better (or better for people generally), and moral vices might be identified with those character traits possession of which tends to make things generally worse.

Finally, *virtue ethics* takes virtue and vice to be at least as basic as moral duty and the goodness of situations. Many versions of virtue ethics take character traits to be basic. For example, one version supposes that the goodness of a situation (at least, how good it is for people in general) has to do with the extent of human flourishing it involves, where human flourishing requires full possession of the morally virtuous character traits. Being a virtuous person is identified with being a person in full possession of the virtuous character traits. This version explains moral duty in terms of a virtuous person: what one ought morally to do in a particular situation is to do what a virtuous person would do in that situation.[6]

In recent work, Judith Jarvis Thomson has also been developing a moral theory that in some ways resembles or sounds like virtue ethics, although it differs in significant ways from the standard version.[7] The purpose of the present paper is to discuss certain aspects of this theory of Thomson's.

My purpose is quite limited. I do not discuss Thomson's objections to consequentialism, for example. Instead I am concerned entirely with her virtue ethics. In particular, I want to examine the extent to which Thomson's version of virtue ethics avoids objections that seem to me to be conclusive against a different version. So, I begin by describing that other version and the serious objections that have been raised to it. Then I describe some aspects of Thomson's view and consider how it does with respect to those objections.

One Version of Virtue Ethics

In one version of virtue ethics,[8] moral virtues are robust character traits possessed by ideally morally virtuous people. The character traits in question are acquired robust habits of perception, motivation and action: habits of perceiving situations in certain ways, habits of being motivated to act in certain ways, and habits of actually acting in those ways. On this view, to specify a moral virtue is to specify the relevant perceptual, motivational, and behavioral habits.

I quickly list some points about character traits. First, they are to be distinguished from possession of certain knowledge or skills, innate temperament, or psychological illness. Second, people are thought to differ in what character traits they possess. Third, the traits are supposed to be robust in the sense that they are relatively long lasting and are or would be exhibited in a variety of circumstances. Fourth, character traits are supposed to be explanatory in the respect that it will at least sometimes be correct to explain actions in terms of character traits and not just in terms of features of the situation. For example, it will at least sometimes be correct to explain an honest action by appeal to the honesty of the agent and not just to features of the situation that would lead anyone to act honestly in that situation.

Possession of moral virtue is often supposed in this approach to be a necessary condition of leading the best sort of life for a human being; in other words, possession of the moral virtues is often taken to be part of what is involved in human flourishing. Even if a person were materialistically successful and content with life, if the person lacked an important moral virtue, he or she could not be leading the best sort of life and could not flourish in the relevant sense, on this view.

On this view, ideally virtuous people are robustly disposed to do what they ought morally to do. Other people should try to become so disposed and should in various situations imitate virtue. In a typical situation of moral choice, an agent ought to do whatever a virtuous person would do in that situation.

However, on this view the goal is not just to do the right thing. It is to be the right sort of person. One needs to develop a virtuous character. So, the moral education of children should be aimed at such character development and might consist in describing to them the ideal virtues as they are expressed in action[9] together with the sort of training that will lead children to acquire virtuous habits.[10]

Objection to Explaining What One Ought Morally to Do in Terms of What an Ideally Virtuous Person Would Do

One obvious objection to the standard form of virtue ethics is to its account of the relation between what a person ought morally to do and what it is to be a virtuous person. The objectionable claim is that what one ought morally to do in a given situation is to do what a virtuous person would do in that situation. The objection is that this cannot cover all cases, because sometimes a nonvirtuous person will be in a situation that a virtuous person would never be in.[11]

To some extent the point is acknowledged in the idea that a person who is not yet virtuous should try to develop the virtues. That is something a virtuous person does not need to do; so, developing the virtues is a way that the nonvirtuous person should act that is not just to imitate the way a virtuous person would act. But there are various other cases as well.

For example, a person who has done something wrong often ought morally to apologize to those affected by his or her action. However, an ideally virtuous person would not have done the wrong thing in the first place, and so would have nothing to apologize for.

Similarly, consider a person who is aware that he or she tends to be weak-willed and to give in to temptation. Should such a person make plans with others that will be undermined if the person gives in to temptation in the midst of carrying out the plans? Perhaps not; but an ideally virtuous person would not suffer from weakness of the will and could make plans with others without fear of ruining everything by giving in to temptation at just the wrong moment. In this sort of case a person should precisely not do what an ideally virtuous person would do, because that would in a way be to pretend that he or she had the sort of character that he or she does not have.

Doing What a Virtuous Person Would Advise One to Do

One might try to modify the account of what a not wholly virtuous agent ought to do by saying that an agent ought morally to do what a virtuous person would advise the agent to do. This would be to move some distance from the original version of virtue ethics in the direction of a critic-centered or spectator-centered moral theory, and it has its own problems. A morally virtuous agent might think that he or she ought not to give another person advice about certain matters, perhaps because it would be better for the other person to figure things out for him or herself, or for other reasons. Furthermore, an agent who is good at acting virtuously might not be good at advising others what to do, just as some people are good at giving advice but not good at doing the right thing themselves.[12]

Objection to Reliance on Character Traits

A less obvious but in my view more important objection to any appeal to what an ideally virtuous person would do comes from current social psychology. It seems that, when people attribute robust character traits to other agents, they do so on the basis of minimal evidence and tend completely to overlook the relevance of features in agents' situations that help to explain why they act as they do. And, although people routinely explain the actions of others by appeal to robust character traits, there is no scientific evidence for the existence of the sorts of traits that people standardly attribute to others. What a person with a seemingly ideal moral character will do in a particular situation is pretty much what anyone else will do in exactly that situation, allowing for random variation.[13]

This is not to deny all individual differences. People have different innate temperaments, different knowledge, different goals, different abilities, and tend to be in or think they are in different situations. All such differences can affect what people will do. But there is no evidence that people also differ in robust character traits or that differences in goals, knowledge, etc. are to be explained by differences in robust character traits.

People unfamiliar with social psychology find these conclusions incredible, just as psychoanalysts find it incredible when they are told that there is no evidence that psychoanalysis has therapeutic value. But our ordinary convictions about differences in character traits can be explained away as due to a "fundamental attribution error" together with "confirmation bias." I have discussed this elsewhere and won't try to say more here.[14]

Similarly, there is no evidence that moral education via "character development" is required for ordinary moral behavior or indeed that it ever happens. The thought that such training is necessary is similar to the thought that children normally have to be taught their first language.[15]

Thomson's Version of Virtue Ethics

To appreciate Thomson's approach, it is important to observe, first, that we use the terminology of particular virtues and vices not only to specify character traits but also to describe particular acts. A person who is not generally honest or dishonest may yet act honestly or dishonestly on a particular occasion. Similarly, someone may act generously on one occasion only, or be conscientious on one occasion only, or be unkind on one occasion only. In developing her account, Thomson starts with a person's acting virtuously or viciously rather than with a person's possessing one or another character trait.

Second, Thomson distinguishes moral virtues, properly so-called, from all-purpose virtues, like courage, industry, prudence, and loyalty, that are useful for both moral and evil purposes. An evil act might be courageous. A villain can be prudent and industrious. One can be loyal to bad companions. Such courage, industry, prudence, and loyalty are not by themselves moral virtues.

Thomson suggests that the proper moral virtues fall into two groups. *Reliance virtues* include justice and honesty (at least if honesty is not just "a sheer unwillingness to lie, come what may," which is "a peculiarly unattractive form of self-righteousness, and thus a minor vice".)[16] *Virtues of concern* include generosity, kindness, and considerateness.[17]

Courage, industry, loyalty, and prudence can be morally praiseworthy if they are exhibited in conduct that is virtuous in one of the basic senses, but not otherwise. Praise of courage, industry, loyalty, and prudence in action is "parasitic on there being other grounds for welcoming the act."[18]

Thomson flirts with a utilitarian virtue ethics in suggesting that the true moral virtues might be distinguished from the all-purpose ones like courage in that "the fact of there being people who possess the virtues is good for us."[19] It is good for us that there are kind and just people. It is not in the same way good for us that there are courageous people, unless those people are also kind and just.

The next point is to specify what morality requires. On the supposition that for each true moral virtue there are corresponding moral vices that are contraries of the virtue, such as being unjust, mean, cruel, etc., Thomson proposes that we identify what morality requires with the avoidance of these contraries. "Morality requires us to *do* a thing if and only if not doing it would be unjust, or mean, or cruel, and so on. Morality requires us *not* to do a thing if and only if doing it would be unjust, or mean, or cruel, and so on."[20]

How Thomson's Version Avoids Problems for Standard Versions of Virtue Ethics

Thomson's version of virtue ethics is concerned in the first instance with virtuous action rather than virtuous character traits. Her version is compatible with the existence of robust character traits, but it does not require that people actually have robust character traits.

It is true that she says she is tempted to identify the virtues by noting that it is good for us that there are virtuous people. So, her idea may be that the virtues are those robust character traits that it is good for us that people have. But the point is really that it is good for us that there are people who act virtuously. It is compatible with this that people do not and maybe even could not have corresponding robust character traits.[21]

Thomson's way of explaining moral requirement also avoids the problem that a person might be in a situation that a fully virtuous person would never be in. She does not explain moral requirement in terms of what an ideally virtuous person would do in a given situation. In such a situation, an agent might still be able to avoid acting cruelly, or unjustly.[22]

Furthermore, Thomson's version is not committed to supposing that "moral education" consists in "character development."

Thomson's Virtue Ethics versus Ross's Theory of prima facie Duties?

What distinguishes Thomson's theory from a deontological theory like Ross's that sees two families of prima facie duties, duties of justice and duties of benevolence? There seems to be a strong parallel between the two views. Wherever Thomson sees a virtue in one or another possible action, Ross sees a prima facie duty, and wherever Ross sees a prima facie duty, Thomson sees a virtue in one or another possible action.

Perhaps there is a disagreement about the order of explanation. Maybe Thomson thinks we have a better grip on what it is for someone to act unjustly or to be inconsiderate on a particular occasion, and Ross thinks we have a better grip on what is involved in the prima facie duty to be honest or benevolent.

One difference is that Ross's duties are prima facie, whereas Thomson's virtues and vices are all or nothing. In Ross's view there may be a conflict in prima facie duties. In Thomson's view there cannot be an analogous conflict. So, for example, Thomson takes it to be impossible to be in a situation in which, if one does A, one will be unjust, and if one does not do A, one will be cruel.[23]

There certainly are cases in which there appears to be a conflict between justice and kindness. A student has written a worthless paper. If the teacher gives the student the failing grade that the paper deserves, the student will not graduate, which will be a hardship both to the student and to the student's family. It would seem not to be fair to the other students that they are held to a higher standard than this student. It might seem to be unjust to give the student a passing grade yet cruel to give the student a failing grade.

How to resolve this apparent conflict? Thomson holds that both these things cannot be true. It cannot be both unjust to give the student a passing grade and also cruel not to do so. It cannot be unjust to do something that it would be cruel not to do and it cannot be cruel to do something that it would be unjust not to do. So, we have to choose between these two possibilities. Which is it? Cruel to fail the student or unjust not to?

Ross would say that we must decide between two prima facie duties, the duty not to be unfair to the other students and the duty not to harm the poorer student. If the duty not to be unfair wins out, then we are not really violating a duty not to harm the student if we fail him. If the duty not to harm the student takes precedence, then that really is our duty and we do not in this case have a duty of fairness to fail the student.

For myself, I find it hard to say whether either of these ways of looking at the issue makes more sense than the other does.

Objectivism

Thomson is an objectivist about the requirements of morality. She says, "a person's having done what morality requires him to do turns on success rather than on intentions—just as, for my own part, I believe we should accept an objectivist view of the virtue properties (and their contraries), that is, a view according to which an act's possessing a virtue property (or its contrary) turns on success rather than on intentions."[24] Does this mean that intentions are irrelevant or just not enough?

Suppose Joan is morally required to return a book to Max. Unconcerned with this requirement, she leaves the book on a bench in the park. It happens that Max is the next along. He finds the book and assumes it has been left there on purpose for him. Has Joan satisfied the moral requirement to return the book? Has she acted justly? Wasn't she careless to leave the book on the bench and isn't carelessness a vice? Perhaps the answer is that carelessness is not a *moral* vice. Carefulness is an all-purpose virtue, not a moral virtue. And, perhaps, it was not unjust of her to leave the book on the bench, given how things worked out!

But can't someone do the wrong thing through a failure of one of the all-purpose virtues? Must this always involve a failure in one of the moral virtues also? To be sure, if Ophelia fails to return the book *she* owes to Max through imprudence, maybe then she has acted unjustly to Max because of her imprudence. But if she wrongly allows Max to be harmed because of her lack of courage, has she acted unkindly?

Here I am neither sure what the best view is nor sure what Thomson's view is.

Conclusion

Philosophers attracted to virtue ethics should consider the account of ethics that Thomson has been developing. Thomson's account focuses on properties of particular actions and so avoids what seem to be serious problems with versions of virtue ethics that focus on robust character traits.[25]

Notes

1. "Utilitarianism and the Virtues."
2. "The Right and the Good"; "Evaluatives and Directives"; and "Goodness" and "Moral Requirement," from her 1999 *Tanner Lectures*.
3. Ross and Nisbett, *The Person and the Situation*; Railton, "Made in the Shade: Moral Compatibilism and the Aims of Moral Theory"; Doris, "Persons, Situations, and Virtue Ethics"; Harman, "Moral Philosophy Meets Social Psychology: Virtue Ethics and the Fundamental Attribution Error."
4. Thomson, "The Right and the Good"; Ross, *The Right and the Good*.
5. Rawls, *A Theory of Justice*.
6. E.g., Hursthouse, "Virtue Theory and Abortion," p. 225. However, Hursthouse immediately goes on to modify her initial account of what someone ought to do.
7. See note 2.
8. For further elaboration see Harman, "Human Flourishing, Ethics, and Liberty," pp. 307–322, and references included there.
9. Bennett, *The Book of Virtues*.
10. Hursthouse, "Virtue Theory," p. 227, fn. 2.
11. Harman, "Human Flourishing," p. 315. Hursthouse, "Virtue Theory," p. 227, notes a related point: "as if the raped fifteen-year-old girl might be supposed to say to herself, 'Now would Socrates have an abortion if he were in my circumstances?'"
12. We might suppose that being a good moral adviser is one of the virtues that an ideally virtuous person must possess. But then the account would seem to become circular and trivial. One ought morally to do what one would be advised to do by someone who advises one to do something if and only if one ought morally to do it.
13. See note 3.
14. Harman, "Moral Philosophy Meets Social Psychology."
15. Harman, "Moral Philosophy and Linguistics."
16. "The Right and the Good," p. 283.
17. Wallace, *Virtues and Vices*, similarly distinguishes three classes of character traits: (1) courage, cowardice, self-indulgence; (2) conscientiousness; and (3) benevolence. His analysis derives in part from Brandt, "Traits of Character: A Conceptual Analysis," pp. 23–37.
18. "The Right and the Good," p. 286.
19. "The Right and the Good," p. 282.
20. "The Right and the Good," p. 286. Wallace says, "It is a plausible thesis generally that the faulty actions philosophers lump under the heading of 'morally wrong' are actions fully characteristic of some vice . . ." (p. 59). Hursthouse, in "Virtue Theory," says, "Every virtue generates a positive instruction (act justly, kindly, courageously, honestly, etc.) and every vice a prohibition (do not act unjustly, cruelly, like a coward, dishonestly, etc.," p. 227. For Thomson, the prohibition against acting like a coward would not be a moral prohibition.
21. Merritt, *Virtue Ethics and Social Psychology of Character*.
22. Hursthouse takes this approach in discussing applications. See also Hursthouse, "Applying Virtue Ethics."
23. Compare Hursthouse's discussion of a similar case, in "Virtue Theory," p. 231: "Someone hesitating over whether to reveal a hurtful truth, for example, thinking it would be kind but dishonest or unjust to lie, may need to realize, with respect to these particular circumstances, not that kindness is more (or less) important than honesty or justice, and not that honesty or justice sometimes requires one to act unkindly or cruelly, but that one does people no kindness by concealing this sort of truth from them, hurtful as it may be."

24. "The Right and the Good," p. 286, fn. 10.
25. I am indebted to Ralph Wedgwood for useful comments.

References

Bennett, W. J. *The Book of Virtues* (New York: Simon & Schuster, 1993).

Brandt, Richard. "Traits of Character: A Conceptual Analysis." *American Philosophical Quarterly* 7 (1970), pp. 23–37.

Doris, John. "Persons, Situations, and Virtue Ethics." *Noûs* 32 (1998), pp. 504–530.

Foot, Philippa. "Utilitarianism and the Virtues." *Proceedings and Addresses of the American Philosophical Association* 57 (1983), pp. 273–283.

Harman, Gilbert. "Human Flourishing, Ethics, and Liberty." *Philosophy and Public Affairs* 12 (1983), pp. 307–322.

———. "Moral Philosophy and Linguistics," in Klaus Brinkman (ed.), *Proceedings of the 20th World Congress of Philosophy: Volume I: Ethics* (Bowling Green: Philosophy Documentation Center, 1999), pp. 107–115.

———. "Moral Philosophy Meets Social Psychology: Virtue Ethics and the Fundamental Attribution Error." *Proceedings of the Aristotelian Society* 99 (1999), pp. 315–331.

Hursthouse, Rosalind. "Virtue Theory and Abortion." *Philosophy and Public Affairs* 20 (1991), pp. 223–246.

———. "Applying Virtue Ethics," in Rosalind Hursthouse, Gavin Lawrence, and Warren Quinn (eds.), *Virtues and Reasons: Philippa Foot and Moral Theory* (Oxford: Clarendon, 1995), pp. 57–75.

Merritt, Maria. *Virtue Ethics and Social Psychology of Character*. Ph. D. Dissertation, University of California at Berkeley, 1999.

Railton, Peter. "Made in the Shade: Moral Compatibilism and the Aims of Moral Theory," in Jocelyne Couture and Kai Nielsen (eds.), *On the Relevance of Metaethics* (Calgary: University of Calgary, 1995), pp. 79–106.

Rawls, John. *A Theory of Justice* (Cambridge, MA: Harvard, 1971).

Ross, L., and R. E. Nisbett. *The Person and the Situation: Perspectives of Social Psychology* (New York: McGraw-Hill, 1991).

Ross, W. D. *The Right and the Good* (Oxford: Clarendon, 1930).

Thomson, Judith J. "Evaluatives and Directives," in Gilbert Harman and Judith Jarvis Thomson, *Moral Relativism and Moral Objectivity* (Cambridge, MA: Blackwell, 1996), pp. 125–154.

———. "The Right and the Good." *Journal of Philosophy* 94 (1997), pp. 273–298.

———. *Tanner Lectures*, delivered at Princeton University, March 24–25, 1999.

Wallace, James D. *Virtues and Vices* (Ithaca: Cornell, 1978).

Chapter 7

Rethinking Kant's Hedonism

Barbara Herman

. . . advise him of his happy state—
Happiness in his power left free to will,
Left to his own free will, his will though free
Yet mutable.
—Milton, *Paradise Lost*

At the very center of the argument in the *Critique of Practical Reason* Kant makes a pair of claims that have been hard to live with (or live down). In his terms they are: (1) that all empirical practical principles are of "one and the same kind," falling under "the principle of self-love or one's own happiness" (*KpV* 22),[1] and (2) that in acting on such principles, the determining ground of action is in every case pleasure.[2] When we add the rule of deliberation that is supposed to follow from (1) and (2)—that when choosing among nonmoral options of action, a *quantitative* measure of expected pleasure is the only possible principle of choice (*KpV* 23)—we get the full flower of Kant's hedonism. Nonmoral action is about pleasure; the rule of choice is to maximize it. In marked contrast to his transformative approach to moral action and choice, Kant's embrace of hedonism seems poorly thought out, something of an embarrassment, better ignored than taken seriously.

To be sure, friendly interpretations of the relevant texts have been offered that would save Kant from the infelicity of hedonism.[3] I no longer think that is the right strategy, primarily because the reading of the texts that tags Kant with a hedonist account of nonmoral action and choice is so clearly correct. Since I have no desire to interpret Kant as embracing a foolish view, in dealing with Kant's hedonism I take a different tack: namely, to suggest that his reasons for putting forward the view, when and as he does, *are* worth taking seriously.

In the discussion that follows I have two aims. One I have just mentioned—to make some sense out of Kant's employment of hedonism.

The other is larger, and will run in the background of the discussion. Kant's hedonism, as I see it, plays a methodological role. It sets the terms for an exploration of the limits of subjective theories of value. Whether they derive from the cruder forms of psychological hedonism or from the sophisticated endorsements of complex valuing, Kant argues that *all* subjective theories are really single-valued. They give rise to views of happiness that are all formally the same as hedonism. And because hedonism can provide a remarkably sophisticated account of action and choice, it cannot be dismissed out of hand. The threat is that in the absence of access to objective values, or values derived from some other authoritative source, hedonism is the *true* theory of motivation and choice. Kant's argument in the *Critique* is that escape from hedonism—theoretically *and* practically—is to be had only through a correct appreciation of the value inherent in the moral law. Trying to figure out how he could think this, and also retain a clear distinction between the concerns of morality and those of happiness, will be the subject of the last part of this essay.

I will start off by examining each of the elements that set up the hedonism: the claim that all empirical practical principles are of the same kind; that the determining ground of nonmoral action is a feeling of pleasure; and last, the quantitative principle of choice. About the first I will argue that even if it is not a successful view, it is not altogether implausible. The second will require some further thoughts about the place of pleasure in Kant's theory of mind and action. And about the third, I want to look closely at the examples Kant uses to illustrate the deliberative principle—what I call the hedonism of choice. They indicate the place where we can begin to see the larger issues that hedonism raises for him.

1 Happiness and the Principle of Self-Love

Hedonism enters early in the *Critique* as part of an argument to show that because the principle of happiness is a material principle, and therefore empirical, it cannot be the basis of any practical law, and so a fortiori, cannot be the basis of the moral law. The first two theorems and their arguments set the stage (*KpV* 21–22):

> *Theorem I*: All practical principles that presuppose an *object* (matter) of the faculty of desire as the determining ground of the will are, without exception, empirical and can furnish no practical laws.

Kant argues: a material practical principle determines the will by virtue of a subject's pleasure in the possible reality of some object; and since there is no necessary connection between any object and a rational agent's capacity to feel pleasure or displeasure, no material principle can be a law. He then advances a twofold claim:

> *Theorem II*: All material practical principles as such are, without exception, of one and the same kind and come under the general principle of self-love or one's own happiness.

The argument for Theorem I introduces a psychological basis for hedonism; Theorem II and its argument connect the hedonism to a theory of happiness. There is much that is puzzling in these texts. Since the most accessible point of entry is through the connection between self-love and happiness in Theorem II, we will start there. So, first off, we need to ask why Kant would hold that all material practical principles are of the same kind.

One might think that by self-love Kant just means concern for one's interests, whatever they are. Then in saying that all material practical principles are of the same kind Kant could be making no more than a formal point. To say that one acts on a principle of self-love is just to say: whatever the object, it is an object of action because, and only because, one has a subjective interest in its existence as an effect of action. Kant would then be a motivational internalist about actions on material principles. There is at least nothing puzzling about that.

But if this were right, Kant should not go on to identify self-love and happiness. All of the actions that fall under self-love, so understood, would outstrip any reasonable conception of human happiness. In fact, Kant does not identify self-love and happiness, but the *principle* of self-love and the *principle* of one's own happiness. He says that someone acts on a principle of self-love when the source of her action is feeling (receptivity), not understanding or rational concepts of value. The claim that the *principle* of happiness is the principle of self-love is therefore trivially true. Kant defines happiness as "a rational being's consciousness of the agreeableness of life uninterruptedly accompanying his whole existence" (*KpV* 22). It is a state or condition we necessarily desire. The idea of my life going well—however I understand that—is pleasing or agreeable to me. If happiness itself is a material object of desire, someone acting on a *principle* of making happiness the object of his will acts on the *principle* of self-love: feeling or receptivity—pleasure felt in the representation of the reality of an object—is the condition of desire and so of choice.[4] We might see this as no more than an elaboration of Kantian internalism.

If there is no immediate textual problem with the identification of the principles of happiness and self-love, the account highlights other features of the argument that call for explanation. One is the role played by pleasure in explaining the connection between self-love and happiness; another is the rather odd conception of happiness.

Now the mere fact that pleasure has entered the story does not by itself signify much. Considered most generally, pleasure is an element in the Kantian account of mind as it bears on action, signifying a subjective relation between agent and object: a relation of fit.[5] It can precede active desire or it can be an effect of the determination of the faculty of desire by something else. As Kant sees it, for *all* determinations of the will and *all* action, there is pleasure in the representation of the *agreement* of an object or action and the faculty of desire or choice. Pleasure is the empirical mark of caring about something. Without it— that is, unless there is a "representation of agreement of an object or action with the subjective conditions of life"—there is no action.[6] (Mutatis mutandis for aversion.)[7] This is true whether we are talking about animals or beings with a rational will, or about nonmoral or moral action. In its primary role, pleasure is not a piece of an hedonic theory of value, but an element in the metaphysics of action. The nature and purpose of pleasure, of feeling, belongs to the account of all action of all things possessed of what Kant calls "life."

Therefore, when Kant assumes psychological hedonism as the truth about nonmoral actions, it is *not* because pleasure is part of the causal history of nonmoral action, but because he holds that in action on a material principle, pleasure always precedes and *determines* the activity of the faculty of desire. Material practical principles determine the will with respect to an object as a function of "the agreeableness . . . expected from the object, which impels activity to produce it" (*KpV* 23). This is a further specification of why all such principles are of the same kind, and it is why Kant can make the claim that the principle of happiness is the *unique* principle of self-love. That is, if, in our nonmoral actions, we always act toward pleasure, and pleasure in what we do (as we go along) is the measure of happiness, then when we act toward what will please us, as we do when we act on any material practical principle, we act on the principle of happiness.

Let us turn now to the conception of happiness. There are various ways in which Kant's talk about happiness is odd. Sometimes Kant describes happiness as an end, indeed as a *necessary* end for human beings; sometimes he describes it as a state. I will suppose he means it is both. It is an unusual state, more like a tone or quality: "a rational being's consciousness of the agreeableness of life uninterruptedly accompanying his whole existence." That is—whatever happiness is materially, in thinking of one's life as happy, one thinks of it as being and feeling agreeable as it goes along. (The source of this notion seems to be the Stoic ideal of self-sufficiency—a state of never wanting any-thing, and in that sense being satisfied [*KpV* 25].) For us, the idea of happiness as a state of satisfaction is "a problem imposed on [every rational but finite being] by his finite nature itself, because he is needy." Given my original set of desires, and the tastes and interests I develop, I just will be moved to plan and live so that as much as possible things go well for me, and I get (or feel) satisfaction from what I do. Now if happiness is also supposed to be an end, or an idea of an end, it cannot, so conceived, provide determinate guidance. There is no predeter-mined set or order of desires that will yield satisfaction, no necessary objects. The formal idea of the satisfaction of whatever ends one chooses for their own sakes is not an idea of an end at all. Kant says that the concept of happiness is *indeterminate*: it sets a task that is in significant ways open-ended.[8]

But if happiness is any kind of end, in what sense can it be neces-sary? Were the necessity natural, then it would be a physical or psy-chological tendency (a purpose) and not an end. The very idea of a naturally necessary end seems to conflict with Kant's idea of an elec-tive will. So the necessity must be rational. Yet if reason is to make hap-piness a necessary end, it must do so in virtue of what we are like as natural beings: as finite rational beings with desires.[9] But what sort of *natural* fact would be the basis for *reason* setting us an end of happi-ness? Why should reason care whether we are happy or not?[10]

Here is a possible story. Given the organization of our faculty of desire, we cannot help but be interested in our welfare, because we cannot be indifferent to our state of agreeableness. But what puts hap-piness on the table for us is something more than this. Because we are rational *and* possess imagination, we not only can conceive of doing and feeling otherwise than we do, we recognize that we have a future whose shape we are able to affect. We come to have the concept of our life, something that we foresee will go along and be pleasurable, or not, depending (partly) on the wisdom of our choices. Happiness is a problem imposed on us in that each of us has to decide how to live *a life*, even if our choice is to do no more than satisfy this or that pre-senting desire. Given our natures as rational and sensible beings with the concept of a life, we have the end of happiness. It is a (quasi-)con-stitutive feature of the way in which we conceive of our material ends, and in that sense a necessity of our human nature.

Beginning with a variety of needs, desires, and interests, work needs to be done with and among them: develop some, defer others, subli-mate, repress—the whole battery of techniques, conscious and uncon-scious, by which we come to be the specific individuals we are. In this way the demand for satisfaction with one's existence drives a process of individuation.[11] And reciprocally, in and through becoming a particular person, we partially resolve the indeterminacy of our conception of happiness. (Only the *idea* of happiness is indeterminate; each of us perforce works out a more determinate conception.) This is part of the explanation why our happiness is a "commission from the side of sensibility" that reason cannot refuse (*KpV* 61). It is only through a finite rational being's formation of a relatively determinate conception of happiness as an end she pursues in her actions that she becomes an agent: namely, a person with reasonably stable and mutually adjusted interests, second-order desires, executive capacities, and the rest.[12] But if we are in the business of "person construction," it will matter a great deal what tools we have. If we are restricted to a hedonism of choice, there will be questions about the shape, or the kind of unity of self we could hope to achieve.

2 The Hedonism of Choice

Kant's full-blown hedonism consists in the view that, for all nonmoral action, we act according to a principle that represents possible objects of choice in terms of their expected pleasure or agreeableness. The range of the hedonism is wide, applying not only to the usual material choices but also to the satisfactions we find "in the mere exercise of our powers, in the consciousness of our strength of soul in overcoming obstacles opposed to our plans . . ." and on to any conception of virtue as a discipline promising a higher kind of satisfaction (*KpV* 23–25). As we have seen, even our happiness is an object of interest only because we represent it as a state of agreeable feeling.

Hedonism is usually taken to be implausible because it conflicts with important claims we make about value and choice. We want to say: some objects are worth choosing because of what they are: beautiful, expressive of some truth, or in some other way of intrinsic value. We might in fact choose such objects as we thought they would give us greater overall satisfaction or make our lives worthwhile, but we think we *ought* to choose them (and ought to be able to choose them) because of what they are—beautiful, or true. Kant seems to hold that we *cannot* do that, not just that we sometimes do not.

In coming to terms with Kant's view, I want first to push the hedonism as far as it can go. It is important for the larger argument that the hedonism not fail prematurely. We need to find the place where it becomes inescapably implausible, since, if I am right, it is Kant's own location of this limit that sets the stage for his more complete view of the relationship between happiness and the moral law. For a while, then, I will try to defend a sophisticated hedonism that might well be Kant's.

Consider the truisms of friendship. We say: we should care about friends because they are our friends, and not because the activities that caring involves promise pleasure. And we should care about friendship because it is one of the goods of human life. Life without others we care about is defective, even when isolation is something we don't mind. When we spend time with a friend it is not because we expect more pleasure than we would get from a visit to the local multiplex. We spend time with friends because that is what friends do.

But a sophisticated hedonism does not imply that every *action* is performed for the sake of the pleasure it separately provides. We can only be moved by the sense that a proposed action or end is agreeable, but we can just as well be responsive to the agreeableness of complex ends as to simple ends or immediate satisfactions. Where ends are rich and complex, they dictate complex courses of action to be taken for their sake. In having a friend one has a range of commitments and interests structured by the kind of thing friendship is. My deciding to spend time talking with a friend rather than going to the movies need not be explained by the pleasure I expect from the time talking. Of course sometimes a choice to spend time with people is best explained by an interest in the pleasure of their company—and sometimes we spend time with friends for that reason. One of the values of friendship is that it increases our opportunities for these and other pleasures. A hedonism can be sensible in these ways. And it can be sensible because the agent's representation of his proposed action is *as* friendship-promoting, which he finds pleasurable.

What of the election of friendship as an end? If our idea of happiness is caught by the thought of "consciousness of the agreeableness of life uninterruptedly accompanying [one's] whole existence," and if we choose friendship for the sake of happiness, then we would choose to have friends because we thought having them would make our life better, in the sense of containing more enjoyable, more satisfying experiences. Surely this makes *some* sense, partly because of the special pleasures of friendship, but also because with good friends, some of the hardships of life are more bearable. And with the best friends, one has access, it is said, to some of the higher forms of feeling that we are capable of having.[13] If this is not the right view of happiness, or of friendship, it is neither foolish nor self-evidently false.

Abstracting, we can say that once we allow for complex ends, we create room *within the hedonism of choice* for the idea of acting for the sake of something other than our pleasure in the immediate object of that action. I take my dog to the vet, not for the pleasure of the trip, but because I care about her health and well-being. Kant will say my interest in her well-being is explained by my feelings for her; but then I often say that too. *Why* we have the ends we do is left unexplained. Some things move me; others don't. Individual characteristics, education, and cultural variations can explain some of the variation in our ends, but explanations of ends in these terms don't get us beyond the causes of differences in receptivity.

What we cannot do on this account is have friends for nonmoral reasons other than that having them gives us pleasure, or read instructive books not for the pleasure of it (immediate or instrumental), but for the sake of the truth to be gained. Given Kant's insistence that the division between material and formal determining grounds of the will is exhaustive—that everything that is a possible principle or object of action belongs either to the sphere of autonomy or to self-love—it would appear that we (necessarily) care for everything that is not a part of morality as an element or way of securing an hedonically satisfying life. Lost, then, one wants to say, are the values of things for their own sakes as a basis of choice—painting, playing music, friendship, learning, the beauties of nature. Is the thought, though, that it is good to have and value these things whether or not they make our lives (*any* lives?) go better? But couldn't one dispute this? The question is about the experience of, say, beautiful things—why we should choose to have such experiences. And then it is certainly not the most foolish thing to say that we should bring the experience of beauty into our lives because a life lived with beauty is a more fully enjoyable one. Aesthetic pleasure may be disinterested, but our interest in having such pleasures is not. They give us, directly or indirectly, satisfactions that contribute to an agreeable life, and, moral considerations aside, that is why we seek to have them.

If we can in these terms understand how we could have and pursue distinct ends as contributing to an overall satisfying life, they give little sense of where these ends come from for us, or why they have the weight they do prior to our grasp of their fit in our lives. Since we cannot appeal to the intrinsic value of ends, we might be left with no more than the instrumental connection of ends to the various biological and psychological elements of our constitution. The form of explanation would be Humean: investigating why we care about what we do, we would regress to some finite list of things that just do matter to us.

Kant has some resources for a principle of end-adoption that fits with this sort of hedonism. As part of the account of our psychological nature as dependent rational beings in *Religion Within the Boundaries of*

Mere Reason, he introduces a capacity that he calls our "predisposition to humanity": an original feature of human nature that leads us to "judge ourselves happy or unhappy only by making comparison with others" (*Religion* 22).[14] Following Rousseau, Kant assumes an initial comparative impulse that seeks equality with others (that no one be superior to me); but our having no independent measure of worth, it is converted into an inclination to "acquire worth in the opinion of others" (*ibid.*): no one should be in a position to judge me less worthy. Since this is a judgment best secured by each striving to be better than the others, and in terms that each will recognize, we gain a social source for ends. Of course, it is a problematic source of things to be valued. The ends one takes on may or may not fit with what one needs; one will come to prefer ends that satisfy a "more is better" rule; and, having a comparative basis of self-worth, one will be drawn into a futile race for competitive superiority.[15] Worse still, it is a basis of self-value that encourages feelings of jealousy and envy, which prompt vice and wrongdoing.[16] But at this stage of the story, that is beside the point. What matters here is that, consistent with the hedonic story, our predisposition to humanity gives us reason to accept ends as our own because they are valued by those whose judgment of our worth matters to us. By itself, this social source of ends does not add a great deal. However, as we will see later on, it plays a key role in the argument that makes dignity, rather than pleasure, a source of value for (some) nonmoral actions. Let us return now to the main discussion. There is more to be said in defense of a sophisticated hedonism.

It is often argued that the inadequacy of any hedonism is easily shown by its inability to countenance actions for ends the agent knows she will not experience (effects at a distance, posthumous effects, etc.). Now, it is quite normal for us to act when success is uncertain. The representation of the value of an end along with the degree of uncertainty of its occurring is part of the calculation of choiceworthiness of actions. So either I am able to choose in conditions of uncertainty, or I can never act for an effect that is not immediate. In cases of effects at a distance and posthumous effects, there is of course no uncertainty about the effect of the end on the agent. But the issue is in important ways the same. In Kant's terms, we act when we judge there is an appropriate relation of fit between the representation of an end and our active powers. Suppose that on my deathbed I create a bequest that will in ten years' time provide scholarship funds for some group of deserving students. What gives me satisfaction—all the satisfaction I need to act— is the setting in motion of the train of events that will yield the desired effect ten years hence. The setting-in-motion is something I can do; its trajectory pleases.

Kantian theory of action is in an important way holistic: motive, action, and end are connected in the agent's principle, or maxim. To act under uncertainty is to judge the chance of an end worth some expenditure; it is the whole—action, end, uncertainty—that strikes the agent as agreeable. Likewise, where we act for a distant end, it is the representation of the whole—my action and its eventual effect—that pleases. Kant is in this way able to accommodate a general feature of action: the frame of an action *outstrips* our activity and willing.

There are various modes of outstripping. My actions initiate sequences of effects that outstrip my intentions (sometimes extending my responsibility beyond my intentions as well). My plans often outstrip anything I can do here and now. And likewise my intentions can outstrip my life, extending my agency past my death. Sophisticated hedonism can include all this. However I make determinate the content of happiness, I make choices that I believe will together make my life an agreeable one. My activity is directed at giving a shape to the world that I find pleasing.[17] Thus we are brought to view our lives in different ways: we do think of our lives in terms of moments or passages of time, but we also think of it as a creative force—something that makes things happen. That is why one can have satisfaction in acting for ends one won't live to see. The story of a life—its effect on the world—can have more extended temporal boundaries than the life itself. So along with fame and monuments, courses of action that carry our agency beyond our life-span allow us to be present in, by giving shape to, the future. Such actions contribute as much to the sense of a life going well as do actions for ends that one expects to see realized. The representation of a world where my action has this creative effect pleases—not as a wish, but as an end engaging my agency and activity. For this reason, faced with the devil's choice between helping her child but believing she has not, and leaving her child to suffer but believing she has helped, the sophisticated hedonist can make the right choice. It is the whole—acting for the welfare of her child—that pleases her. When she represents the future her actions will bring about, she will represent the relevant concerns correctly.

What she cannot do, of course, is take the needs of her child as a per se reason for action. But since what the hedonist theory entails is that there cannot be such a basis for choice, its absence in the account is hardly an objection. There would be a problem if the theory could not countenance acting for ends that outstrip expected experience; but since it can, the basic theoretical commitment of hedonism is not, so far, challenged.

The remaining issue is the hedonism of choice as a principle of deliberation. This is the view that, in choosing between options for action, the only thing that concerns an agent "if the determination of his will rests on the feeling of agreeableness or disagreeableness that he expects from some cause . . . in order to decide upon a choice, is how intense, how long, how easily acquired, and how often repeated this agreeableness is" (*KpV* 23).[18] Kant has almost always been read as accepting this hedonism of choice. I now think he may have had something else in mind: namely, to use the unpalatable consequences of a hedonism of choice to show the limits of empirical practical reason (i.e., the principle of self-love) as a fundamental principle of will, even in its own domain of nonmoral choice.

The hedonic principle of choice is introduced to make sense of cases where we trade what is, in our own considered opinion, a "better" for a "worse" option. Here are Kant's examples:

> The same human being can return unread an instructive book that he cannot again obtain, in order not to miss a hunt; he can leave in the middle of a fine speech in order not to be late for a meal; he can leave an intellectual conversation, such as he otherwise values highly, in order to take his place at the gaming table; he can even repulse a poor man who at other times it is a joy for him to benefit because he now has only enough money in his pocket to pay for his admission to the theater. (*KpV* 23)

And why do people do such things? It is usually assumed that Kant reasons this way. To so choose among courses of action, we must be using a calculus of pleasure. Then all that must matter to us about books, speeches, charity, or the theater is the amount of pleasure to be gained from each. The proof is in what we do. However, there are warning signs that things are not so simple. The list of paired choices are ones that Kant, and presumably we, disapprove of. But on what grounds could he disapprove of them if hedonic fungibility is true? And what's the point of its being "the same human being" who makes these choices? The pairs are also familiar examples of practical irrationality: weakness of will or some other misvaluing of goods. It seems strange that Kant is silent about this.

Suppose one did find the pairs disturbing, and wanted to explain them. People *do* make such choices, and they do not always on reflection regret them. Kant's question could be: how could this make sense? Perhaps the idea is this: *if* someone reads instructive books for the enjoyment of them, then other kinds of enjoyment will sometimes be more pleasurable, and when they are, preferable. And *if* someone has friends because spending time with them makes him feel good, then at those times when other things would make him feel better, he will ignore a friend for the sake of the more agreeable activity. Choosing the worse over the better in these cases is not an instance of weakness of will. It is explained by the principle of choice underlying the agent's more specific maxims, a principle that he takes on in his adoption of ends for their contribution to his happiness. More generally: if all of my ends are embedded in maxims that have the same form (if, that is, they are valued in the same terms), then it may at times be difficult for me to see why I should stay with a pursuit that is arduous when another is immediately available and easy. It may be *irrational* to choose otherwise. So if we find such choices disturbing, as Kant clearly does, perhaps he has identified the source of concern.

Of course, such choices are not always wrong. Contingent circumstances and the nature of one's character may warrant acting with an eye to satisfactions. One cannot be a friend at all if one does not give friendship a certain prominence in one's choices. But for someone for whom friendship comes hard, or who lives among thieves, choosing to balance the satisfactions to be had from other ends with that of friendship as an end might even be best. The problem is that in the normal course of things we cannot appeal to the hedonic principle to distinguish cases like these from cases we want to say exhibit practical irrationality. Taking only the perspective of empirical practical reason, our wills look like animal wills. So if empirical practical reason were all there was, we would lack the resources to *achieve* weakness of will—or strength of will, either.

The absence of an account of weakness, or strength, of will is a symptom of a larger problem. Under the rule of self-love, there is no principle that could show the choices in Kant's examples to be irrational or imprudent. We may have complex plans of life that usually direct our choices, but we can have no *reason* to prefer them in the face of stronger inclination or momentary change of heart. Neither the principle nor the end of happiness can play a regulative role; the former is just another material practical principle, and the latter, indeterminate in content. The importance of happiness to us, as the importance of any end, is a function of our receptivity—of whether and how much we find the idea of its realization pleasing. If our desires happen to be calm and the environment friendly to them, we will act in stable ways, and feel our lives accumulating meaning and satisfaction. But this will be an accident, a function of good fortune. The principle of self-love, with its hedonic principle of choice, lacks the practical resources to give us more.[19] This, finally, is the place where hedonism runs out.

3 Happiness and the Moral Law

We are left with what I shall call "the problem of natural happiness." We have an idea of happiness; the desire that things go well for us moves us to make this idea determinate. But the guidance provided by any such determinate idea or end is always defeasible, since the only principle of construction is hedonic and idiosyncratic. Neither one's own settled ends, nor any wisdom drawn from the lives of others can provide a rational counterweight to strong attractions. The comparative measure of value offers some structure, but no well-founded direction—nor much freedom, if envy, jealousy, and competition are the motivational bases that shape our lives. So while we can, in a sense, imagine life going well, we gain no rational purchase on our choices based on that idea. What we can imagine outstrips the resources of practical deliberation.

In the absence of any independent domain of nonmoral value, the remaining possibility for a solution to the problem of natural happiness is that the structure of nonmoral choice can somehow be affected by the moral law, or by what happens when we acknowledge the law as the fundamental determining ground of our will. If we rule out the moralization of all choice as a possible solution, what's left is the idea that the moral law can somehow alter our character with respect to the content of *nonmoral* action and choice. To do this, it would have to make possible the rational transformation of (some) desires, and the enabling of (some) distinctly human modes of valuation so that we no longer had to regard all nonmoral ends as hedonically fungible. New resources of rational structure would be necessary to support ends that we had nonhedonic reasons to adopt and sustain. These are ends that might, in turn, provide release from the strains of comparative self-valuation.

The moral law may not look like much of a resource because we tend to mischaracterize its charge. Especially given Kant's philosophical preoccupations, it is natural to think that the sole effect of the moral law on our character is to enable action from duty. But its effect is much more wide ranging. For example: moral agents require a wide range of rational capacities, of planning and organization, deferral and recall, responsiveness to change, and so forth, in order to do what morality requires of them. Under the aegis of the moral law we will develop general capacities of agency that we otherwise might not. I say "might not," for all sorts of higher-order capacities may develop if one happens to be so inclined that what one cares about most demands them. But we can imagine environments so friendly (or so hostile) to our natures that it does not make sense that we would be motivated to develop a wide range of complex practical abilities.[20] By contrast, the moral law gives us noncontingent and authoritative reasons to develop practical capacities and to be mindful of the effect of generic and idiosyncratic weaknesses.[21]

Like most acquired practical abilities, exercise is required to maintain use. So if I am to be capable of effective planning, I must plan. And since to plan I must have longer-term projects, there are, odd as this may seem, moral reasons to live a life of greater rather than lesser complexity. Of course this seems backwards. There is a seamlessness to ordinary development that usually makes attention to reasons of this sort unnecessary. But the reasons are there, and they have priority. (We can see this in worries about children who for too long remain dependent on their parents. It's not just their welfare and dignity that are at issue. We think they need to do things to prepare themselves to take their place as members of a public moral culture.) That our psychology is such that we typically enjoy the exercise of higher-order rational capacities is a further feature of the seamlessness. The idea is not, of course, to go for practical complexity tout court. But we can see why Kant maintains that, other things equal, for most of us there is moral value to living in social settings that are intellectually and practically demanding.[22]

Having the ability to pursue complex projects does not by itself resolve the problem of natural happiness. We still have no noninstrumental reason to prefer one kind of activity over another, nor reason to stay with the discipline of a complex end when another appealing activity is available. So even though the practical impact of the moral law is not cabined off from the structure of our rational agency generally, we do not yet see how the law could alter the reasons we have, or are capable of having, in the pursuit of happiness. To get to this, we need to look at two often neglected features of Kantian rational psychology. The first is that rationality is not an "add-on" to an independent, nonrational course of development. The fact that we are rational alters the desires we come to have: not just which objects we pursue, but the content and structure of the desires we act on. The second feature builds on the first: there is a connection between the development of higher-order rational capacities, *reason*-based pleasures, and our *dignity* as rational agents. It supports something like a Kantian version of Mill's doctrine of the "quality of pleasures," and is for Kant, as it was for Mill, the pivotal element in a solution to the problem hedonism poses for a theory of happiness.

About the first feature: we allow into our story notice of the fact that desires do not lie outside the sphere of normal development. New desires are created, and old ones are (at least partially) transformed as we mature. The thirst of a newborn and that of an adult are likely connected, but they are hardly the same thing. Much of our developing system of desires is both fact and reason responsive. We may cease desiring what we see is impossible; a general desire becomes a desire for some specific object; we desire some things only as our acting for or having their object does not violate this or that constraint (that is, sensitivity to constraint can be internal to the desire itself).[23] Because the object and internal structure of desires change as we mature, we get some prereflective yet rational organization, and the elimination of some sources of potential conflict, in the course of normal development of the system of desires.

Although all of this may happen to us, it does not follow that we have reason to prefer more complex desires, nor reason to *value* ones we might happen to have. In just this regard, Kant praises Epicurus for his honesty in recognizing that even if the source of an activity were in the representation of a "higher cognitive faculty," so long as our principle of action appeals to the satisfaction we expect, the action (and its reasons) remain of the same kind "as those of the coarsest senses."[24] Neither fancy liking, nor endorsement, nor reflective commitment to ends gets us beyond one mode or another of our passive receptivity. But it does make us open to changes in desire that might be prompted from another source of value, were there one.

This brings us to the second feature—the idea that the moral notion of *dignity* might provide the link to happiness. I mentioned Mill a moment ago because he, like Kant, thinks the route of escape from crude hedonism is via an account of higher pleasures supported by a notion of the dignity of rational persons. The difference between them on this is instructive. Mill introduces a "sense of dignity" to explain the preference for activities and ways of life that involve the exercise of rational capacities: they not only provide access to a broader palette of more durable satisfactions—interesting work and enjoyments in the usual sense—we see and value ourselves in exercising powers commensurate with our dignity.[25] Indeed, Mill notes, a sense of dignity is "so essential a part of the happiness of those in whom it is strong that nothing that conflicts with it could be otherwise than momentarily an object of desire to them."[26]

Mill's "sense of dignity" explains why it is not *hedonically* irrational to prefer a way of life that engages the mind, for it names a special source of self-referential pleasure. This is enough if you think, as Mill does, that "next to selfishness, the principal cause which makes life unsatisfactory is want of mental cultivation."[27] But because Millian dignity merely extends the domain of satisfactions, it provides no solution for the problem Kant has with natural happiness (Mill does not disagree).[28] By contrast, because Kant can provide a separate and nonhedonic foundation for the value of (or inherent in) dignity, if there is a way to connect dignity with nonmoral choices, then it is a possible candidate for the solution.

The problem from the Kantian side is getting the notion of dignity—which has its basis in the moral law as a law of our will—first, to have application in the domain of happiness, and second, to provide some form for the happiness we seek. The Kantian notion of dignity is a status concept: it expresses the fact that rational nature as an end-in-itself constrains, both negatively and positively, what may be willed. But once I satisfy the moral law, what difference can it make whether I spend my leisure time constructively or sybaritically, have solid friendships or a host of casual acquaintances, have work that productively engages my rational capacities or instead just spend my time filling out forms?

Certainly it makes some difference that our nonmoral activities have causal consequences for our moral character. If my work (or my play) deadens my powers of judgment, or creates in me a dependence on the wills of others, then I have moral reasons to alter my situation or in other ways resist these effects.[29] But if this were the extent of the penetration of the moral law into the domain of happiness, after satisfying constraints of permissibility, obligatory ends, and concerns for the health of our moral character, it would leave the hedonic principle of choice, constrained by the effects of social competition, as the final arbiter of the content of happiness.

Dignity can affect the content of happiness first and most directly through the effect of the recognition of the authority of the moral law on feelings. To a happiness-pursuer, the encounter with the moral law involves a shock of self-recognition.[30] We see that what we had taken to be first in the order of value—our satisfaction—is not. We are also revealed to ourselves to be persons of moral standing or dignity: our own rational nature as a source of value that has authority over all action and choice. This confrontation with "the sublimity of our own nature" gives rise to a strong, positive feeling—a kind of self-approbation, whose source is not in desire or our passive receptivity, but in the moral law itself. Not because of its strength, but because of its source, this feeling in turn affects the structure of material incentives: by altering our sense of who we are, it changes what we count as our well-being.

Although happiness and morality remain distinct, we gain a decisive interest from the side of happiness in keeping them correctly aligned. For one thing, I can get pleasure from a dignity-based conception of myself only if I live up to it. There are various ways I can fail to sustain a commitment to the priority of the moral, but there is no way that is rationally defensible. And if out of weakness or self-hatred I reverse the order of value of morality and self-love, I cannot rationally value myself for doing so. It would be as if I allowed a self-serving mistake to persist in an argument and for that reason claimed pride in my philosophical powers.

The second way that dignity enters the account of happiness is by providing closure to the comparative impulse. We gain an autonomous and not merely comparative measure of self-worth. Given an idea of happiness that now includes the moral powers as defining who I am, how could that not matter to the way I live? To think of myself as in any way important gives rise to a desire to express that value—to make it real through my actions. In addition, the self-conception and sense of worth that comes with recognizing that I am a being with dignity will change the terms of recognition I want from others. From the perspective of morality, our equality as persons with dignity is a non-discretionary and prior demand. That is, morality requires each to accord all others their status as persons, and we must likewise insist on it for ourselves. We are, and are essentially, equal. But from the perspective of happiness, where in desiring not to be or seem to be less worthy than others one was drawn into an open-ended and escalating pursuit of tokens of public esteem (wealth, power, etc.), once dignity is in the picture, there is a different value I will want recognized, and it will be satisfied by the respect to which I am entitled.

However, even if the moral law in this way provides conceptual closure for the comparative impulse, it does not thereby fully solve the problem of natural happiness. The new source of self-valuation is independent of the judgment of others, but it is also ours without regard to how we live.[31] Even living a morally good life, in the duty-attending sense, is not the answer. On the one hand, if we will want our life activity to be and be seen as expressive of our dignity, the opacity of virtue, as well as the contingency of the occasions for its visibility—some lives are morally pretty quiet—can render even a deep moral commitment invisible. And on the other, as a happiness-seeking creature whose practical identity is formed in the interplay of abilities, dispositions, circumstances, and the ordering work of the hedonic principle of choice, living a good life leaves most of what I do and care about separate from the dignity-based sense of my value. If in large portions of my life I am indifferent to the exercise, expression, and development of my moral, or reason-related powers, my life will express some other value. The Kantian "two natures" problem will have moved from philosophy into the life of the individual agent.[32]

If, analytically, there are separate principles that regulate the volitional activity of human beings, we should not be surprised if what is analytically the case is empirically realized. That is, we may in fact live our lives divided, responsive to the strictures of morality, but for the rest, under the sway of an at best sensible hedonism. The ambition of

Kant's argument cannot be to show that dignity *necessarily* solves the problem of natural happiness, but that it *can*. In the last part of the paper, I want to take a brief look at how this might be made to happen. One striking feature of the account is that, in the normal course of things, the solution to the problem of natural happiness is a developmental achievement, and one that is dependent on the availability of the right kind of external, social support.[33]

4 *Kantian* Paidea

We start with the recognition that the solution to the problem of natural happiness does not follow from the moral law. It is not knowable a priori; it is not part of the concept of dignity. The solution belongs to the domain of what can be made or constructed—that is, within the purview of moral education. Now, moral education can, indeed it should, aim at more than sensitization to standards of moral correctness. Children can be brought up *to* the idea that their value as persons lies in their dignity. And if they are confident that their social world is an arena for its expression, they will, as they can, make choices that reflect and express their sense of their value. In this way they will come to understand what the value of dignity is. Knowing that persons are to be treated as ends-in-themselves sets children a task, but the knowledge genuinely informs their moral understanding only as they can safely experience and work through the temptations and vulnerabilities of different sorts of relationships. They thereby gain a concrete sense of who they are, making their dignity real.[34]

Such experiences will give shape to a person's idea of happiness. If we imagine an upbringing that attuned children to the ways persons who recognize one another's dignity act together, it is reasonable to suppose that in the normal course of things they would be drawn to relationships that offer the opportunity to explore and enjoy a life in which respect and intimacy are mutually enhancing. Likewise, we might think, forms of work, structures of family life, and relations to art and culture that are respectful of dignity would be sought out by persons whose idea of happiness was given shape by their sense of themselves as persons with dignity.[35] Of course, not everything should be valued in the same way. Some of what we do properly belongs to the sphere of the hedonic principle—it would be perverse to make every choice and preference an occasion for the display of refined taste. On the other hand, not everything we enjoy is good for us—and one sense in which there are attractive relationships, kinds of work, and kinds of leisure, that we should nonetheless forgo, is in this way explained.

It is a chronic error in moral psychology to investigate the limits of what is possible from the perspective of the "however formed" adult. Not a great deal follows from the fact that many are indifferent to some set of concerns—choose abusive friends or relationships that flatter. The best explanation may be, as Mill argues it often is, the want of a certain sort of education, or the early and stable provision of opportunity. Kant differs from Mill in the foundation he offers for the value of dignity, but they are one in their view of the profound difference there is for human life when the value of dignity is given room to be central to persons' conceptions of their happiness.

To come to value friendship as an occasion to explore the ways mutual dignity can play out in ordinary life is not to regard such relationships as a stage for specifically moral action. Brought up within morality, we become a different sort of person. We care about different things than we would have if differently educated, and we also may care about some of the same things in a different way. The picture is not that the person of good upbringing has special access to a class of nonhedonic, objective reasons. (As if, like an expert, she could report to the rest of humankind on the truth about the good life.) What she has is a self-conception that becomes an aspect of the content of activities and relationships she values. This is part of the reason why an agent whose choices are shaped by dignity-based concerns can have reason to resist the blandishments of immediate pleasures. She has such reasons because (some of) her nonmoral choices now express her own objective value. (It is the presence of such reasons that also creates the possibility of ordinary weakness of will. Both analytically and phenomenologically, weakness of will requires more than one value or principle of choice, and a standard of correctness that goes beyond subjective commitment to ends.)

I don't think there is anything psychologically extravagant here. The recognition that one is a person with dignity gives rise to a desire to organize wants and aspirations *as* the wants and aspirations of that kind of a self. This then carries outward. Discovering that some forms of work or friendship or even leisure fail to underwrite our self-regard, we prefer others. There is nothing strange in this. The man whose pride is based in his physical prowess will choose activities that give him opportunities for its development and expression. Someone who values her musical gifts will not ignore them, not if she is normal and otherwise well circumstanced. We can have abilities and talents that mean nothing to us, and which it is not unreasonable to ignore. But we cannot (normally) value ourselves for having some capacity or ability and live without the desire to involve it in our activities, if we have a choice.[36] And unlike features of ourselves that we value or not as we will, someone brought up to an awareness of her dignity, cannot, with good reason, ignore it. So we say: dignity is not of value because a subject values it; it is to be valued for its value. But that's not the whole story. When valued for its value, dignity transforms subjectivity. There are activities, kinds of work and kinds of relationships that, when freely chosen, express either lack of self-regard or self-contempt. These are different faults. At the extreme, both may lead agents to impermissible activities, especially to the violation of duties to oneself. But only someone who knows her value can have self-contempt.

Two things direct this account of dignity-shaped happiness beyond the individual and outward to social institutions. Respect for ourselves and for others *as pursuers of happiness* gives us reason to create and support social arrangements in which the relevant rational capacities of persons are developed and have wide opportunity for expression. Second, the fact that we are affected in our self-regard by the judgment of others gives us reason to seek a social order of value in which the equal status of persons is publicly acknowledged and secure. Taking both together, we should not be surprised to find that Kant argues for a form of public institutions in which social esteem is related to the conditions of equal, autonomous agency. Indeed, in his full political view, Kant embraces a modernized version of the classical ideal: participation in a political order of the right sort—a republic of equal citizens under law with a progressive public culture—will complete the process of human development, and provide the best conditions for human happiness.

Kant's ideal is that through active citizenship in a republican form of government, persons can express their free, legislating personality in a context of equal regard. The voting citizen of a republic can regard the law as an expression of her own activity and will, not merely as a source of command and protection. Making law for herself and with others who are free and equal citizens, she both gains insight into her own autonomy and she sees herself as a co-producer of a rational order. Seeing herself and others in this light, the citizen gains reasons to support public education and welfare, and to seek peace—as the empirical conditions appropriate to the pursuit of happiness informed by a sense of dignity.[37]

Though Kant's conception of politics is not ours, in his embrace of the moral possibilities in republican citizenship we at least gain a concrete idea of what might be involved in seeing rational agency expressed through institutional forms, and a sense of why it matters. We may find Kant's view of politics naive, and think about the social circumstances for the self-expression of our rational agency in more modest terms. There are many activities and institutions rich in opportunity for the development, exercise, and display of our rational powers. Work, art, social relationships—all may provide avenues for expression and mutual recognition of our fundamental value as rational agents. But because there is a fair amount of chance in the "fit" between a person's talents and the social world she happens to inhabit, the loss of confidence in public or civic life as an avenue of self-expression is not just a loss of one possibility among others. Where political life is a real possibility, we can act together as equals, making law for ourselves that brings into being what Kant calls the "ectypal world"—nature transformed by reason "determining our will to confer on the sensuous world the form of a system of rational beings" (*KpV* 43). One of the deeply appealing motivations of John Rawls's political vision is the formulation of terms for a scheme of social cooperation that returns this possibility to the political world. It is, of course, a moral ideal. But it is not just that. According to the Kantian arguments I have been examining, it may be a necessary goal if we are to bring reason to our pursuit of happiness.[38]

Notes

In the course of writing this paper, I would from time to time hear in the background a reprise of a conversation I had with Judy Thomson in 1979. Patiently and firmly, she tries to explain to me why my writing isn't clear enough, how I need to argue things out more fully, and every so often would I please "talk about what I am going to talk about." I am still trying to get it right. For more than twenty-five years it has been my good fortune to know Judy Thomson as an exemplary model, teacher, and friend.

1. References to the *Critique of Practical Reason* are by the page number of volume 5 of the Prussian Academy of Sciences edition of Kant's collected works (cited as "*KpV*"). The text used is translated by Mary Gregor, Cambridge University Press, 1997. Other in-text references are to *The Grounding of the Metaphysics of Morals* (cited as "*G*"), volume 4 of the Prussian Academy edition (translated by James Ellington, Hackett, 1981); and *Religion within the Boundaries of Mere Reason* (cited as *Religion*), volume 6 (translated by A. W. Wood and G. di Giovanni, Cambridge University Press, 1996).

2. Considerations about pleasure are meant to include displeasures and pains. Kant seems to hold the standard view that pleasures and pains are of the same kind (modifications of some single sensibility), and therefore can straightforwardly be compared.

3. The best of these tries to salvage the initial pair of claims by relegating the ubiquitous role of pleasure to the causal history of our desires and interests, not their objects—we value our ends for various reasons—and then account for the hedonism of choice by treating happiness as the idea of the maximal sum of expected satisfactions to which the various activities and projects contribute different amounts. (See, for example, Andrews Reath, "Hedonism, Heteronomy, and Kant's Principle of Happiness," *Pacific Philosophical Quarterly* 70 [1989], pp. 42–72.) This separation of value in a deliberative principle from the value of ends is not always benign. It's not that we can't separate them; we often have to make choices on grounds that don't reflect the values that make alternatives options for us. When this happens, deliber-

ation is not so much about adjudicating between the options or their values, but about the introduction of a third value that for one reason or another has greater "say" in determining what we should do. Then the saving strategy would give us this: what makes X of interest to me may be its feature α, but what makes me choose X over Y is the *satisfaction* I get from engagement with an α-featured object or activity. So if a summative pleasure or satisfaction conception of happiness plays the role of the third value, the saving strategy does not take Kant very much off the hook.
4. Here is the full remark about happiness and self-love.

> Now, a rational being's consciousness of the agreeableness of life uninterruptedly accompanying his whole existence is *happiness*, and the principle of making this the supreme determining ground of choice is the principle of self-love. Thus all material principles, which place the determining ground of choice in the pleasure or displeasure to be felt in the reality of some object, are wholly *of the same kind* insofar as they belong without exception to the principle of self-love or one's own happiness. (*KpV* 23)

5. Consider the long footnote in the preface of the second *Critique* where Kant offers what he calls a "neutral" account of the faculty of desire: neutral because it leaves it "undecided at the beginning" whether the supreme principle of practical philosophy can be empirical. It gives the pieces of the practical psychology in their sparest form. Separating out the sentences, we get the following formulations:

> *Life* is the faculty of a being to act in accordance with laws of the faculty of desire.

> The *faculty of desire* is a being's *faculty to be by means of its representations the cause of the reality of these representations*.

> *Pleasure* is the *representation of the agreement of an object or of an action with the subjective conditions of life*, i.e., with the faculty of the *causality of a representation with respect to the reality of its object* (or with respect to the determination of the powers of the subject to action in order to produce the object). (*KpV* 11n)

So, suppose an active being (person or animal) is thirsty. Seeing water nearby, and other things being equal, it is able, by means of its representation of the water as thirst-relevant (as the result of an habitual or conceptual association of drinking water and the relief of thirst), to be moved to drink. For this to happen, a being need only be a thing possessed of "life"—that is, capable of acting from representations and as a cause of the object it represents. A moral being recognizes a duty-invoking need. She is able, other things equal, by means of her (suitable) representation of the need, to help. We will not know until later in the argument whether the principles/laws of these two types of action are of the same kind. At this point, as Kant says, the account is neutral. But then what is also neutral is the place of pleasure in the operation of the faculty of desire. In both cases, pleasure comes from the representation of the fit between object and active powers. What is left undecided is "the question whether pleasure must always be put at the basis of the faculty of desire or whether under certain conditions pleasure only follows upon its determination. . . ."
6. Here I am intimating a distinction between determination of the will and empirical conditions of action that will be developed a bit later.
7. In the sense at issue, aversion is a special case of pleasure, not a distinct mode of feeling. The pleasure is in the avoidance of the object of aversion.
8. That happiness is an idea of the imagination, and not of reason, partly explains this.

9. In the *Groundwork* Kant says that the purpose of happiness is one that "can be presupposed a priori and with certainty as being present in everyone because it belongs to his essence" (G 416)—which is to say, is true of us, as finite rational beings, by necessity.

10. Of course, if reason's demands typically gave us a life of pain, or permitted few satisfactions, we would find its object difficult to love. But these are second-order considerations. As are those that depend on the fact that morality requires that we be concerned with the happiness of others. Happiness already has to be in the orbit of reason's concerns for duties of beneficence to make sense.

11. Choice involves giving structure to the material of maxims via a conception of the good.

12. Moreover, if there is a reciprocal relation between the pursuit of happiness and self-individuation, and if self-individuation is a necessary condition for rational agency in finite rational beings with needs, then the *actual* satisfaction of (some) desires and inclinations that are part of an agent's conception of happiness is also necessary. That is why the right relation of morality to happiness is rational self-love. For its own reasons, reason cannot ignore our desires. So, contrary to what one might have thought, the problem sensibility poses for morality is not that desires tempt us away from virtue. The problem arises from a feature of our *rational* natures, from self-conceit—a flawed rational principle of desire-satisfaction.

13. It is not just piety to the ancients that has Kant pointing repeatedly to Epicurus.

14. The three practical dispositions are for animality, humanity, and personality. The first presses us toward procreation and living with others; the last is the disposition to make the moral law the fundamental maxim of our will. They are all said to be in some sense good.

15. An interesting upshot of this is that extreme individualism in the pursuit of happiness is tempered by the fact that the happiness we pursue must be coordinate in kind. Since by nature we live together, and by nature we care about how we stand in the regard of others, we must live in ways that are mutually intelligible. (This is a condition of having a culture.) The facts of difference we prize tend to be in style or mode, or in features of life that do not directly challenge defining cultural norms. But such convergence of direction does not produce a determinate concept, and, of course, does its work at the very high cost of arbitrary cultural oppression. The lack of a value-norm for happiness is not exclusively a philosopher's problem.

16. Where the highest goal is to be comparatively best, morality is an obstacle. It prompts not just immoral actions, but a tendency to reverse the priority of moral and non-moral incentives. See *Religion* 24–25.

17. Although the work of articulating a conception of happiness takes place as life goes along, the point of view that anchors the conception is not similarly ongoing. We do not regard each moment in life as having the same weight; there are factors of aging and reflection, but also features of the kinds of experiences we have that provide abiding points of reference (not all of which are as sustaining as we may at the time think they will be).

18. Essential to the hedonism of choice is the claim that all pleasure is of one kind, "not only insofar as it can always be cognized only empirically but also insofar as it affects one and the same vital force that is manifested in the faculty of desire, and in this respect can differ only in degree from any other determining ground" (*KpV* 23).

19. This will be a problem with any theory that tries to get normative purchase out of hierarchically structured desires.

20. This is the point of Kant's south sea islanders example (G 423): the demands of instrumental rationality are contingent.

21. It's not that we must develop all the powers that we could possibly have; rather, we may not neglect specifically moral abilities, nor those general executive capacities that enable us to initiate and carry out complex projects. The injunction not to neglect amounts to a requirement that we be mindful of the conditions and circumstances of our agency. There are faults and weaknesses to which all of us are prone to some degree (a tendency to exaggerate the importance of our own interests, for example), and there are idiosyncratic deficiencies and shortcomings—ways we are prone to be lax in our actions or inattentive to certain sorts of morally salient facts. These may not be matters of indifference to us, and we are obliged to resist or overcome those flaws of character we detect. Further, we need to acquire and maintain some flexibility and openness to change: we cannot be rule-bound, nor can we assume that practices through which we learned morality are impervious to criticism and change.

22. See, e.g., the essays "A Conjectural Beginning of Human History" and "Idea for a Universal History from a Cosmopolitan Point of View," both in *Perpetual Peace and Other Essays*, trans. Ted Humphreys (Indianapolis: Hackett, 1983).

23. For more on this view of desires, see my "Making Room for Character," in S. Engstrom and J. Whiting (eds.), *Aristotle, Kant, and the Stoics* (Cambridge: Cambridge University Press, 1996).

24. (*KpV* 24–25). This is an occasion for one of Kant's rare philosophical jokes. He compares those who take them to be different ways of determining the will to when "ignorant people who would like to dabble in metaphysics think of matter so refined, so super-refined, that they make themselves giddy with it and then believe that in this way they have devised a *spiritual* and yet extended being."

25. And since one can have a sense of dignity to the extent that one has access to one's higher faculties (some mix of capabilities and developed abilities), the claim is not specific to any one way of life or mode of culture.

26. J. S. Mill, *Utilitarianism*, p. 9 (Indianapolis: Hackett, 1979). Other things equal, work that engages understanding is better—that is, preferred—to work that is mindless. It is preferable to participate in decisions than merely to follow orders. We find it better, other things equal, to be able to discriminate among a variety of tastes than simply to eat to satiety. And so on.

27. *Utilitarianism*, p. 13.

28. This will be so whether the source value is hedonic or the more neutral post-Humean hierarchical commitments.

29. And so for our commitment to morality too. Thus Kant argues for the indirect duty to promote our own happiness: "for discontent with one's condition under many pressing cares and amid unsatisfied wants might easily become a great temptation to transgress one's duties" (*G* 399).

30. This recognition is the empirical side of the Fact of Reason. For more on the effect of the moral law on our feelings, see my "Transforming Incentives" (forthcoming). The account is drawn from chapter 3 of the second *Critique*: "On the incentives of pure practical reason."

31. We do not lose dignity in acting immorally.

32. The "two natures" view of human agency and the problem of natural happiness are at bottom the same; when we understand how we can be "one," we will have solved the problem of natural happiness.

33. This would be consistent with the view we have of those whose nonmoral activities and ends are formed "naturally": we do not see how the recognition of the moral law could have any effect, beyond constraint, on the shape of a person's conception of happiness.

34. Friendship is a particularly significant relationship for this sort of learning. The intimacy and mutual regard in some sorts of friendships lets us go further in exploring what our dignity amounts to. I can act respectfully toward a stranger. But outside the sphere of negative duties and necessary kindness or beneficence, we are constrained. The boundaries of another's dignity are not always clear, and the possibilities for reciprocal acknowledgment extremely limited.

35. Though it may be next to impossible to explain to one's adolescent child that what he does now will look different to him later, and that it is the point of view that he now lacks that ought to determine his choices, one might hope that a child brought up to value his dignity *because* he has been so valued can resist some bits of fashion, or some exploitative relationships, for the sake of what is valuable to him now.

36. Self-valuation based on unexpressed gifts—what I could do or be if I wished—is, other things equal, more like magical thinking than normal choice. It can be a mark of regret—what I could have done, if I'd had the chance; it is more likely a sign of disorder.

37. These views are presented in the second essay of Kant's "Theory and Practice" and in part 1 of the *Metaphysics of Morals*. Their connection with canonical Kantian moral theory is the topic of my "Training to Autonomy: Kant and the Question of Moral Education," in A. Rorty (ed.), *Philosophers on Education* (New York and London: Routledge, 1998).

38. A version of this paper was presented to the MIT Philosophy Colloquium. My thanks to that audience for interesting discussion, and to Miles Morgan and Seana Shiffrin for their good advice.

Chapter 8

Toward the Essence of Nonconsequentialism

F. M. Kamm

In this article, I will try to provide an account of the nonconsequentialist constraint on harming innocent, nonthreatening persons. I begin
by examining other principles that have been proposed to rule out
harm to such people. I consider objections to them and ways to revise
them. In particular, I consider the Doctrine of Double Effect and offer
as a revision of it the Doctrine of Triple Effect. I try to show how it
may explain a version of the Trolley Problem introduced by Judith
Thomson known as the Loop Case. I raise problems for the Triple Effect
Doctrine and then develop the Doctrine of Initial Justification, which,
I claim, reveals certain crucial distinctions between permissible and
impermissible harm.

1 Principles and Problems

When may we significantly harm innocent, nonthreatening people
who would not otherwise be harmed? In a case known as the Transplant Case, five people can be saved from dying of organ failure if
and only if we kill one person to get his organs. (He is an innocent
nonthreat, not himself under any grave threat and not responsible
for the problems of the five.) Act consequentialists say this act is permissible, given that there will be no additional bad consequences. Nonconsequentialists say it is not permissible. Among the reasons they
have offered for its impermissibility is the priority of not harming
over aiding: we would harm the one if we kill him, but only not aid
the five if we did not give them the organs. Another nonconsequentialist reason is the priority of not intending harm over merely foreseeing harm: we would intend harm to the one if we kill him, but only
foresee harm to the five if we did not aid them. Some supporters of this
intention/foresight distinction support the Doctrine of Double Effect
(DDE), according to which we may not intend evil as a means to a
greater good or as an end in itself, but it is permissible to pursue a
greater good as an end by neutral or good means even if a lesser evil

is a certain, foreseen side effect (if there is no other way to achieve the greater good).[1]

Problems can be raised for the moral significance of the harming/not aiding distinction and intending/foreseeing distinction. Consider first problems for the former: (a) In a version of the Trolley Case, a trolley is headed toward killing five people, but a bystander can save them (only) by redirecting the trolley. However, if redirected it will go off in a direction where it will definitely kill one person. Typically, nonconsequentialists think it is permissible (though not obligatory) to divert the trolley even though this involves harming some in order to aid others.[2]

(b) In another case, five are dying of organ failure. If we let one person who is suffering from pneumonia die by not giving him the penicillin he needs to be cured, we can use his organs to save the five (Penicillin Case). It seems impermissible to do this, even though it involves letting him die rather than harming him.

Now consider problems for the moral significance of the intention/foresight distinction: (c) Suppose a doctor is called and told that organs—innocently acquired—have arrived and must be transplanted quickly into his five patients. He drives to the hospital but on the road finds an immovable person in his path. If he takes a different route, he will be too late to do the transplants, and as he is the only one who can do them, the five will die. If he runs over the person on the road, he foresees, but does not intend, the death of the one. However, he knows (suppose) that if he gets to the hospital, he will save the five (Car Case). It seems impermissible for him to proceed.[3]

(d) Consider again the Trolley Case. Suppose it is a not very good person who sees the trolley headed to the five. He has no interest in saving the five per se, but he knows that it is his enemy who will be the one person killed if he diverts the trolley. He does not want to be accused of acting impermissibly, however, and so while he turns the trolley in order to kill the one, he does so only *because* he believes that (i.e., on condition that) a greater good will balance out the death. Hence he would not turn the trolley unless he expected the five to be saved (Bad Man Case). His turning the trolley is still permissible, I believe. This raises doubt about the correctness of principles such as the DDE if they would determine the act to be impermissible on the basis of the bad intentions of the agent.[4]

(e) In the same vein, we may consider a case where someone wants to do something on a whim but foresees that someone will die as a side effect. However, he also foresees another side effect: a massacre of twenty people will be stopped. He allows himself to act on the whim, only because he believes that (i.e., on condition that) the greater good will outbalance the lesser evil (Whim Case). He does not act with the ultimate aim of producing that greater good (any more than in the Bad Man Case the agent acted with that aim).[5] It is permissible, I believe, to act in the Whim Case, even though the agent does not aim at the greater good. But the DDE says that we may produce lesser evil as a side effect only if we are *pursuing* a greater good.[6]

(f) Finally, as an objection to the DDE it has been suggested that, in many cases where acting is impermissible, we need not be intending harm strictly speaking. For example, although we must intend the removal of the organs in Transplant Case, we need not intend the death of the person, since if he survives the removal of his organs that would not interfere with our saving the five.

2 The Counterfactual Test and the Doctrine of Triple Effect

A great deal of contemporary nonconsequentialism has been concerned with trying to revise moral principles employing the harming/not aiding distinction or the intending/foreseeing distinction to meet objections (a), (b), (c), and (f). Possibly objection (d) and almost certainly (e) are new. Let us first consider changes that might be made to a principle involving the intention/foresight distinction so that it meets some of the objections to it.

To deal with objection (f) (the narrowness of intention), Warren Quinn[7] suggested that we focus on the wrongness of *intending the involvement of a person without his consent in a way that we foresee will lead to significant harm to him*. This is instead of focusing on the wrongness of *intending the harm* to him, as the DDE says. Let us say that Quinn's revision results in the DDE Revised (DDE(R)). Henceforth, to mark my acceptance of this revision without adding words, I shall use evil* to mean "evil or involvement without consent that we foresee will lead to evil."[8]

Possibly, we can deal with objection (d) (the Bad Man Case) by rephrasing the DDE or DDE(R) so that it requires that we not do an act that *could only be deliberately done* by someone who intends evil*. Then acts (such as turning the trolley) that could be done for other reasons would be permissible even when done by someone with an improper intention.

I suggest that one way to deal with objection (e) (the Whim Case) is to revise the DDE or DDE(R) to permit actions done because one believes that a greater good than an evil will occur, even if that greater good is not intended as an end (or even as a means). In discussing the

DDE, *so much attention has been paid to the issue of whether or not we may intend a lesser evil that none has been given to whether we must intend a greater good.*

But now notice that if we can distinguish conceptually between intending an effect and acting because we believe it will occur, a common test used to distinguish conceptually between intending and merely foreseeing an effect is shown to be inadequate. The Counterfactual Test says that to see if someone acts intending or alternatively merely foreseeing an effect, we should imagine (counterfactually) that the effect will not occur but everything else remains the same. If the person would not act because the effect would not occur, this shows, it is said, that he intended the effect. But in the Whim Case, if the greater good did not occur and all else remained the same, the agent would not have acted. He only acts because he believes that this good will occur—he will not act unless he believes it will occur, his act is conditional on his belief that it will occur—but he is still not intending this good. So we see that the Counterfactual Test fails to distinguish effects the belief in which is a condition of action from effects that are intended.[9]

I have been trying to draw the *conceptual* distinction between acting because I believe something will happen and acting with the intention that it happen. What is the *moral* distinction between acting because I believe a greater good will occur and acting in order to produce a greater good? It shows that it is possible for someone to be concerned with justifying his behavior without being concerned per se with what it is (the greater good) that does the justifying. The reasons that justify his act are not his reasons for acting, though the fact that they justify his act is a reason for his acting. (It is interesting to consider this point in connection with a contractual moral theory such as T. M. Scanlon's that emphasizes one's concern to justify oneself to others.)[10] An agent who allows himself to act if he produces greater good as an effect may then do more good than someone who insists that intending the greater good for its own sake is a condition on acting with a bad side effect. Furthermore, if someone would find in the expected existence of a greater good a mere opportunity for doing what he really wants to do, this may (though it need not) lead him to create new links between what he wants to do and a greater good, for the latter can justify the evil side effects of what he wants to do. If he creates these links, he would be intending the greater good as a means to doing what he wants. But these agents would also be seeking excuses for acting, and the facts that would justify their acts would not be their reasons for acting. These may be at least nonmoral defects in an agent's practical reasoning.

I have suggested that we can distinguish conceptually and morally between acting because we intend greater good and acting because we expect greater good. Perhaps we can also distinguish conceptually and morally between acting because we intend an evil* and acting because we expect an evil*.[11] Consider the Party Case. I intend to give a party in order for me and my friends to have fun. However, I foresee this will leave a big mess, and I don't want to have a party if I will be left to clean it up. I also foresee a further effect of the party: if my friends have fun, they will feel indebted to me and help me clean up. I assume that a feeling of indebtedness is something of a negative for a person to have. I give the party because I believe my friends will feel indebted and (so) because I will not have a mess to clean up. These expectations are conditions of my action. I would not act unless I had them. But I do not give the party even in part in order to make my friends feel indebted nor in order to not have a mess. To be more precise, it is not a goal of my action of giving the party to do either of these things. I may have it as a background goal in my life not to have messes (just as it is a background goal not to violate constraints), but not producing a mess is not an aim of my giving the party. Indeed, if I see that my friends are feeling indebted, as a good host I may try to rescue them from these feelings (while expecting that I may not succeed). I might try to rescue them from these feelings because I do not want it to be the case that I fail to do so only because I *intend* their feeling indebted. This would not be inconsistent with giving the party *because of* my belief that they will, as a side effect, feel indebted. (The Party Case could also be used to show that the Counterfactual Test fails as a test for intention.)

What is the *moral* distinction between intending that something bad occur and acting only because one believes it will occur? If I intend something bad, as a rational agent I am committed to doing other things to bring it about (if there is nothing per se objectionable with those other things). But if I take advantage of a bad effect that an act of mine will have and decide to do the act because I can take advantage of the bad effect, that does not commit me to doing anything else to bring the bad effect about or to make it the case that my act brings it about. In this way, it is like merely foreseeing the evil*. Furthermore, I will have some other reason (even if not a sufficient one) besides producing the bad for doing the act that has the bad effect. For example, giving the party will lead to fun.

If we combine what I have said about the cases of unintended greater good and unintended lesser evil, we can revise the DDE(R) further. These cases show that in addition to intending an effect or merely foreseeing it, one can also act because of it. Even if intending an evil is wrong, acting only because one believes it will occur may not be wrong. On account of this third relation we can have to an effect, I suggest the Doctrine of Triple Effect (R): A greater good that we cause and whose expected existence is a condition of our action, but which we do not necessarily intend, may justify a lesser evil and involvement leading to it that we must not intend but the expectation of which we may have as a condition of action.

3 The Loop Case

The Doctrine of Triple Effect (R) may help us with the Loop Case, another version of the Trolley Case introduced by Judith Thomson.[12] In this case, the trolley is headed to killing the five and can be redirected to a side track, but that side track loops around toward the five. Hence the trolley would kill the five from another direction, but for the fact that there is one person on the side track to which we redirect whose being hit by the trolley stops it from looping to the five. In this case, one person's being hit is causally necessary to the trolley stopping. I shall assume we would not turn it unless we thought that the one would (with some probability up to certainty) be hit, for (let us suppose) turning takes much effort and there would be no point in doing it if the five would shortly be killed anyway by the looping trolley. Does this mean that we intend the hitting of the one person and thus that turning in the Loop Case violates the DDE(R) on account of our intending the hit that kills him?

I suggest "no" to both questions. To support these claims, I wish to make clear how I (intuitively) see the structure of the Loop Case. The only threat that faces the five that prompts my act to help them is the trolley heading toward them from one direction. This is the first problem. If this threat is not taken care of, they will die; to save them, it must be taken care of whatever else we do, though that does not mean that it is sufficient to save them. The problem that would exist (if the one on the side track were not there) of the trolley coming at the five from a somewhat different direction *only arises* because I turn the trolley away from the five: One way to see this *new problem* is as a *second threat* facing the five because I have taken care of the only threat that faced them to begin with.

It may be thought that this cannot be true, since it is the same trolley and in that sense the same, not a second, threat that faces them when it loops toward them. But it might be argued that the fact that the device is the same is irrelevant. The case in which the same trolley comes at them in a new way has the same structure as a case in which *a differ-*

ent entity comes to threaten the five as a result of my removing the trolley threat. Consider the Wagon Case: The trolley is headed to killing the five. We divert it and as it goes on the side track it stops. But we know that it will stop on a button whose depression will cause a wagon on the side track to be set in motion. The wagon will head around the loop toward killing the five, but it will be stopped by hitting one person on the side track. The wagon is a new threat in the obvious sense that it is a new threatening entity that was threatening no one previously. Nevertheless, *the case is (intuitively) the same for moral purposes as the Loop Case*. It does not matter for moral evaluation whether a new threatening entity is created or the same trolley hits from a different direction.

Still, it may seem odd to say when I divert the trolley in the original Trolley Case so that it threatens the one person that I have created a new threat. After all, we might say that I have *diverted the threat* in diverting the trolley and that implies it is the same threat. Instead of worrying about this point, I will say that in diverting the trolley in the Loop Case I have created *a new problem* (the trolley directed to the one and, potentially, to the five). It should be morally the same, whether I create the new problem by setting the wagon in motion in the Wagon Case, or by setting the trolley to one person and potentially to the five from a new direction.[13]

A proponent of the DTE(R) may argue that turning the trolley in the Loop Case is permissible for the following reasons: We turn the trolley in order to remove from the five the only threat that faces them when we are prompted to act. We do this only *because we believe* they will not soon die from another problem anyway *because we believe* the one person will be hit, thereby stopping the trolley. Because these other things will happen, the five will be saved from all threats. *This* makes turning the trolley worth doing; and that is different from its being worth doing in order to hit the one. Although the expectation of hitting and nonlooping are conditions of our action, that does not mean we turn the trolley even in part in order to hit the one or even in part in order to stop the trolley looping. (It even seems odd to say that we turn the trolley in order to stop it from looping; in part, this is because the threat of the trolley looping only arises because we turn the trolley. However, I do not claim the oddity of speech is definitive.)

As evidence that a rational agent who turns the trolley because it will hit the one need not thereby have intended it to hit the one, we could note that he need not be committed to doing anything extra (not in itself objectionable) in order to get the trolley to hit the one. For example, suppose that an extra push is not necessary to divert the trolley, but without it the trolley would jump *over* the one and head toward the five (Extra Push Case). Unlike a person who aims at the hit as a means of saving the five, the agent I have in mind need not be committed to giving the extra push. Indeed, like the host in the Party Case, he might even, consistent with turning the trolley because he believes the one will be hit, try to rescue the one if this became possible rather than omit aid in order that the one be hit. The reasoning of an agent who does these things might be as follows: I may turn the trolley so long as I am not aiming at the hitting of the one. I must not refuse to rescue the one if my only reason for not rescuing him would be that I aim at his being hit as a means. But I may fail in my rescue, and so long as this is true, it still makes sense to turn the trolley (Rescue Case).

To reinforce these claims, here is a further analogy to the Loop Case: I need a pair of shoes. I have just enough money to buy them, but I am poor and I do not have enough money to also pay for the gas bill I will run up by driving to and back from the store. I would not have my new shoes for long as I would have to sell them to get the money to pay the bill on my gas credit card. Then the store announces automatic reimbursement at the end of the month of gas bills of anyone who buys a pair of shoes. I do not like the idea of reimbursement as I am proud and would do nothing extra to get it, but I go to the store anyway to buy the shoes, given that I will be reimbursed (Gas Reimbursement Case). (The structure of this case is in many ways similar to the Loop Case: means used to get rid of a problem [being shoeless] leads to a new problem [gas bill], which will lead to my being shoeless anyway unless something else [reimbursement] occurs.) In this case, I have it as a background goal in my life not to fall into debt, and I go to the store because I believe I will not fall into debt, since the threat to my finances (gas bill) that arises as a result of my going to get the shoes will also be eliminated by my getting the shoes. But I do not go to the store and come home in order to get the reimbursement or to prevent myself from having to sell my new shoes.

This Gas Reimbursement Case also shows that even when another background condition of my action (to wind up with shoes when all is said and done) has the same character as the goal of my action (to get shoes), the goal and condition can still be distinct. Similarly, when I turn the trolley in order to save the five from the first trolley-threat problem, I am interested in their being saved when all is said and done (as I am interested in having shoes when all is said and done). Yet, my goal in action (to save them from the trolley's first hit) can still be distinct from the condition of action (that they be saved when all is said and done).

If we need not intend or aim to hit the one in the Loop Case, we need not violate the no-intending-evil* component of the DDE(R), let alone the DTE(R). Why then, it may be asked, do we need the DTE(R) at all? Do we refer to the DTE(R) *only* to help us see that acting "because of" is consistent with *not* acting "in order to" and thus does not violate the DDE(R)? No; for another component of the DDE(R) says that we may produce a lesser evil* *foreseen* as a side effect if we use neutral or good means with the aim of achieving a greater good. But the lesser evil* we produce in the Loop Case is not a mere foreseen side effect; we act because we believe it will occur. Furthermore, it is possible that turning the trolley in the Loop Case fails to involve aiming at the greater good, which alone can justify the evil. This is because (as I have argued above), we may not be doing anything with the aim of achieving the greater good of the five being saved when all is said and done (i.e., being saved from all problems involving threats to their lives that are present *and* will arise). We may act only *because* this will occur. (Clearly, though, the ordinary agent who acts because the five will be saved from all problems does not treat that good as a mere excuse for acting as the agent in the Whim Case treats the greater good. Furthermore, in the Whim Case, the small good provides some reason for action independent of the greater good. In the Loop Case, although turning from one direction is necessary if the five are to be saved at the end of the day, it only produces any good worth acting for because of the condition that other problems are eliminated.)

Hence the act in the Loop Case may fail to satisfy the DDE(R) not because we aim to hit the one person, but because the evil* is not merely a foreseen effect and (more surprisingly) because we do not have as a goal in action achieving the greater good that can justify the evil*. The DTE(R), by contrast, does not require that evil* be a mere foreseen side effect. It also does not require that we act in order to bring about the greater good that justifies the lesser evil*.[14]

The DDE has been used to distinguish morally between (1) terror bombing civilians in wartime and (2) bombing military targets while foreseeing with certainty that civilians will be killed. The first is impermissible, the second may be permissible. The DTE(R) helps us see that there is an in-between type of case which I will call Munitions Grief: If we bomb military targets and they are immediately rebuilt, it will be pointless to bomb. It is only because civilians are killed as an (unavoidable) side effect of our bombing, that other citizens, consumed by grief, are unable to rebuild. Hence, if we bomb, it would be *because* we know the civilians would die. But this does not mean that we aim at their deaths. Though we take advantage of a side effect of our act (A) to provide us with a reason for doing act (A), we need not be committed (as rational agents) to doing anything especially to make our act have that side effect. I believe bombing in Munitions Grief can be permissible even if terror bombing is impermissible.

4 *Toward the Essence of Nonconsequentialism*

There are still problems with the DTE(R). First, like the DDE(R), it is a state-of-mind principle, that is, one that tries to derive the permissibility of acts from the state of mind of someone who does them. If the bad person who turns the trolley away from the five would have turned it on his enemy even if (counterfactually) the five had not been there, then his behavior does not satisfy the DTE(R) even when the five are there. Yet, contrary to this implication of the DTE(R), his act of turning the trolley from the five is still permissible. As with the DDE(R), one might try to remedy this problem by revising the DTE(R) so that it rules out acts that could only have been done by someone who does not meet its conditions.

Second, there are several cases in which the DTE(R) may fail to give the right results. Consider the Multiple Track Case. The trolley is headed to killing the five. We can divert it onto either track A or track B. Both tracks loop back to the five, but only on track A is there a person whose being hit stops the looping. In this case, one has *an extra choice* to make between two tracks that one did not have in the Loop Case. Everything one must do only to get the trolley away from its first hit on the five would be done if one diverted to B as well as to A, but there would be no point in going to B since the five would die from the diverted trolley. If one *picks* track A over B, is one doing it in order to prevent the looping and at least in part aiming at hitting the one? If so, the DTE(R) says one should not divert the trolley at all. This seems puzzling.

A clear problem for the DTE(R) is that (like the DDE(R)) it would permit the doctor to drive over the person in the Car Case, since it allows a means to a greater good to have a lesser evil as a side effect.

Finally, the DTE(R) may fail to distinguish between the permissibility of turning the trolley in the Loop Case and (what I believe is) the impermissibility of turning the trolley in the following Tractor Case: The trolley is headed toward killing the five. It can be redirected and there is no way for it to loop back. However, there is another threat, a deadly tractor, also headed to killing the five. We know that if we turn the trolley, it will gently hit and push (without hurting) one person into the path of the tractor. His being hit by the tractor stops it but also kills him. In this case, is it possible to say we turned the trolley in order to stop its hitting the five because we knew the one would be pushed and so stop the tractor, but not (even in part) in order to push him and to stop the tractor? If so, then the DTE(R) will allow us to turn the trolley in the Tractor Case. However, I believe this act is impermissible; the Tractor and the Loop Case are, intuitively, morally different, and the DTE(R) may not explain this.

Let us now try to inch our way by steps to an alternative theory that does better. This theory is intended to apply only to cases in which we will harm innocent, nonthreatening persons who are themselves not already under a comparable threat. It is a non-state-of-mind theory, unlike the DTE(R) and DDE(R). I believe we can discover it by considering intuitive responses to cases and trying to explain their underlying deep structure. However, rather than strictly follow the order of discovery, I shall first present each component of the theory, followed by discussion of cases in which intuitions can be accounted for by the component. Finally, I shall offer a doctrine that both summarizes the components and tries to provide an underlying, morally satisfying rationale for them.

(1) The first thing we can show on the basis of intuitions in cases is that it is permissible for greater good already achieved to cause lesser evil*. Then, the good that justifies lesser evil* causes it. For example, suppose the trolley is headed to the five, and though we cannot redirect the trolley, we can move the five. Unfortunately, we know that we can only move them to land that is loosely packed and that their presence in this threat-free area will cause a landslide. We know this landslide will kill one person below. Intuitively, I believe it is permissible to move the five, foreseeably causing the lesser evil*. This is accounted for by the permissibility of greater good causing lesser evil*.

If *only* greater good might permissibly cause lesser evil*, a principle of our morality would be that *the good that justifies evil* should cause it.* (Acts that cause the greater good that, in turn, causes lesser evil* are, of course, permitted.) This would be a strong version of nonconsequentialism, since the good is not a causal consequence of evil* or of means that have evil* as a side effect. Nonconsequentialism is usually understood minimally as the *denial that all that matters to the rightness or wrongness of acts is the goodness of the consequences.* But it also denies that all that matters is the state of affairs, including *the act itself* and its consequences. For example, it claims that an act of killing A that will prevent more acts of killing B, C, and D may be impermissible, even if the state of affairs including that act and its consequences is better than the state of affairs without that act and its consequences.[15] (Perhaps nonconsequentialism should instead be called non-state-of-affairsism.) If it were a requirement that the good that justifies evil* should cause it, nonconsequentialism would be concerned that the *greater good not be the causal consequence of evil**. It would involve a "downstream" principle, in that evil* would have to be causally subsequent to good.

(2) We can go further, however. Although greater good may permissibly cause lesser evil*, it is not required that evil* only come about in this way. *Events that have greater good as (what I will call) a noncausal flip side or aspect may cause, or lead to events that cause, lesser evil**. By "noncausal" I mean something tighter than causation, sometimes identity, sometimes constitution. Another way of putting this is that events that per se cause lesser evil* should either (a) be noncausally related to the greater good or (b) be caused by events that are noncausally related to the greater good.[16] Other events may only lead to lesser evil* by way of such events. These claims account for intuitions in several cases. In the Trolley Case, intuitively we think we may turn the trolley that causes the death of one. In the context where only the trolley threatens the five, the turning of the trolley threat away from them—by which I mean the moving of the trolley itself away—is the same event as or consists in their becoming free of threats, and this is the same event as their becoming saved. Hence there is a noncausal relation between the turning away of the trolley and the five becoming saved. Furthermore, the state of affairs of their being saved is noncausally related to these events in that context.[17] Because this is true, I will say that the five being saved (the greater good) is the noncausal flip side of the turning of the trolley. Intuitively, I mean to distinguish this noncausal relation from a less "tight," ordinary causal relation that could connect the turning of the trolley and the saving of people, as in the following Van Case: A van is headed toward killing twenty people. If we turn the trolley away from hitting five, the diverted trolley will gently push into those twenty and move them away from the van. Here the saving of the twenty is simply a causal consequence of the moving trolley. It contrasts with the relation between the five being saved and the moving of the trolley away from them. This is the contrast, as slim as it seems, that I think is crucial.[18]

Intuitively, it is permissible to do acts (e.g., push a button that redirects the trolley) that cause the event that has greater good as a noncausal flip side and lesser evil as an effect. We can explain this by noting that pushing the button—an event that per se does not have greater good as a noncausal flip side or aspect—also does not per se cause the death of the one. It causes the death of the one *by* causing the trolley to be *diverted*, and *this* diversion has the greater good as its noncausal flip side.

If pushing the button that turns the trolley away from the five itself sent out a death ray killing one, intuitively, I think, it would be impermissible to push the button. What underlies this intuition, I think, is the fact that the event that per se causes the death would not have the greater good as its noncausal flip side, nor be caused by an event that does, nor would it be an event that causes the death by way of either of these two sorts of events. Rather, the event that per se causes death would have the greater good as a further *causal* consequence, since it would *cause* the trolley to be diverted and this would have the greater good as a noncausal flip side.

In a similar vein, consider the Wiggle the Bridge Case: The trolley is headed under a bridge to the five. We know that if we wiggle the bridge, this will stop the trolley. However, we also know that wiggling the bridge will, as a useless side effect, topple a person over the bridge to his death. Intuitively, I think wiggling is impermissible. Wiggling the bridge causes a death, just as the moving trolley does, but unlike the moving trolley, it has only a causal relation to the greater good, since it leads to the greater good by causing the trolley to move away from the five. Furthermore, wiggling neither is caused by an event with a noncausal relation to the greater good nor causes the death solely by way of causing such an event. I think this is what underlies the intuition that wiggling the bridge is impermissible.

The relation between the existence of the greater good and the turning of the trolley in the Trolley Case may also be compared with the relation between the five being saved and the moving of a Lazy Susan–type device with them on it. In the Lazy Susan Case, we cannot redirect the trolley, but we can move the five away from the oncoming trolley by turning the Lazy Susan. The relation to the good here also seems noncausal insofar as, in the specific context, the five being saved is not a separate event that is a causal consequence of the moving of the Lazy Susan; rather it is an aspect of it. Here is an analogy: When I raise my arm, the area under it is greater than it was. The relation between my arm going up and the increase in space under it is noncausal. The relation between the space becoming larger (an event) and its being larger (a state of affairs) is also noncausal.

If another person is seated on the other side of the Lazy Susan from the five when we turn it he will be moved into, and be hit by, the trolley as the five are moved away. Intuitively, it is still permissible to turn, I believe, because means that have greater good as a noncausal aspect cause, or lead to the cause of, the lesser evil*. Notice this implies that it is not only permissible to turn a threat from the five and to turn five from a threat. It is also sometimes permissible to *push one into a threat*. How does this case differ from the following Pole Case: A person is on a side track and cannot move off it. If we move a pole, it will push him gently into the trolley headed to the five; his being hit will stop that trolley and kill him. Intuitively, it is impermissible to do this. I suggest that this is because, unlike what is true in the Lazy Susan Case, the one being hit (which foreseeably leads to his death) is causally necessary for producing the greater good. Evil* in this case is a causally necessary means that has greater good as a further causal effect.[19] The same reasons that rule out acting in the Pole Case explain the impermissibility of acting in the Transplant Case. (Sometimes people say nonconsequentialists are squeamish, and therefore they will not push the bystander into the trolley. But this will not explain why they will push the person on the Lazy Susan into the trolley.)

The idea that it is permissible to use means that have a noncausal relation (as explained) to greater good even though the means cause, or lead to events that cause, lesser evil* is again nonconsequentialist, in the sense that it is concerned with *how* good comes to be a consequence. First, *the greater good must be noncausally related* to what causes (or to what leads to what causes) evil*, and second, the greater good may be *causally* related to what causes evil* when it is causally related by way of means noncausally related to that greater good.

The first component of the theory permits cases where the greater good itself causes a lesser evil*. Is this second component similar, in that the only cases that it does not permit are those in which the greater good lies causally downstream from evil*? Possibly evil* lies downstream when the greater good is noncausally related to means that cause, or lead to causes of, evil* as well as when greater good itself causes evil*. (Suppose, by contrast, that good is a *causal* effect of means that cause evil*, but it is a causal effect not by way of what has a noncausal relation to that greater good. Why is evil* then *not* downstream from good? After all, in the *temporal* sense, the good may still come about before the evil. But, evil* and good are *both* causally downstream from the means, *and* the good [or what has it as a noncausal flip side or aspect] does not cause the evil*. Hence evil* and good are causally parallel.)

(3) However, what if *evil* itself* had a noncausal relation to greater good? It would then not be downstream from it (or causally parallel to it). Would it then be impermissible to bring the good about? Here is a possible example: Suppose the trolley directed away from the five might have but did not reach the one. Would we say something bad had happened to the one nevertheless, namely, he was placed under a threat even if it was never fulfilled? If being under a threat is itself an evil*, then, in the context of the (original) Trolley Case, the greater good of the five saved is the noncausal flip side of the one being threatened. This evil* is not causally downstream from the good; but it is still permissible to act. *This suggests that in nonconsequentialism, the noncausal*

relation to the good is crucial, not the downstream position of evil*. More evidence for this: Evil* is not downstream when a greater good has evil* as one of its aspects; this is also a case where an evil* has greater good as one of its aspects. Yet, here acts leading to evil* are permitted. Further, if means have evil* as an aspect and greater good as an aspect or noncausal flip side, evil* is not causally downstream from the greater good. Yet, it is permissible to act.

(4) The next step is to see that it is *permissible for lesser evil* that is an effect of greater good (or of means noncausally related to it) to sustain that greater good*. This is so even if it is not permissible for evil* *to produce* that greater good. If it *sustains* greater good, the greater good is not *produced* by it. Is evil*, then, in that sense, causally downstream from the good? However, *an evil* that sustained a greater good could also be an aspect of it or a flip side of it*. For example, suppose being under the threat of the diverted trolley is itself an evil* and having the one under a threat for a while sustained the greater good. Then the evil* might be a flip side of the good it sustained and not downstream from it. Once again, it seems that in nonconsequentialism, greater good having a noncausal relation to evil* or to something involved in producing evil* takes priority over any supposed requirement that evil* be downstream from greater good.

Consider the Loop Case: for the second problem (looping trolley) to exist, the further causal consequences of our turning the trolley would have to exist, since the turning causes the looping of the trolley. Independent of this further causal consequence of turning the trolley in the Loop Case, *the noncausal flip side of turning the trolley* exists; that is, the five being rid of the first problem involving the trolley. (This is the problem of the trolley's being headed to them from one direction and this problem existed independent of my doing anything to save them.)[20] Their being rid of the trolley headed to them in one direction leaves them free of the original problem that *prompted my rescue* to begin with. This noncausal flip side would completely justify bad effects for others of turning the trolley—the one hit and dead—*unless some new problem arose for the five as a consequence of my turning* and this *new* problem were not itself eliminated. That is, we would have achieved a state that, when described *independent of further causal consequences for the five* of removing the trolley as it was initially, would justify the lesser evil*. I shall call such a state the *structural equivalent of the justifying good* (structural equivalent for short). This is because it has the structure of the ultimate good (the five free of threats all said and done) that justifies the death of the one.[21] This structural equivalent provides us with a possible rationale for turning the trolley, for we see that the structural equivalent of the justifying good involves something that could outweigh *certain* of the evils* that are effects of what we do (or that remain despite what we do) to save the five. Which evils*? Those that would *not* affect the condition of the five as it is in the structural equivalent, but all those that would affect other people (like the one hit).

Still, having achieved the structural equivalent, we may not be at all justified in turning the trolley (and hitting the one) unless we know that the five will not die shortly anyway. So justification for turning can depend on how the further causal consequences of turning are likely to affect the condition of the five as it is in the structural equivalent. It is a prerequisite of being justified in turning that *there be a prospect that the condition of the five as it is in the structural equivalent will remain*, thus becoming the greater good that all things considered justifies the lesser evil*.[22]

Another causal consequence of turning the trolley is that it would threaten the five's survival were it not that the one would be hit. Since the stopping of the trolley by its hitting one is a matter of physical causality, it is possible that it will not stop and all six will be killed. Still, we could be justified in turning if it were likely to save the five, even if the good that would ultimately justify the death of the one does not occur. When we are justified in acting on the structural equivalent, I shall say it provides an *initial sufficient justification* for turning; the turning and the hit it causes are initially sufficiently justified. "Initial" refers to what exists independent of further possible causal consequences to the five of turning; "sufficient" refers to the fact that five is a large enough number of lives saved to outweigh the death of one.

Consider the first problem that existed independent of my action to help and the removal of that problem, separate from the further causal *consequences for the five* of my act. This provides an initial sufficient justification for acting if it involves a structural equivalent of a greater good that ultimately (i.e., including effects of my act on the five) justifies the lesser evil*. This identity connection between the structural equivalent of the greater good and the greater good that ultimately justifies the evil* rules out a certain type of different greater good (call it greater good (2)), which could be caused by the turning trolley, from justifying the harm done by turning the trolley. For example, suppose we knew that turning the trolley away from the five caused the one to be hit and die, but we knew it did not stop the trolley looping back to the five. However, on its way back to the five, the trolley depresses a button that prevents another trolley from running over three different people. Intuitively, turning the trolley should be ruled out as impermissible. I think what accounts for this is that there is no initial sufficient justification for turning; we know that the structural equivalent that leads to harm cannot be sustained. Turning is merely a means to hitting the one and causing good. Here we see that although the requirement that "the good that justifies evil* causes it" is dropped, something of it remains: *the good that justifies evil* E has a structural equivalent that either causes E or is noncausally related to what causes, or leads to the cause of, E.*[23]

Suppose that at least the initial sufficient justification for turning is present. Then the hitting of the one does not *produce* the structural equivalent of the good. Rather, it stands outside the structural equivalent and prevents new threats to it that arise from what I have done to rescue the five. *In that sense, the evil* prevents the undoing of the good, rather than bringing about or producing the good.* This is a further nonconsequentialist feature connected with how the good is a consequence. (I have already noted [p. 163] that although there is a sense in which this puts the evil downstream from the good in the Loop Case, this is *not* the crucial factor.)[24] The evil* plays a part in justifying the turning, and hence plays a part in there being an initial sufficient justification. But it plays a part by helping sustain the structural equivalent in the face of *new problems I produce;* not by producing the structural equivalent.

Consider by contrast the Tractor Case. In it the tractor threat exists independent of the further causal consequences of turning the trolley.[25] Given the existence of the two threats initially, we have no initial sufficient justification for turning the trolley from its initial hit on the five. For *when we turn the trolley and abstract from any new problem for the five thereby created*, the five are still subject to a fatal threat. That is, the structural equivalent of the justifying good does not yet exist as a flip side of turning the trolley. In the Tractor Case, the structural equivalent depends, in part, on the *causal effects for the five* of the removal of the trolley. This is because it is the moving and hitting of the one that causes the tractor to stop from the direction of its initial hit. This, I believe, is what underlies the intuition that turning in the Tractor Case is impermissible. (As it turns out, in the Tractor Case the *ultimate* justifying good comes into being when the structural equivalent does, as no further problems for its continuing existence are produced by what we do. But this fact that our turning the trolley can lead to the justifying good does not mean that we have an initial sufficient justification for turning, for we lack the structural equivalent without the evil*.) When some evil* is causally necessary for the structural equivalent that helps provide an initial sufficient justification of that evil*, the structural equivalent is *produced by an evil* that is not already initially sufficiently* *justified.* The evil* does not stand outside the structural equivalent of good and merely prevent its being undone by consequences of our intervention.

For the same reason that we may not turn in the Tractor Case, it would be impermissible to turn the trolley away from five people each of whom shortly was going to die of organ failure, even if we know that the death of the one hit by the trolley would make available the organs we need to save them.

Yet, the fact that bringing about a structural equivalent requires an evil* does not always make acting impermissible. For example, an evil* E may permissibly produce a structural equivalent of what justifies greater evil* F if E is caused by what at least initially sufficiently justifies *it*. This involves (at least) a structural equivalent of that greater good which can justify E, a structural equivalent that has some chance of being maintained. (E could also be caused by means (or their effects) noncausally related to the greater good or its structural equivalent.) For example, suppose a trolley is headed to five people. We can only push it to the right a bit. We know this will save one person and also cause a bystander to be hit, paralyzing his leg. His being hit stops the trolley from hitting the remaining four, but the trolley comes to rest where it causes a rock slide that kills one. Intuitively, this is permissible. The underlying structure is that the paralysis (E) is caused by means non-causally related to one being saved. Hence paralysis (and the act causing it) is (at least) initially sufficiently justified already. The hit then helps produce the good of four being saved, which justifies the death of the one. In this case, the existence of the structural equivalent is not caused by the very evil* that is to be (initially) justified. The evil* that causes another greater good is already (at least) initially sufficiently justified by a lesser good (saving one).[26]

In sum, (1), (2), (3), and (4) together suggest that much is said for the permissibility of a harmful act when (at least) the structural equivalent in an initial sufficient justification of an evil* E is *not* produced by other evils* that are *not* themselves produced by what initially sufficiently justifies them (or by means [or effects of means] that are noncausally related to what initially sufficiently justifies them). This is a requirement that there be *internal purity of causal chains.* It expresses a concern that the causal chain that leads to a good G, where G justifies evil* E, does not involve evils* that are not at least initially sufficiently justified by what causes them (or by what is noncausally related to what causes them, or by what is noncausally related to what causes the cause of them). We can capture this idea more easily in a positive version as the Doctrine of Initial Justification (DIJ) (omitting "sufficient" for brevity's sake): *Lesser evils* to innocent, nonthreatening people not already facing com-*

parable threats should be caused by what at least initially sufficiently justifies them (which involves [at least] a structural equivalent that can become what ultimately justifies them) or by means (or effects of means) having at least that structural equivalent as its noncausal flip side or aspect. I think this is the essence of the deep structure of nonconsequentialism in the area with which we are concerned. Its motto is: Initial sufficient justification all the way down. The DIJ(R) can be used like the DDE(R) and DTE(R) to test acts for permissibility and is intended to supplant them for this purpose.[27]

Should we translate the DIJ into a thesis about rights? The DIJ is a doctrine that tells us a good deal about when actions that cause significant harm are permissible. This could mean that it tells a good deal about when we are permissibly *infringing* a right not to be harmed; it need not be telling about when there is no right not to be harmed. Yet I think that the result is stronger—there is no right not to be harmed if we act according to the DIJ, other things equal. (Things will be unequal, for example, if the one in the Trolley Case had extracted a promise that he would not be killed in any way to save the five.) This could explain why the saving of even one additional life is enough to justify turning the trolley, when it would not be enough to justify pushing a bystander in, and is not, therefore, enough to override a threshold on a right not to be killed.[28]

It also explains why, I think, compensation would not be owed to the one (if it were possible) just for turning the trolley in a way that hits and kills him. (This does not mean there could not be other reasons that one owes the one compensation. For example, if we had a duty to all six people to see to it that the problem faced in the Trolley Case never arose and we failed in that duty, we would owe the one (or his survivors) compensation if we directed the trolley to him. He would have been wronged, even if we did the right act in turning the trolley.)

How could we translate the DIJ into a thesis about rights? Here is a rough suggestion for a right to initial justification (RIJ): (1) A person has *no* right not to be the victim of a threat to his protected interests as an effect of the elimination of a sufficiently greater problem affecting others' protected interests (nor as an effect of means [or their effects] having the elimination of a sufficiently greater problem as its noncausal flip side or aspect). This is so even when his being the victim of such a threat plays a causally useful role in dealing with greater problems that will face others, including new problems that arise from our efforts to eliminate an initial problem. (2) Except as in (1), a person has a right not to be the victim of a threat to his protected interest *as an effect of or as part of what is done to* cause the elimination of sufficiently greater problems for protected interests of others. (That does not mean this right is absolute.) (1) and (2) say, *roughly, one can have no complaint if one suffers as an effect of the greater good of others, but one can complain if one's person is used to produce that good in a way that harms one or if part of the world we all share is used to produce that good in a way that harms one.* To distill the DIJ and the RIJ even further, it is as if beings who are ends-in-themselves can only be subordinated by a superior condition of others who have the same status, but cannot necessarily be subordinated for their sake.

We now see the deeper meaning of the sort of inviolability against harm that is provided by nonconsequentialism when there are conflicts of interests between people. (I take inviolability to be a status expressed by what it is permissible or impermissible to do to people.) The nature of persons requires that they be related to the good of other persons only in certain ways. It is not greater or lesser inviolability alone that is important thought of quantitatively, but interpersonally respectful or disrespectful violability.[29] We also see that *the DIJ is how the RIJ is expressed in terms of the causal relations between goods, harms, and events leading to them.* Hence, a moral theory of persons and their rights has a very specific expression in the causal relations that should hold between goods, harms, and events leading to them.[30]

Notes

1. I accept that there is a delicate distinction to be drawn between intending and aiming such that all intendings involve aimings but not the reverse. I also accept that those who are against intending an evil should be against aiming at it even when this does not involve intending it. (I owe these points to Michael Bratman.) Hence I shall consider aiming at an evil to violate the DDE even when it does not amount to intending. Nothing I say in this paper should depend on distinguishing intending from aiming.

2. The one person is typically envisioned as on a side track, but this is not necessary. He could be in another part of the country and the redirection of the trolley that leads to his being hit would still be permissible, I think.

3. This case is modeled on one described by Philippa Foot in "Killing and Letting Die." It is also modeled on a case she used as an objection to the DDE (in "The Problem of Abortion and the Doctrine of Double Effect"): We must operate on five to save their lives, but doing so requires that we use a gas. It is harmless to the five, but it will unavoidably seep into a neighboring room, there killing an immovable patient. We may not operate, she concluded.

4. Judith Thomson also raises objections on these grounds to the DDE but uses cases in which action may be required to help someone. See her "Physician-Assisted Suicide: Two Moral Arguments."

5. He does not even act intending to stop the massacre as a means to his acting on his whim. He need not do this as the massacre will stop without his intending that it do so, just if he acts on his whim. To say that he intends to stop the massacre as a means to his acting on his whim suggests that if his act did not cause the massacre to stop,

he would, as a rational agent, be committed to doing something (in itself unproblematic) in order to make it the case that his act would cause the massacre to stop. But, as a rational agent, he need not be committed to doing this just because he wishes to take advantage of a connection that already exists between his acting on a whim and the greater good.

6. This I believe is the standard way in which the DDE is presented. Different philosophers, without drawing attention to what they are doing, have described the DDE differently with respect to whether we are to intend the greater good. The traditional rendition requires aiming at a good greater than the evil side effect (not just any good). Here are three sample renditions: (1) "The agent acts with a good intention and seeks to realize a good end. . . . [T]he good end that the agent seeks to realize is not morally disproportionate to the bad consequence" (Nancy Davis in "The Doctrine of Double Effect: Problems of Interpretation"); (2) "(a) the intended final end must be good . . . and (d) the good end must be proportionate to the bad upshot" (Warren Quinn, in "Actions, Intentions, and Consequences: The Doctrine of Double Effect"); and (3) "the good effect is the intended effect" (Baruch Brody, "Religion and Bioethics"). In (3), Baruch Brody is pointing to the fact that the intention/foresight distinction in the DDE's account of permissibility is meant to distinguish the two effects—one good, which is intended, the other bad, which is foreseen. If this is the correct way of understanding the "double effect" point of the DDE, then the doctrine does not so much distinguish intending a bad effect from foreseeing a bad effect, as it distinguishes intending a good effect from foreseeing a bad one. If this is so, and the good must be proportionate to the bad, this implies that we must intend a good greater than the evil.

   One account of the DDE that does not point to an intended greater good says that the conditions that must be met if it is to be permissible for one to produce a bad effect include "(1) one's action also had a good effect . . . and (4) the good effect was important enough to outweigh the bad" (*Cambridge Dictionary of Philosophy*). (This entry also requires that one "did not produce the good effect through the bad" in addition to "not seeking the bad effect as an end or means." However, this is wrong as the DDE does not require that the good that justifies the bad not come about through the bad, only that we not intend that it do so.) This version of the DDE, which I think is unrepresentative and inaccurate, only says that a greater good need occur; it is not necessary that we intend it. Moreover, this account also does not state that our act is permissible only if we act *because* there was (expected to be) a greater good. For it is quite possible that we would have been willing to act even if a greater good would not have occurred. Yet, this would not make our act impermissible, according to this version of the DDE, if a greater good did in fact occur. Even if a nonstandard version of the DDE required that we *expect* a good effect great enough to outweigh the bad, this state of mind is not the same as acting because of that expectation. For we might act, while expecting a greater good, even if we would have acted without the expectation and so did not act because of it. According to this nonstandard version of the DDE, this act might still be permissible. This nonstandard account represents the DDE as a non-state-of-mind principle.

7. In "Action, Intention, and Consequences: The Doctrine of Double Effect."

8. The revision is not unproblematic, as it radically changes the apparent point of the DDE. Those defenders of the DDE (like Thomas Nagel) who focus on not aiming at evil per se should be reluctant to accept it, I think.

9. The Counterfactual Test would also fail to distinguish side constraints on action (that are not strictly effects of action) from intended effects (as Michael Bratman pointed out to me). For example, suppose I will not drink some water if it would involve

violating someone's right; not violating the right is a side constraint on my act. Hence, if I believed that, counterfactually, I would violate the side constraint, though all else would remain the same, I would not drink the water. According to the Counterfactual Test, I drink the water with the intention of not violating (in order to not violate) the side constraint. But it is not my goal in acting not to violate someone's right; my goal in acting is to quench my thirst. Rather, it is a condition on my acting to quench my thirst that I believe I will not violate rights. Acting on condition that I believe I will not-x is not the same as acting in order to not-x.

10. See T. M. Scanlon, *What We Owe to Each Other*.

11. I first discussed this possibility in *Morality, Mortality*, vol. 2.

12. In "The Trolley Problem." I first tried to apply the distinction between acting because of an effect and in order to produce an effect to the Loop Case in *Morality, Mortality*, vol. 2. I discuss the DTE(R), its application to the Loop Case, and what it implies about instrumental rationality in more detail in "The Doctrine of Triple Effect and Why a Rational Agent Need Not Intend the Means to His End," in *The Proceedings of the Aristotelian Society* (2000).

When Thomson introduces the Loop Case, she compares it with Transplant. Here is what Thomson says:

> Let us now imagine that the five on the straight track are thin, but thick enough so that although all five will be killed if the trolley goes straight, the bodies of the five will stop it, and it will therefore not reach the one. On the other hand, the one on the right-hand track is fat, so fat that his body will by itself stop the trolley, and the trolley will therefore not reach the five. May the agent turn the trolley? . . . [W]e cannot really suppose that the presence or absence of that extra bit of track makes a major moral difference as to what an agent may do in these cases, and it really does seem right to think (despite the discomfort) that the agent may proceed.
>
> On the other hand, we should notice that the agent here needs the one (fat) track workman on the right-hand track if he is to save his five. If the one goes wholly out of existence just before the agent starts to turn the trolley, then the agent cannot save his five—just as the surgeon in Transplant cannot save his five if the young man goes wholly out of existence just before the surgeon starts to operate.
>
> Indeed, I should think that there is no plausible account of what is involved in, or what is necessary for, the application of the notions 'treating a person as a means only', or 'using one to save five', under which the surgeon would be doing this whereas the agent in this variant of Bystander at the Switch would not be.

I believe that the intuition that it is permissible to turn the trolley in the Loop Case need not be based on assuming that the five's being hit if we did not turn it is what would stop the one from being killed by the trolley. To keep this point in mind, I wish to revise the case as Thomson presents it so that there is a semipermeable brick wall behind the five. It is coated on one side, so that it would stop the trolley if the five were not there, but not coated on the other side, so that if the one were not on the side track, the trolley would go through the wall, killing five. Thomson says the following about this problem:

> There are two facts about what he does which seem to me to explain the moral difference between what he does and what the agent in Transplant would be doing if *he* proceeded. In the first place, the bystander saves his five by making

something that threatens them threaten the one instead. Second, the bystander does not do that by means which themselves constitute an infringement of any right of the one's. [Thomson repudiated this explanation in *The Realm of Rights*.]

However, I think there are cases of permissible harming that do not satisfy these two conditions. For example, consider the following Lazy Susan Case: A trolley is headed toward five people seated on a large swivel table. We are physically unable to redirect the trolley, but we can turn the table so that the five are moved out of reach of the trolley. However, turning the swivel table causes it to bang into and kill a bystander near the table who cannot be moved. Furthermore, the only way to turn the Lazy Susan involves our throwing a rock at and damaging (though not stopping) the out-of-control trolley, which is owned by the bystander. The rock bounces off at an angle that releases the lock on the Lazy Susan.

In this Lazy Susan Case, we do *not* make something that threatens the five threaten the one instead. Arguably, we also infringe a property right of Joe's in damaging his trolley. Yet it seems permissible to turn the Lazy Susan. So these two conditions are not necessary for permissibly killing. Nor are they sufficient, for suppose a bystander is on a bridge. If we wiggle the bridge this will cause an electrical discharge that turns the trolley. Unfortunately, the wiggling also topples the bystander off the bridge and in front of the diverted trolley by which he is hit and killed. Though the two conditions Thomson mentions are present in this case, it is impermissible to do what kills the bystander. So, I suggest, there is still a problem distinguishing Loop and Transplant.

The solution Thomson offers to the Trolley Problem in *The Realm of Rights* would justify turning in Loop if the following were true: It was to the advantage of each of the six before they knew who would be among the five and who would be the one that the trolley be turned, even when it would not be to the advantage of the one that it be turned at the time of the turning. The problem is that this proposal could also justify pushing someone into the trolley to stop it in order to save the five. For example, suppose all six were railroad workers (as Thomson imagines) and five will be assigned to work on the tracks and one to clean up the bridge over the track. It would be to the advantage of each, before they know their assignments, for someone to push the one off the bridge if this is the only way to stop the trolley. See my discussion of her proposal in *The Realm of Rights* in "Nonconsequentialism, the Person as an End-in-Itself, and the Significance of Status."

13. The trolley need not even be coming from a different direction for there to be a new problem. We could imagine a Loop Case in which the diversion results in the trolley going in a perfect circle right back to where it was originally (A) and then heading to the five. (See figure 8.1.) I still believe it is proper to see the trolley's coming back to A as a second problem that arises from what we did to take care of the first problem.

14. There is another possibility that is consistent with the Loop Case violating neither the "seek greater good" nor the "do not intend evil" conditions of the DDE(R). This is that our aim in acting is that we achieve the greater good of the five being really saved, but we do not intend all the means causally necessary to achieve this. If this were possible, it would show that, contrary to a so-called Principle of Instrumental Rationality, a rational agent need not intend what he believes are means causally necessary to an end he continues to intend. I discuss this possibility in "The Doctrine of Triple Effect and Why a Rational Agent Need Not Intend the Means to His End."

15. Judith Thomson notes this in *The Realm of Rights*.

16. Being noncausally related is not the same as merely not being causally related.

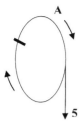

Figure 8.1
Another Trolley Case

17. I thank John Gibbons for his suggestion that there are two descriptions of the same event and they are noncausally related to a state of affairs.

18. The analysis I have provided of the Trolley Case shows that diverting a trolley headed to the five is morally the same as deciding to turn a trolley at a crossroads, which must be turned somehow, to one rather than five.

19. Suppose evil* (caused by our act) actually causes the greater good, but evil* need not have come about in order for our act to lead to the greater good (i.e., if it had not come about, something else due to our act would have caused the greater good). Then acting to produce the greater good can be permissible even when this act leads to evil* causing good. For a case like this see the Track-Trolley Case in *Morality, Mortality*, vol. 2.

20. In this trolley case, the noncausal flip side is the trolley's being away from the front of the five; their being free of the trolley from that direction is not a *further* causal effect of turning the trolley away from them.

21. Actually this requires more than is needed, since the initial sufficient justification could have a minimally sufficient part of the ultimate greater good (e.g., two of the people saved) or the ultimate greater good could be a minimally sufficient part (e.g., two of the people saved) of an even greater initial sufficient justification (e.g., seven people saved). Strictly, the structural equivalent of the minimal good that would justify evil* E must be included. I shall simplify by bypassing this strict condition and working with a complete structural equivalent.

22. Notice that even in the following case, the structural equivalent (as I have defined it) is the noncausal flip side of diverting the trolley: We turn the trolley away from its hitting the five from the right, and this causes a missile previously aboard the trolley to detach and head toward them also from the right. (This case is based on one described by Kaspar Lippert-Rasmussan in "Moral Status and the Impermissibility of Minimizing Violations.") Even though there is no time during which the five do not face a threat, the missile threat arises because of what we do to save them from the trolley. Hence it does not affect the character of the structural equivalent.

23. Recall again that actually this is too strong a requirement in two ways. The final greater good might include the structural equivalent *plus even more good*, but this is not a necessary condition. On the other hand, the greater good might involve only a part of the structural equivalent that is still large enough to help justify the evil*. If this happens, the initial sufficient justification for evil* includes more than what is structurally equivalent to the good that ultimately justifies the evil*. Strictly speaking all that is needed is that *the structural equivalent of the minimal good that would justify evil* E must be included in the initial sufficient justification.*

24. Recall that the Multiple Track Case made problems for the DDE(R) and even the DTE(R). This was because choosing one track over the other seemed to involve intending the hit and doing something not necessary to get the trolley away from the first hit on the five especially in order to hit the one. By contrast, if means that have the structural equivalent of the greater good as their noncausal flip side cause (or lead to what causes) the lesser evil, my theory permits turning to track B where the one is hit. If we went down A where no one would be hit and the trolley would loop, there would be no initial sufficient justification for turning, since there is no hope of the justifying good. Suppose there were yet another track, C, where the probability of hitting the one (and stopping the trolley) was smaller than if we went to B. Again, my theory raises no objection to turning to B.

25. Though it is true that the five people are alive and so vulnerable to the threat only because I turn the trolley away. In the sense that is morally pertinent, I do not think this means that whether the tractor was a threat to them at the start depends on whether we would turn the trolley or not.

26. Indeed, we could go further. Consider the Component Case: A trolley is headed toward five people. Moving the trolley to the right saves one person and has several side effects. It causes two bystanders to be hit and die, but their being hit plays no causal role in saving the four others. Moving the trolley is also foreseen to lead to a hit on a bystander that paralyzes his leg. His being hit causes the trolley to stop. *Here, the structural equivalent that is part of the initial sufficient justification for turning the trolley only comes by way of considering the further causal consequences for the five of turning the trolley.* This is because saving one right away does not justify killing two, which it causes. It does justify the paralyzed leg. Yet, I think, it is intuitively permissible to turn the trolley. I believe this is because the bad consequences (bystander pushed and leg paralyzed) that would cause (at least) the initial sufficient justification for the death of two is justified by saving one life *and* saving one is a component of a good (saving five) great enough to justify the deaths of two. So long as each component (or its structural equivalent) is at least an initial sufficient justification of an evil whose further causal consequences are required to produce the greater good, other evils that those components cause but do not justify may be justified by the greater good as a whole (or be provided with an initial sufficient justification by the structural equivalent of that greater good). For an illustration, see figure 8.2.

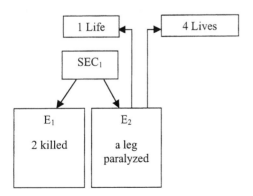

Figure 8.2
Modeling of causal chains and components. SEC = structural equivalent of component. E = side effect.

Notice that on this analysis, there is a big moral difference between a component of a greater good causing an evil that it itself cannot even initially sufficiently justify and a mere means to a greater good doing so. The former may be permissible; the latter is not.

27. I have omitted a step intervening between consideration of cases and the DIJ. It is (what I call) the Principle of Permissible Harm (PPH). It provides principles summarizing case judgments. The DIJ provides the underlying rationale of the PPH. Possibly, for some readers, considering the PPH first may make understanding the DIJ easier. A version of the PPH follows:

I. In thinking about the greater good (G) that will justify a particular lesser evil* (E) to innocent, nonthreatening people not under comparable threat already, it speaks in favor of permissibility of acts if:

  (i) E is caused by G or its structural equivalent;

  (ii) E is caused by events that have G or its structural equivalent as their noncausal flip side or aspect (or by effects of such events); and

  (iii) E is caused by components of G (or their structural equivalents) or by events that have such components (or their structural equivalents) as their noncausal flip side or aspect (or effects of such events), and that lead to G via good/neutral effects or evils* smaller than the good of the components.

It speaks against the permissibility of acts if:

  (iv) the only possibility provided by that act is that E is a cause of G unless E is an effect of the structural equivalent of G, or of an event that has this as its noncausal flip side or aspect (or of effects of such events) (as in (ii));

  (v) the only possibility provided by that act is that a cause of G is an event that has E as a side effect and G as a *mere causal effect*, unless the production of E is mediated by (i), (ii), or (iii). (I speak of "the only possibility" to take account of what was discussed in note 19.)

II. It speaks against acts involving or causing E, if there is no G. It speaks for the permissibility of acts if it is reasonable to believe that they would have (i), (ii), or (iii), when they do not. It speaks against the permissibility of acts if it is reasonable to believe that they would have (iv) or (v), when they do not. (This version of the PPH differs from the one I presented in *Morality, Mortality*, vol. 2.)

28. This conclusion differs from Thomson's view that the right of the one who is killed by the trolley is infringed, and the permissibility of harming does not signal any diminishment in the stringency of his right. See *The Realm of Rights*.

29. So quantitatively greater inviolability would exist if we needed more people to be saved in order to justify turning the trolley. But this is not necessary.

30. For comments on earlier versions of sections of this paper, I am grateful to Michael Bratman, Ronald Dworkin, Thomas Nagel, Derek Parfit, Susan Wolf, and members of (1) the N.Y.U. Colloquium on Law, Philosophy, and Political Theory, (2) Philamore, (3) the Chapel Hill Colloquium on Philosophy, and (4) the Departments of Philosophy at the University of Vermont, UCLA, and Brown University.

References

Audi, Robert, ed. *Cambridge Dictionary of Philosophy* (Cambridge: Cambridge University Press, 1995).

Brody, Baruch. "Religion and Bioethics," in H. Kuhse and P. Singer (eds.), *A Companion to Bioethics* (Oxford: Blackwell, 1998).

Davis, Nancy. "The Doctrine of Double Effect: Problems of Interpretation," in J. Fischer and M. Ravissa (eds.), *Problems and Principles* (Fort Worth: Harcourt Brace Jovanovich College Publishers, 1992).

Foot, Philippa. "Killing and Letting Die," in Jay Garfield and Patricia Hennessey (eds.), *Abortion: Moral and Legal Perspectives* (Amherst, Mass.: University of Massachusetts Press, 1984), pp. 178–185.

———. "The Problem of Abortion and the Doctrine of Double Effect," reprinted in her *Virtue and Vices* (Oxford: Blackwell, 1978).

Kamm, Frances. "The Doctrine of Triple Effect and Why a Rational Agent Need Not Intend the Means to His End," *Proceedings of the Aristotelian Society* (2000).

———. *Morality, Mortality,* vol. 2, (New York: Oxford University, 1996).

———. "Nonconsequentialism, the Person as End-in-Itself, and the Significance of Status," *Philosophy and Public Affairs* 21 (1992).

———. "Harming Some to Save Others," *Philosophical Studies,* Nov. 1989.

Lippert-Rasmussan, Kaspar. "Moral Status and Impermissibility of Minimizing Violations," *Philosophy and Public Affairs* 24 (1995).

Quinn, Warren. "Action, Intention, and Consequence," in his *Morality and Action* (New York: Cambridge University Press, 1993).

Scanlon, T. M. *What We Owe to Each Other* (Cambridge, Mass.: Harvard University Press, 1998).

Thomson, Judith J. "Physician-Assisted Suicide: Two Moral Arguments," *Ethics* 109 (1998): 497–518.

———. *The Realm of Rights* (Cambridge, Mass.: Harvard University Press, 1990).

———. "The Trolley Problem," *Yale Law Journal* 94 (1985).

Chapter 9

What Do Fathers Owe Their Children?

Claudia Mills

This paper grows out of a story. A friend of mine got his girlfriend pregnant, in the usual way. He did not want to be a father, though he was willing to help pay for her abortion and to support her emotionally through the experience of abortion (his first choice); or (his second choice), he was willing to help pay her medical expenses for the birth and support her through the experience of giving birth and then relinquishing the child for adoption. What he got, however, was his non-choice, what he did not choose at all: she had the baby, kept the baby, and he became a father, with financial and emotional responsibilities to meet for the rest of his life. Throughout the decision-making ordeal, he became increasingly frustrated that his fate, his future, depended almost entirely on her choice. He had to wait to see what *she* would decide to find out whether or not *he* would have a lifelong identity that he wished to reject. If she chose abortion, he would have no obligations to this child, for there would be no child; if she chose adoption, he would have no obligations to this child, for such obligations would be willingly (joyfully) borne by others. But if she chose parenthood, he would have the full (though perhaps partly attenuated) obligations of a father, to provide both financial support and emotional support for the indefinite future. And so he waited: what would she choose? And now he is struggling to live with the results of her choice.

The philosophical problem this generates points to a seeming asymmetry in our intuitions about choice. Many of us want to hold the following, seemingly inconsistent views. When it comes to the area of reproduction, women have a right to choose whether or not to become mothers—whether or not to abort, to give up their babies for adoption, or to keep their babies. The reason often given is that obligations to particular other persons follow (only) from one's voluntary choices. And although the woman may have made a voluntary choice to engage in sexual activity, she didn't make a voluntary choice to become pregnant; she didn't choose to enter into the relation of mother with a child she was creating. But in the same area of reproduction, we want to hold that men do not have a right to choose whether or not to become fathers—whether or not to opt out of paying child support or to otherwise refuse paternal duties. While far too many do so, this is something we not only criticize morally, sometimes in the harshest possible terms, but also seek to thwart through the power of law. The reason often given here is that actions have consequences, and that we are often faced with obligations we did not explicitly assume. He should have thought of *that*, we say to ourselves, before he unzipped his pants! But, as Keith Pavlischek writes, "It certainly would seem strange to suggest that the mother could be relieved of potential parental burdens and responsibilities in *all* situations but the father could not under *any* circumstances. To some this may even appear sexist."[1]

Why the asymmetry? Perhaps this kind of admittedly gender-sensitive response is just a legacy of past sexism in the other direction, where men forced themselves on women, pressured women to have sex with them, and then blithely walked away, leaving 100 percent of the consequences of their mutual act to be borne by the woman alone. Hers was the stigma of unwed motherhood, hers were the shattered dreams, hers was the life of poverty—with her child forever labeled as bastard. He waltzed off scot-free, merely enhancing his delightfully wicked reputation as a rake and scoundrel. We may feel that it's only fair that this far more egregious asymmetry of the past be redressed by current practices that privilege women's choice. But it takes only a moment's reflection to feel uncomfortable with this. If our aim is chiefly retributive, surely it is the wrong men who are being punished by it— as, for example, my friend who deeply regretted his role in an unplanned conception and was sincerely willing to bear whatever part of the burden he could bear.

In this paper, I want to explore this asymmetry further and in the process partially (but only partially) to reject it. Along the way we will need to answer questions about what we all—fathers *and* mothers— owe to our children, willingly or unwillingly conceived, and the role that choice plays in determining our deepest and most abiding obligations.

The Choice to Abort

I think it is helpful to look in turn at a series of choices to be made by the partners to an act of unplanned conception.

The first is the choice, once the child is conceived, to abort or not to abort. Here it seems obvious to me that the choice to abort or to carry a child to term has to belong to the mother, and to the mother alone.

I do not wish in this paper to attempt to put forward an unassailable argument for pro-choice abortion policy more generally, though what I have to say below about the role of choice in child-bearing and child-rearing may well have implications for abortion policy. I want to say only that if we permit choice, it is the choice of the mother, not of the father, that is central.

Three points here:

First, unlike the choices we will consider below, the choice to abort or not to abort an early-term fetus is, in my view, the choice of whether or not to bring a person into existence. It is not the choice of whether or not to provide support to an existing person. It is certainly helpful, for the sake of argument, to see what follows if we assume that the fetus is indeed a person at this stage of development, as Judith Jarvis Thomson so famously has done. But it is important never to forget that the fetus is not a person. What is at issue is precisely whether or not there is to be a person, a child to whom the parents will have obligations.

Second, just about all the burden of either carrying a child to term or of having an abortion falls upon the mother. The father may (help?) pay for the costs of the abortion or the costs of the birth, but whatever financial contribution he makes is dwarfed into near-insignificance by the physical contribution she makes. There is no comparison whatsoever between going through pregnancy or having an operation and merely paying (some portion of) the bill for the same.

Third, focusing now on pregnancy, the contribution the mother makes is unique, so that it is difficult to compare any other burden to it, even the burden of providing financial and emotional support for a child from birth to adulthood. Pavlischek claims "one would hardly be thought irrational to think that forced appropriation of the father's time and labor over almost two decades counts for less than the physical burdens of pregnancy for a mere nine months."[2] Francis Beckwith, pressing a similar point, describes the burdens of pregnancy as involving "some bouts with morning sickness, water retention, and other minor ailments."[3] To this David Boonin has replied convincingly that the burden borne by the pregnant woman is "fundamentally different" from that borne by the man: "The woman is required to suffer a distinctly intimate and physical burden while the man is required only to hand over some money."[4] Boonin asks whether we would ever accept an obligation on the part of the father to have artificially induced in him "a pseudo-zygote which would develop into a pseudo-embryo and then a pseudo-fetus" and then to give "birth" to it "in a manner that parallels the nature of childbirth as closely as is anatomically possible." He concludes, "It goes without saying that no court would order him to undergo such a procedure."[5]

I want to add that it is not so much that the burden of unwanted pregnancy is quantitatively greater, which it is, but that it is qualitatively different. Compare the case of rape. Suppose that a rape is relatively brief—over in a "mere" ten minutes or so. Suppose also that it is relatively nonbrutal, leaving no significant physical damage, and causing no pregnancy or sexually transmitted disease. Are we to dismiss the seriousness of the crime committed against the woman because of its brief duration and negligible physical consequences? What makes rape so terrible, among other terrible things, is that an act that should be the most intimate, based in love, consented to joyfully by both partners, is turned into a savage violation.

I want to say something similar about unwanted pregnancy. Although here there is no analogy to the crime, brutality, and violence of rape, we have the same result that an event in a human life that should be the occasion of joyful, loving anticipation is instead the occasion of misery and dread. A central human experience is turned in upon itself. This is *not* comparable merely to paying child support for the rest of one's life. There is no single scale on which the two "inconveniences" can be measured. Just as we do not judge the harm suffered by a rape victim by comparing the experience of involuntary sex to the "inconveniences" (few as they are) of voluntary sex, so we should not judge the harm suffered by an unwillingly pregnant woman by assessing the relatively minor "inconveniences" of ordinary pregnancy. That voluntary sex and voluntary pregnancy can both be joyful experiences, with few if any unpleasant side-effects, does not mean that involuntary sex and involuntary pregnancy can be judged in those terms. The lack of voluntariness changes—indeed, inverts—everything.

Thus, if the woman chooses abortion, whereas the father would have chosen to have a child; if the woman chooses childbirth, whereas the father would have chosen abortion; this has to be her choice. There is no workable way that it can be his. Yes, it is unfortunate, even tragic, if he desperately longed to have and raise the child that is to be aborted; yes, it is unfortunate, even tragic, if he finds himself trapped forever in the role of father (and we shall examine below the extent to which he should be thus trapped); but if the only alternative to these tragedies is for a woman to be forced to submit to an unwanted abortion or to an unwanted pregnancy, that alternative is simply unacceptable.

Should the man at least be "involved" in the woman's choice? Should he at least have some voice? And have his voice heard? Ideally, yes, certainly, though there is no way that this ideal can be made legally operational. I can't imagine any "notification" requirement being workable, or helpful. If the couple is sufficiently estranged from each other that they have severed all communication about the pregnancy, I can't imagine that their court-ordered conversations mandated by a legal notification requirement would be at all fruitful. But yes, I would hope that two people who conceive a child together would be able to talk together about its, and their, future. If the man desperately wants a child, and the woman has at most a weak desire not to have it, I would hope that she would at least consider making the choice to give birth. In fact, following Thomson, we might say that it would be indecent of her not to. But the choice here has to be hers.

The Choice to Give Up One's Child for Adoption

Suppose now that the mother decides against abortion and carries the child to term; she now faces the choice of whether to give up her child for adoption or to raise it herself. Suppose she wants to keep it, but he (like my friend, wanting to avoid paternal responsibilities) wants to give it up. Now, switching genders in the example, suppose he wants to keep it, but she wants to give it up. To whom should this choice belong?

I think the answer here is also an easy one and this time involves rejecting any explicitly gendered asymmetries. Here I answer: it is more terrible to have to surrender a child one wants to keep than to have to assume responsibilities to a child from which one would want to distance oneself. So I privilege the choice to keep the child, whether made by the mother, *or* made by the father.

I don't know if I can give an argument for this. Am I simply measuring costs in some crude utilitarian way—calculating the pain of unwillingly relinquishing one's child, added to the costs of subsequently mourning its loss, compared against the costs of keeping the child with all the attendant stresses and strains of parenthood? I don't think so. Indeed, I think that if one were simply to add up utilities here, the costs of keeping the child would be greater. It is rather that one has a right to keep one's child, if one wants to keep it, and one is not demonstrably unfit. This seems to square sufficiently, I think, with most people's intuitions that I don't think the view requires further defense.

This view is bolstered by our also thinking it is generally in a child's best interest to be raised by a biological parent, at least where the biological parent loves it and wants it. The hunger that many adopted children express for their biological roots and for some knowledge of and contact with their biological parents suggest that this kind of biological connection is an important good, at least in a culture in which children are standardly raised by their biological parents.

This means that if the mother wants to keep the child and the father doesn't, she gets to keep it. If the father wants to keep the child and the mother doesn't, he gets to keep it. Neither mother nor father can surrender the child to a third party if the other biological parent is willing to keep it and raise it.

This, then, leads us to the difficult questions that will occupy me for the remainder of the paper. If the mother decides to keep the child, over the objections of the father, who would have chosen adoption or abortion, or if the father decides to keep the child, over the objections of the mother, who would have chosen adoption (remember, if she chooses abortion, her choice here is final), does the other parent, the objecting parent, now owe child support? Is he or she required to assume, however unwillingly, the responsibilities of parenthood?

The Choice to Become a Parent

My first claim is that whatever our answer here will be, it should (with one possible exception to be discussed below) be the same for fathers and mothers. If the mother chooses to keep the child, or if the father chooses to keep it, the obligations of the other parent should be comparable, regardless of the gender of the parent. Only in the case of abortion can I see any justification for treating these differently. Only there is a unique burden biologically imposed upon the mother. However, I will argue that the nature of our final response will be rightly shaped by the fact that at present it is overwhelmingly mothers who choose to keep the child, and not fathers. Should this fact change, our response should perhaps change as well.

So our question now becomes: what *do* we owe children we do not choose to have, simply because they exist, and because our partners in their conception have chosen them as theirs?

Here is an argument that the "other parent" should have no parental obligations. After all, the argument goes, just because *you* choose to be a parent—when you could have given the child up for adoption (or, said by the father, when you could have had an abortion)—why do *I* have to be parent, when I would have chosen to give up the child for adoption (or paid for an abortion)? I respect your right to make these choices for your life; why can't you respect my right to make them for mine? If you can choose to be a parent, why can't I choose *not* to be a parent? Indeed, how can *you* make not only the choice that *you* be a parent, but that *I* be a parent? What gives one person license to make such a deep, abiding, life-affecting choice for another?

I think this response, for which I confess considerable initial sympathy, is most plausible in the following kind of circumstance. Suppose either parent—let's say, for simplicity, the mother—simply has a strong desire to be a parent. So far, I've been focusing on unplanned pregnancy, but let's change the case: suppose one parent has a strong antecedent desire to be a parent and actually plans the pregnancy. On one scenario (Scenario 1), she plans it with the explicit permission and cooperation of the other partner (on the understanding that she alone will bear parental responsibilities); on another scenario (Scenario 2), she plans it without enlisting the explicit permission of the other partner (she simply has unprotected sex with him, on purpose, deceiving him about her nonuse of contraception, and hopes for conception to follow). Why, then, should the other partner bear any subsequent responsibility for the child created?

On Scenario 1, presumably both partners made some kind of (perhaps written, perhaps merely oral) agreement in which the mother waived any claim for further contributions from the other partner—else why would he have agreed to proceed, given that he doesn't want to enter into the role of parent and assume any parental responsibilities? On Scenario 2, if there has been (at worst) actual deception of the other party, or (at best) deliberate using of him as a means to her end, why should he now bear the costs of being deceived and used, given that clearly the deception and arguably the using was a wrong to him in the first place?

My answer is that we need to proceed carefully here in sorting out the obligations of the reluctant father. We need, first, to distinguish between his obligations, if any, to the mother, to assist her in bearing the financial and emotional burden of child-rearing, and his obligations, if any, to the child he has created.

I think we can agree that in both Scenario 1 and Scenario 2, the reluctant (and wronged) parent has no obligation to the other parent, to assist her in her task of child-rearing. She has explicitly excused him from any obligation in Scenario 1; in Scenario 2, her wrongdoing in deceiving and using him causes her to forfeit any claim she would have otherwise had against him. When we turn to potential obligations to the child, however, we must remember that the child has been no party to any agreement between the parents, nor has the child committed any wrongful act. So the possibility remains open that the father has obligations to the child, although he has none to the mother. My conclusion here will be that although we do have prima facie obligations to the children we create, simply from our committing voluntary acts that predictably lead to their birth, under some circumstances these obligations can be assigned to others. I believe that the obligation of the father to the child is transferred to the mother in Scenarios 1 and 2.

Let me explain. I think it is implausible to suggest that we have no obligations at all to the children we produce as a predictable outcome of our voluntary acts unless we at some point voluntarily assume these. Where two persons voluntarily have sexual intercourse, knowing that there is always at least some chance of producing children in that way, they have obligations to those children. These obligations do not proceed from mere genetic connection to our children: thus, the rape victim has no obligation to the child she bears, nor would a man whose sperm had somehow been removed from him without his knowledge or authorization, perhaps through some illicit surgical procedure. But when people take actions—such as engaging in voluntary sexual intercourse or, I would add, contributing genetic material to an egg or sperm bank—they act voluntarily in a way that one can expect will lead to the creation of a child. Thus one bears some obligation toward this child, unless this obligation is transferred to another party.

Many philosophers, including most notably Thomson, have claimed that to consent to sexual intercourse is not yet to consent to the creation of a child; to open one's window for fresh air is not yet to consent to the entrance of person-seeds and their subsequent rooting in one's carpets and upholstery. But although I accept Thomson's answer regarding person-seeds, I cannot accept it regarding persons. With person-seeds, and with fetuses, there is as yet no person there to whom *somebody* must owe something; but once there is a person, a helpless child who exists only because of my voluntary actions, I can't accept that this child has no rights against me regarding its support and nurture. Children have a right that their parents care for them, even if the violinist doesn't have a right that I remain plugged to him and I have no right that Henry Fonda place his cooling hand upon my head. I have not created the violinist's need for my kidneys; nor has Henry Fonda created my need for his cooling touch. But in creating a child through my own voluntary actions, I create its helplessness and generate its right against me to relieve that helplessness. (Again, this does not mean that the mother is obligated to bring a fetus to term; an early-stage fetus is not a person and does not have such moral rights.)

Now, the obligations we bear toward our children can be transferred to another. One way that this is standardly done is through adoption. David Boonin has claimed that the existence of adoption as an accepted practice shows that we do not believe that parents have a duty to provide for their children's needs; Boonin claims that a father has no obligation to provide for his son's needs, because "If he no longer wishes to be a parent, it is permissible for him to put his son up for adoption."[6] But the example of adoption shows only that we do not insist on parents' meeting their children's needs where others are willing and indeed eager to do so. If no prospective adoptive parents appear, however, the biological parent is simply stuck with his or her child. Nor are we free to put our older children up for adoption, should we begin to find parenthood more burdensome and wearying than previously expected.

Another case in which parental obligations are transferred to another party is in the practice of sperm/egg donation. The donating party makes an explicit agreement with the fertility clinic and with the receiving party that his or her parental responsibilities will be met by another. We are now approaching the situation of Scenario 1, where the man is little more than a sperm donor, although the method of donation is less clinical and detached than in the typical sperm bank case; here we can say that his obligations to the child are voluntarily assumed by the mother. It is worth noting, however, that it is prima facie suboptimal to have one person assuming obligations of both father and mother, for this is bound to produce some subsequent strain as one individual (the mother) attempts to carry out the obligations of two. In Scenario 2, I would say that the mother can be assigned the father's parental obligations by virtue of her deceitful manipulation of him.

This means, if you will, that the "default setting" is one of parental obligation, but these obligations, again, can be transferred to another. What if, however, the party to whom the obligations have been transferred reneges on those obligations or proves otherwise unable to carry them out? I think we need to conclude that the obligation does not revert to the original parent. Otherwise, biological parents could find themselves years later faced with obligations to children whom they had given up for adoption at birth. No one could live stable lives if obligations kept appearing and reappearing in this unpredictable way.

Most conceptions do not occur as in Scenario 1 and 2. So let us look at a few more typical scenarios to determine what obligations the father in these cases bears to the mother of the child conceived and what obligations he bears to the child itself. In Scenario 3, while there is no antecedent plan to create a child through the sexual act, when conception indeed takes place, one partner, but not the other, is thrilled—welcoming wholeheartedly the opportunity to become a parent. The other party is distinctly *not* thrilled. What do we say here about the obligations of the less-than-thrilled parent?

Once again, the father has obligations to his child, unless we can understand him to have transferred these to another party. But there is no reason to think he has transferred them to the mother; there has been no explicit agreement to transfer these obligations, nor has there been any wrongdoing on her part. Given that she welcomes parenthood while he does not, perhaps it might be a kindness on her part to him to relieve him of parental obligations by assuming them herself, along the lines of Scenario 1. It is less clear that this would be a kindness to the child, however, who would now be raised with fewer resources of parental income and attention.

Although the father has clear obligations to the child in Scenario 3, however, I do feel some pull to say that he has at best limited obligations to the mother. After all, she is embracing a choice that he is not embracing: why should he be bound by her enthusiasm? She is clearly making a choice to bear this child: she wants to be a parent to this child. If he makes a different choice, why should he be bound by what she chooses? I'm not sure in practice how much difference it makes to the father's actual level of contributions if he owes obligations to both mother and child or to child alone. But it might make sense to see the situation of double-obligation, where it exists, as justifying a somewhat greater burden of contribution, as well as making his obligations of support even more securely grounded.

Let us vary the case a bit more. In Scenario 4, neither partner is enthusiastic about becoming a parent, but while one is willing either to accept an abortion or to give the child up for adoption, the other is not. We can imagine a range of reasons one would give for this reluctance to give up one's child, either via abortion or via adoption. A woman might think that abortion and adoption are morally wrong, thus "nonoptions." Or a woman might think that although abortion is morally permissible and should remain legally available, she is unable to abort *her* child. Many people hold the view that although abortion is not wrong generally, it is "wrong for me," that is, it violates my own personal standards. A woman might also think that even if abortion isn't wrong even "for her," nonetheless she would be haunted by— perhaps irrational but nonetheless real—regret afterward. Likewise, in the adoption case, one might think that, however much one doesn't want to be a parent, one just can't make oneself give up one's child, that, again, one would forever be haunted by regret should one do so.

Although there is no necessary gendered asymmetry here—either parent could voice this view—I do think it more likely empirically that it would be women who would think in this way, given the bonds that tend to grow up between mother and fetus through a pregnancy and the expectations our society places upon women to accept and welcome, indeed to define themselves in terms of, the role of mother. I think it is more likely that a woman would say, "I cannot abort this child now growing within my body," or "After spending nine months with this child growing inside my body, I can't give it away."

As we move along the spectrum from Scenario 3 to some version of Scenario 4, my claim is that the other partner increasingly incurs responsibilities not only toward the child (which are present in all scenarios, though transferred in some), but toward the mother as well. Why should this be? Why should *he* be held hostage to her (perhaps unfounded) moral scruples? Why should he be bound by her (perhaps irrational) sense of moral guilt?

One first answer would be that we hold that he is to the extent that we see her moral scruples and moral guilt as justified. If we think it is in fact wrong to have an abortion or to give up a child for adoption, and we see her as simply meeting what we would agree are her clear moral responsibilities, of course we want to see him meeting his moral responsibilities, and being forced to do so if necessary. That she has a legal choice does not mean that she, properly speaking, has a moral choice. But in my own view, (early-term) abortion is permissible, and giving up one's child for adoption is often not only permissible but admirable, a painful and loving act done for the child's best interests. So I think it is important to be able to give an account of how her convictions can generate his responsibilities even if we hold that her moral scruples about abortion and adoption are unjustified, or at the least if we accept that there is room for legitimate disagreement about where the moral truth actually lies.

A second answer, then, is that where the mother (or father) chooses to be a parent only because she (or he) feels in some way morally or personally obligated to do so, there is a different sort of burden involved, or the burden that is involved is chosen under more difficult circumstances. It is still chosen. I have argued elsewhere that we are always making our choices against the background of circumstances not of our choosing: few if any choices are made with complete and unmitigated delight in every detail.[7] Even where the single mother plans her pregnancy (Scenario 1), she may very well have wished things could be otherwise, that she could have found a man with whom she could have joyfully shared a life as partners and parents. Just because you aren't thrilled with the context within which you choose doesn't mean you didn't make a choice.

And yet—I do think our views shift according to whether we see the partner who chooses parenthood as merely exercising a "lifestyle option" or doing what she does because she doesn't see—feel?—any real, viable alternative. In many cases where mothers (in particular) decide not to abort and not to give up their children for adoption, they do not see themselves, at least, as making a choice between two open options, between two genuine alternatives. They can't *not* do it. They see themselves, rightly or wrongly, as having no choice.

Why? One reason is surely based in biology, some kind of deep bond between parent and child that is hardwired into parents of most species by nature. The same reason that led me, above, to say that no one should have to relinquish a child involuntarily also makes it hard, perhaps approaching in some cases impossibility, for parents—especially mothers?—to relinquish a child voluntarily. It is just too hard to do. This is one argument sometimes given for abortion rights—that despite all the talk about adoption as an option, it doesn't really feel like an option; that although one can make oneself submit to a surgical procedure to remove a tiny embryo, one cannot make oneself hand over from one's arms a real live baby, one's own real live baby.

Yet, as having myself experienced the heartbreak of infertility, dreaming of finding a little baby in a basket left on my doorstep, I wish more people could see adoption as an option. I think we are collectively in real danger of fetishizing biological ties, in a way that has detrimental effects on women who feel forced to keep their children, on infertile couples yearning for an adoptable infant, and on children themselves, who live unwanted in one family when another family, perhaps down the street, would have wanted them so desperately. A significant part of why mothers in particular feel they have no option but to keep their children is because of an elaborate complex of societal pressures and expectations that we would do better to revise.

All this said: why should the fact that I see myself as having no option but to become a parent to this child mean that you owe me any kind of support as I carry out my decision? After all, sometimes—often? always?—we think people are just wrong in seeing themselves as having no options. In fact, I am one who thinks that almost every time we see ourselves as having no option, no choice, we are wrong. The claim "I had no choice" is almost always false, and worse than false: it purports to provide an excuse for our fleeing from taking real responsibility for the choices we are indeed making even as we persist in denying them.

And yet—given that it is not unreasonable that women in particular, having spent nine months in pregnancy, feel a bond with their child; given that we do live in a society that has strong expectations that women keep and raise their children—I think it may be too much to expect women to give up their children, and, given that this is so, likewise too much to expect them to raise these children entirely alone. It's hard enough that they bear the burden of raising unplanned and in some sense unwanted children; it would simply be too hard to ask that they do this entirely alone.

I think it does make a difference here that the parent who feels unable to walk away from a pregnancy or a birth is so often the mother. To permit him to walk away, when she—for reasons biological, for reasons societal, but somehow clearly connected to her gender—feels unable to, seems wrong, seems to perpetuate an ages-old system of sexist oppression. In cases (if such there be) where gender roles are reversed, and it is the father rather than the mother who feels the need to keep his child, I still would view the reluctant mother as having obligations not only to her child, but to the father as well. I would not be willing to accept a formal, explicit male-female asymmetry here. If, however, gender roles should sufficiently erode so that we saw roughly the same number of men as women making the choice to keep their children, and if we also saw a more equal number of parents making the choice to keep their children and making the choice to give them to others, then I would feel less insistent that the reluctant parent has an obligation to the other parent, independent of his or her inescapable obligation to his or her child. I would feel more comfortable saying to the "keeping" parent: hey, it's your choice, you could have given up your child, but you chose not to, so you're on your own with this one. I don't feel comfortable saying that now, in our world, in the world in which the context of choice for mothers continues to be so deeply different from that for fathers.

Obligations to Our Children

I have been talking so far about obligations to one's children in fairly general terms, focusing on the question of whether we have such obligations or not, and why. Now we need, in closing, to turn to the substance of these obligations. When we have parental obligations to a child, what exactly is it that we are obligated to do? What *do* we owe our children?

We don't owe them whatever is needed for an optimal upbringing. That would be to weigh their interests too heavily, ours not at all. We don't owe them lots of money, or piano lessons on a Steinway baby grand, or an Ivy League education; thus we have no obligation to surrender them for adoption to families that are able to provide these "advantages." I don't think we owe them a conventional family structure, with two parents of opposite genders in traditional gendered roles; thus the unmarried partners to our hypothetical unplanned conception have no obligation to marry. What we do owe them is a good faith effort to meet their needs—physical, emotional, and educational. And if we fail at meeting these needs, it is appropriate for the state to intervene to see that the needs are met by others. I also would include love among these needs—not just loving behavior, but love itself.

The parent who decides to keep the child should decide to keep it only if she thinks she can provide these things—some reasonable meeting of the child's basic needs, and love. If you don't think you can be an adequate or loving parent, you have an obligation to transfer your parental responsibilities to somebody who can. The noncustodial parent, however, in the cases we have been considering, may well not think he can be an adequate or loving parent, and yet he, though not she, is still stuck in this role. Does he really have obligations to try to love a child he has no desire even to have in the first place? I think he does. Although he can't have obligations actually to love the child, for that may be out of his control, he has an obligation to try. After all, no one ever promised us that meeting all our obligations would be easy.

Conclusions

I began with a puzzle: if women must be allowed to choose whether or not to become mothers, why shouldn't fathers be allowed to choose whether or not to become fathers? If mothers can choose to abort their fetuses, or to give their children up for adoption, why shouldn't fathers be permitted to choose whether or not to pay child support to children who are not aborted and not given up for adoption? Surely it seems as if we should have a consistent view here: either obligations to our children are freely chosen or they are not. It can't be that they are freely chosen by mothers but forced by circumstance upon fathers.

My solution to the puzzle involves several elements.

First, I treat the case of the choice to abort as special: only here do we have the choice of whether or not a person will exist, as opposed to the choice of assuming or refusing obligations to a person who does exist. And only here do we have a necessary male-female asymmetry, for only women can either have abortions or give birth. Thus here there is no obligation to a child on the part of either parent, for no person yet exists to whom obligations can be owed. And the choice of whether or not this child will come to exist belongs to the mother alone.

Second, as for the choice to keep one's child or to give it up for adoption, I argue that the choice here should be the same for both mothers and fathers, but that the choice to keep a child is privileged over the choice to give it up. This is in part because one has an obligation to a child one creates, and the choice to decide to fulfill that obligation oneself reasonably takes precedence over the choice to transfer that obligation to another.

Third, in most but not all cases, when one parent chooses to keep the child, the other parent can be required to provide some level of child support. Parents do have obligations to individuals created as a predictable result of their voluntary actions, unless these obligations can be understood as having been transferred to others, by a clear agreement between the parties or through the wrongdoing of one of the parties. Whether or not the noncustodial parent has obligations not only to the child but to the other parent will turn on the degree to which the custodial parent has made a genuine choice to keep and raise her child, in the face of genuine options to do otherwise. My argument here rests in part on the fact that it is overwhelmingly women who choose to keep their children, under the weight of significant biological and societal pressures. If their partners were not required to help them bear the burdens of unwanted parenthood, the resultant male-female disparity in life burdens would be too great, and too oppressive, for us to accept. However, should the choice to keep a child become more of an actual choice, and exhibit fewer gendered patterns, the obligation of the reluctant parent to provide support to the custodial parent would be less stringent.

So to my friend whose story triggered this discussion, I would say: it is not that she has a choice whether or not to be a mother, whereas you have no choice whether or not to be a father. Although she is the only one who can make the choice to abort, once the child is born, both of you have obligations to your child, unless you can transfer these obligations to another willing party. She did not choose to transfer her obligations, perhaps because she did not view this transfer truly as a choice. Thus, unless you can find someone who wishes to assume your parental obligations (perhaps, in later years, her new partner, for example), the obligations continue to be yours. And insofar as she makes her choice in a context of gender-asymmetrical constraint, you may owe at least some level of support to her as well as to the child you so carelessly created together.[8]

Notes

1. Pavlischek, "Abortion Logic and Paternal Responsibilities," p. 182.
2. Pavlischek, *ibid.*, p. 190.
3. Beckwith, "Arguments from Bodily Rights: A Critical Analysis," p. 144.
4. Boonin-Vail, "A Defense of 'A Defense of Abortion,'" p. 170.
5. Boonin, *A Defense of Abortion*, p. 451.
6. Boonin-Vail, *ibid.*, p. 174.
7. Mills, "Choice and Circumstance."
8. I would like to thank my colleagues and students in the Center for Values and Social Policy in the Philosophy Department at the University of Colorado at Boulder for

helpful comments on an earlier draft of this essay. And above all, I would like to thank Judith Jarvis Thomson for her formative influence on my career as a philosopher. She was my teacher and my mentor when I was an undergraduate at Wellesley twenty years ago, taking philosophy courses at MIT through the Wellesley-MIT exchange program. Her courses were thrilling intellectual experiences, and the wise advice she gave my twenty-year-old self—on philosophy, on writing, on life—is still heeded and cherished.

References

Beckwith, Francis. "Arguments from Bodily Rights: A Critical Analysis," in Louis P. Pojman and Francis Beckwith (eds.), *The Abortion Controversy* (Belmont, Calif.: Wadsworth, 1998), pp. 132–150.

Boonin, David. *A Defense of Abortion*. New York: Cambridge University Press, forthcoming.

Boonin-Vail, David. "A Defense of 'A Defense of Abortion,'" in Louis P. Pojman and Francis Beckwith (eds.), *The Abortion Controversy* (Belmont, Calif.: Wadsworth, 1998), pp. 151–175.

Mills, Claudia. "Choice and Circumstance," *Ethics* 109 (1998), pp. 154–165.

Pavlischek, Keith. "Abortion Logic and Paternal Responsibilities," in Louis P. Pojman and Francis Beckwith (eds.), *The Abortion Controversy* (Belmont, Calif.: Wadsworth, 1998), pp. 176–198.

Thomson, Judith Jarvis. "A Defense of Abortion," in *Rights, Risk, and Restitution: Essays in Moral Theory* (Cambridge, Mass.: Harvard University Press, 1986), pp. 1–19.

Chapter 10

Thomson on Self-Defense

T. M. Scanlon

We all believe that people have a "right of self-defense": when their lives are threatened they are entitled to defend themselves by doing things that would normally be forbidden because of the harm they cause to others. As Judith Thomson has shown, however, it is far from easy to say exactly what this right involves, or to explain why people are permitted to act in self-defense in the ways it seems that they are.[1] As she says, these questions raise deep issues in moral theory.

Like many others, I have learned an enormous amount from Thomson's discussion of these matters. In this paper I will consider some of the questions that she raises, addressing them from the point of view of a contractualist account of right and wrong. This is a point of view that Thomson does not share, so what I will be doing is trying to show how some issues that she has enlighteningly discussed look when viewed from a different perspective.

To begin with, my terminology will be somewhat different from Thomson's. She speaks mainly of rights and claims, a central class of rights that correspond to duties on the part of the person against whom the right obtains. I will speak simply of what is or is not morally permissible, and I will understand permissibility in contractualist terms. According to contractualism, as I understand it, an action is impermissible if and only if any principle that permitted it would be one that someone could reasonably reject, even if that person had the aim of finding principles for the general regulation of behavior that others similarly motivated could not reasonably reject.[2]

According to Thomson, as I understand her, if A has a claim against B that B not do X, then B ought not do X in the absence of special conditions or justifications. This incorporates her thesis that "rights reduce, in a certain way, to what—other things equal—people ought to do or not do, and may or may not do."[3] My inclusion of the qualification about "special conditions or justifications" corresponds to her thesis that rights and claims are "not absolute," that is to say, that it can be true both that *A* has a claim against *B* that *B* not do *X*, and that it would not be wrong of *B* to do *X*.

I agree with all of this, in particular with the thesis that rights are not absolute. I will part company with Thomson, however, in understanding these requirements in contractualist terms. So the thesis that *A* has a claim against *B* that *B* not do *X* will amount, as I will understand it, to the thesis that *B* stands in a certain relation to *A* such that any principle that permitted a person who stands in that relation to someone to fail to do *X* (in the absence of further special conditions or justifications) would be a principle that anyone in *A*'s position could reasonably reject. In particular, I will use this contractualist idea to explain both why there are certain rights in the sense just described and why these are not absolute—what the special conditions and justifications are that limit them.

Turning, then, to self-defense, we begin with the fact that it would be reasonable to reject any principle that left agents free (even in the absence of any special justification) to act in ways that could reasonably be foreseen to cause other people serious injury or death by the impact on their bodies of the agents' bodies or of machinery that the agents control (such as guns, knives, automobiles, trolleys, etc.). We all have strong reasons to want to avoid serious injury or death, and thus have good grounds for reasonably rejecting such a principle. The next question is whether a principle forbidding *all* conduct that can reasonably be foreseen to cause serious injury or death in these ways could also be reasonably rejected. This principle would be supported by the strong reason just mentioned. But there are also good reasons to reject such a broad prohibition, since we also can have strong reasons to behave in ways that it would forbid. Indeed the reason just mentioned might be cited here, since circumstances can arise in which we can avoid serious injury or death only by behaving in ways that can be foreseen to lead to the injury or death of others in the ways that this principle would forbid. So we need to consider how this principle needs to be qualified in order not to be reasonably rejectable.

One very broad qualification would permit us to inflict injury or death on others in ways that this principle would otherwise prohibit whenever doing so is necessary to preserve our own lives or protect us from serious injury. This would include much more than self-defense, since it would allow killing others in order to obtain their organs for transplant, or in order to eat them, if this were the only way to avoid starvation. It would be reasonable to reject a principle incorporating such a broad exception. It is not unreasonable to refuse to regard one's own life and body as "on call" to be sacrificed whenever it is needed to save others who are at risk. A defensible exception to the general prohibition against causing injury or death would have to be more narrowly drawn.

The idea of self-defense, as ordinarily understood, is narrower in several respects. Consider the following case, described by Thomson.[4]

> *Villainous Aggressor*: B and A are in an elevator. B has always hated A and takes this opportunity to get rid of him; B goes for A's throat to kill him. A can save his life only by killing B.

Three features of this case might serve to distinguish it from other examples of the use of potentially deadly force: B is a threat to A, B has chosen to become a threat to A, and B is at fault for having so chosen. These features are distinct and independent. Someone can become a threat to another person without choosing to do so. Suppose, for example, that A and B are victims of a shipwreck, and a wave tosses B, unconscious but still alive, onto the piece of floating debris to which A is clinging. It will not support both of them, so A can save himself only by pushing B off. One can also choose to become a threat but do so without fault, as in

> *Mistaken Aggressor*: B attacks A because he believes, reasonably but mistakenly, that A, who is much larger and stronger than B, is about to kill him and that he can save himself only by a preemptive attack.

The question is what role these three features—being a threat, choosing to become a threat, and being at fault in so choosing—might have in the formulation and defense of an exception to the general prohibition against the use of force.

Consider first the role of choice. According to contractualism, the role of choice in the formulation and justification of principles of the kind we are considering is as a factor that reduces or eliminates a person's reasonable objection to a principle.[5] To illustrate this, suppose P is a principle that would allow others to do something that could affect me in a way that I have reason not to want. Consider two possibilities. The first is that if people do what P allows then I will certainly be affected in this undesirable way. The second is that if they do what P allows I will be affected in this way unless I take evasive action by doing X, where X is something that I could do quite easily and without sacrificing anything important. I take it as obvious that my grounds for rejecting P are weaker in the second case than in the first. It does not follow, of course, that even in the second case P is not reasonably rejectable. If other people have no strong reason for wanting to be able to behave in the way P allows, then I may have good reason to reject P in both cases. Why should I have to be alert to the possibility that I might need to do X to avoid the objectionable effects of their behavior, if they have no good reason to want to be able to engage in it? But if they do have good reason for wanting to do this, then it may well be that I could reasonably reject a principle permitting it if I could not avoid the effects in question, but not if I could easily avoid these effects by doing X.

I believe that this phenomenon, of the reasonableness of a person's objection to a principle being diminished by the possibility of avoiding its effects, is quite common. It is illustrated, for example, in Thomson's discussion of what she calls the Aggravation Principle, the initial form of which holds (with a qualification that is irrelevant for present purposes) that "If X has a claim against Y that Y do alpha, then the worse Y makes things for X if Y fails to do alpha, the more stringent X's claim against Y that Y do alpha."[6] Thomson goes on to note that this principle does not hold if the worsening is brought about intentionally by X. Suppose, for example, that X, foreseeing that Y will violate his rights in some relatively trivial way, arranges for this trivial violation to have much more serious consequences, with the aim of justifying more serious retribution against Y. In such a case, it is plausible to say that neither the stringency of X's claim against Y, nor X's claim for restitution, is increased. On my view this is explained by the fact that Y has reason to object to a form of the Aggravation Principle that would take X's claim to be more stringent in this case and X has no good reason to reject a weaker form of the principle that would ignore such worsenings, since X could easily avoid the additional cost they involve.

Thomson's formulation of the weaker principle excludes " 'worsenings' that X consents to." This is a step in the right direction, but I believe that "consents to" is too narrow. The relevant notion is "has adequate opportunity to avoid," which is broader than "consents to" and more basic. As I will argue more fully below, "adequate opportunity to avoid" can have the legitimating effect that consent often has, and also explains why consent has this effect, when it does.

This will become clearer if we turn to a slightly different kind of case, in which the possibility of avoidance lies in a principle itself rather than in the process through which the actions the principle allows have their undesirable effects. Consider two principles that are related in the following way. The first would permit a person to behave a certain way even if her doing so would affect another person, V, in ways that he has reason not to want. The second would permit this behavior only if V does not do X, where, as before, X is something that V could quite easily do or not do, without sacrificing anything of importance. It seems clear that a person in V's position has stronger reason for rejecting the first principle than for rejecting the second, since the second principle (if others abide by it) allows him to avoid the deleterious consequences of the behavior in question by taking relatively costless action.

Despite this difference, it may be that both principles can reasonably be rejected. If the agents in question have no good reason for wanting to be free to engage in the conduct in question, and if this conduct has undesirable effects on people in V's position, why should people in that position have to do anything, even if it is a relatively costless action, in order to avoid being subjected to this result? On the other hand, if people have very strong reason to want to engage in the conduct in question, then it may not be reasonable to reject even the first, more permissive principle. I might not like it if people come onto my land, and would prefer if they were only allowed to do this with my permission, but I could not reasonably reject a principle that permits them to do so without my permission when this is required in order to save someone's life.

What is important for present purposes, however, is that there are many cases that fall between these two extremes—cases in which it would be reasonable to reject a principle that licensed people generally to act in a way that has undesirable consequences for someone in V's position, but not reasonable to reject a principle that would permit this provided that the person in that position did a certain thing, X, which that person could easily do or not do.

It is natural to think of "doing X" in such a case as giving consent. But this is only a special case. Suppose, for example, that the theater box office is licensed to sell my seat to someone else if I do not pick up my tickets at least a half an hour before the concert begins. If I do not turn up, this does not mean that I have consented to the resale of my tickets, but only that I have not complied with the conditions of sale, thereby releasing the seller from his obligation to me.

One might say in this case that by not turning up I have forfeited my claim to the ticket, and this idea of "forfeiting" a right or claim is one that needs to be considered further. As Thomson points out in discussing criminal punishment, the fact that I have not complied with certain conditions constitutes forfeiture of my claim not to have certain undesirable things done to me only if a policy attaching this consequence to that failure is justified. The criminal's breaking the law constitutes forfeiture of his moral claim not to be deprived of his liberty (i.e., licenses the government to deprive him of liberty) only if the government is justified in having such a law, with this penalty attached to its violation, and my failure to pick up my tickets on time constitutes forfeiture of my claim to them only if this policy is one the theater is justified in having. Similarly, in purely moral contexts (as opposed to these institutional ones) my failure to do X constitutes a forfeiture of my claim that others not behave in a certain way only if the principle restricting that conduct falls in the middle ground described above—only if others could reasonably reject a principle banning such conduct altogether and I could reasonably reject a principle that always permitted it; but I could not reasonably reject a principle that allowed it only when I did X, since such a principle gives me as much protection against the behavior in question as I could reasonably demand.

The important point is that if by doing X I forfeit my claim against others that they not treat me a certain way this is so because of many things, including the reasons that others have to want to act in the way in question, the reasons I have to want not to be treated this way, and the ease and cost to me of doing or not doing X. If these considerations balance out in the right way then doing X constitutes forfeiture of my claim; otherwise it does not. When it is true that giving consent, or just acting or not acting a certain way, constitutes forfeiture, this is a product of a moral argument of the kind just described, not an input into it. What serves as an input into this argument is not the idea of forfeiture, or consent, but what I call the value of choice: the fact that the ability to avoid an unwanted consequence is something one has reason to want. Because this is so—because being faced with an avoidable burden is less bad than being faced with an unavoidable one—the opportunity to avoid an unwanted consequence can diminish the force of one's objection to a principle that would permit others to behave in ways that would bring that consequence about.

The terms 'forfeit' and 'consent' suggest an act of consciously laying down a right, or consciously allowing it to lapse. As the concert ticket example shows, however, this suggestion is misleading. If I do not pick up the tickets by the prescribed time then I have forfeited my right to them even if I am unaware of doing any such thing and never made a decision not to go to the concert. It might be that I simply forgot, or was distracted by something more important.

What, then, differentiates cases in which an agent forfeits a right or claim from the more general cases in which an agent simply ceases to have a claim? It may be that as Thomson says, "The English word, 'forfeit' is really too soft an affair to rest any great weight on."[7] I suggest, however, that we take the difference to be this: it is proper to speak of forfeit in those cases in which the principle that permits some action holds that that action would not have been permissible if the person in question had done (or not done) a certain thing, and it is crucial to the defense of that principle that it allows a person in that position to avoid the consequences of the permitted action by doing that thing. One question before us, then, is whether forfeiture, so understood, plays an important role in explaining the permissibility of actions in self-defense.

Before turning to that question, I want to say something about the idea of fault. As the case of the reasonable but mistaken aggressor clearly shows, fault is not a necessary condition for having forfeited one's claim not to have force used against one. But the account I have just given of the importance of choice in the formulation and justification of moral principles does provide some role for the idea of fault. I mentioned above that the fact that V could avoid an undesirable consequence of another person's action by doing X may undermine V's objection to a principle permitting the other person's action. But whether it does so depends on the costs to V of doing X. If X involves very great sacrifice for V, then the availability of this option may not diminish the force of V's objections. This is where fault becomes relevant. If X is something that V is morally required to do, or, to say the same thing, if V would be acting wrongly in failing to do X, then V could not appeal to the sacrifice involved in doing X in order to argue that the availability of this option does not diminish his objections to the principle in question. Consider, for example, a principle permitting someone whom V wrongfully assaults to defend himself by the use of force. V's objection to the harm he might suffer as a result of the actions this principle would permit is diminished by the fact that he can avoid such harm by refraining from wrongful assaults, and the fact that these actions would be wrongful blocks V from responding that it would be too costly for him to avoid harm in that way. It seems, then, that even if fault does not have an independent role in the justification of self-defense it can play a subsidiary role in an argument appealing to avoidability.

When we speak of self-defense, the cases that are most likely to come to mind are ones like *Villainous Aggressor*, and the fact that it would not be reasonable to reject principles permitting the use of force in such cases is adequately explained along the lines I have been discussing. The grounds that someone in the aggressor's position would have for rejecting such a principle are undermined both by the fact that such a person can avoid being vulnerable to the legitimate use of force by simply refraining from aggression, and by the fact that in so doing he or she would not be making any sacrifice that has weight in moral argument.

But there are other cases, in which these factors are not present, in which it may nonetheless seem permissible to use deadly force to protect one's life. Consider the case Thomson calls *Innocent Aggressor*.

Innocent Aggressor: D and E are in an elevator. E suffers a temporary fit of insanity and goes for D's throat to kill him. D can save his life only by killing E.[8]

In such a case D is justified in attacking E, just as B is justified in attacking A in the *Mistaken Aggressor* case, in which B reasonably but mistakenly believes that A is going to kill him. But in neither of these cases is the person against whom force is used at fault. And even the force of avoidability in qualifying the aggressor's objection to a principle permitting force to be used against him is severely diminished. The mistaken aggressor could have avoided being vulnerable to retaliation by choosing not to attack, but given the available information, this option would reasonably have seemed unattractive. The same is true in the case of the innocent insane aggressor Thomson describes. If we do not think it just to punish people for what they do while in the grip of schizophrenic attack, because they have insufficient opportunity to avoid such punishment, it would not seem consistent to say that the case for using force against them in self-defense rests on the fact that they could avoid being vulnerable to such force by refraining from attacking others. And there are other cases in which Thomson suggests that the use of force in self-defense is justified in which it is even clearer that this cannot be explained by appeal either to fault or to avoidability.[9]

Innocent Threat: A sudden gust of wind blew E' down a well. D' is at the bottom. If D' does nothing, E' will survive the fall but D' will die; D' can use his ray gun to disintegrate E', in which case E' dies but D' lives.

This strikes me as a less clear case than *Innocent Aggressor*, but I am nonetheless inclined to agree with Thomson that it is permissible for D' to kill E' in order to save his own life. To explain this I would need to find some factor that introduces an asymmetry between the reasons that someone in the position of E' has for rejecting a principle that would permit this and the reasons that someone in the position of D' has for insisting on this permission, and rejecting any principle that would exclude it. As I have repeatedly noted, however, it is not always permissible to kill someone else in order to protect one's own life. This is not permissible, for example, in the following case.

Trolley: A trolley is out of control and if it continues on its present track will kill G, who could, however, throw a switch, turning the trolley onto a different track, in which case it will kill H instead.

What is needed, then, is an explanation of the asymmetry in *Innocent Threat* that is compatible with the fact that the opposite asymmetry holds in *Trolley* (that is, the fact that it is reasonable for someone in *H*'s position to reject a principle permitting *G* to throw the switch).

In her most recent writing on the subject, Thomson, who is of course not looking at this as a problem for contractualism, explains the difference between *Innocent Aggressor* and *Innocent Threat* on the one hand, and cases like *Trolley* on the other, in the following way.[10] From the mere fact that unless *X* kills *Y* he himself will be killed, it does not follow that *X* may kill *Y*. But in the former class of cases there is the further fact that unless one person (*D* or *D'*) kills the other (*E* or *E'*), the latter will kill him *in violation of his right not to be killed*. When this is true, she says, it is permissible for the former person to kill the latter in self-defense. This does not apply in *Trolley*, since if the switch is not thrown and the trolley kills *G*, *H* will not have killed *G* or violated any right of *G*'s. *H* is a mere bystander, not causally involved in the threat to *G*'s life.

This account also explains a further asymmetry in *Innocent Aggressor* and *Innocent Threat*. In *Innocent Aggressor*, if *D* uses deadly force to protect his life against deranged *E*, is it permissible for *E*, who will then be threatened, to defend himself, killing *D* if necessary? Thomson argues that the answer is no. Her account can explain this, since although *D* will kill *E* unless *E* defends himself, *D* will not thereby violate any right of *E*'s, since his action is justified. (And this obviously applies in *Innocent Threat* and all other cases in which killing in self-defense is justified on the grounds Thomson proposes.)

This is in many ways an extremely appealing and convincing account (in an area in which not many accounts are so convincing). But there are, nonetheless, some aspects of it that give me pause. First, it may not seem obvious that *E*, the innocent aggressor, will violate *D*'s rights if he kills *D*; and this is even less obvious in the case of *E'* and *D'*. Given that *E* is insane, he is not at fault for killing *D*, and *E'* is not even an agent, but is just thrown at *D'* like a boulder. In Thomson's view, however, rights violation does not entail fault, nor does it require agency. This reflects the fact that she understands rights in what may be called an objective sense.

On her view, a right in the strictest sense is violated when one person does something that another person has a claim against him that he not do. And *X*'s having a claim against *Y* that he not do alpha is equivalent to *X*'s behavior being under a constraint according to which he ought not do alpha under the circumstances, even if this would produce great advantage. (In order to do alpha, *X* ought to seek a release from Y and, failing that, ought, other things equal, to compensate Y for doing it.) Thomson illustrates her idea of a claim, and the sense of ought that is used in formulating it, with the following example:

> *Day's End*: B always comes home at 9:00 P.M., and the first thing he does is to flip the light switch in his hallway. He did so this evening. B's flipping the switch caused a circuit to close. By virtue of an extraordinary series of coincidences, unpredictable in advance by anybody, the circuit's being closed caused a release of electricity (a small lightning flash) in A's house next door. Unluckily, A was in its path and was therefore badly burned.[11]

Thomson believes that in this example B has infringed a claim of A's. We may be inclined to resist this claim since it is clear that B, assuming he has no reason to think that this "extraordinary series of coincidences" will occur, is not at fault, or open to moral criticism for flipping the switch. But Thomson rejects the idea that an agent violates someone's claim only if he is at fault in behaving as he did. The core of the idea of a claim, she argues, is that actions violating it are ones that an agent ought not to do, where "ought" is understood in the "objective" sense that does not entail fault. This is the sense in which we might say, for example, that we ought not to have given the baby aspirin, given that it made him worse, even though there was, at the time, every indication that it would make him better. Using 'ought' in this sense, she says, B ought not have flipped the switch, given that it would cause A serious harm. In support of this thesis she says the following about *Day's End*.

> Wouldn't it be weird in us, knowing what will happen if B flips the switch, to say, "Look B, we know something you don't know. If we tell you, then it will be true to say that you ought not flip the switch, but not if we don't tell you." The weirdness of that performance is a sign that "ought" is at least typically used objectively.[12]

I myself am inclined to deny that B infringes any claim of A's in *Day's End*, or does anything that he ought not to have done in a morally significant sense of 'ought not'. Two principles might be relevant to the case: that one ought not to do what one sees or should see will cause serious harm to someone, and that one ought to take due care not to cause harm to others. But neither of these principles is violated in *Day's End*, given that it was only "by virtue of an extraordinary series of coincidences, unpredictable in advance by anybody" that what B did led to A's being harmed. If it is true that B ought not have flipped the switch, this is only true in a sense of 'ought not' that seems to me to lack moral content. Both *A* and *B* may wish, after the fact, that *B* had not flipped the switch, but this is not a matter of moral right and wrong.

A contractualist account of morality of the kind I favor is concerned with 'ought' and 'ought not' in the "subjective" sense, since it understands the morality of right and wrong as concerned exclusively with the principles that we could ask people to govern themselves by—that is to say, use as guides to conduct. I believe that such an account can, however, explain the phenomena to which Thomson appeals.

In considering principles by which our own and other people's conduct is to be regulated, we are of course centrally concerned with the way in which their actions will affect us. It would be reasonable for us to reject principles that did not require others to take the fact that an action would cause us serious harm as a strong, indeed normally conclusive, reason against it. They can take this as a reason only if they have some reason to think that an action will have this effect, but what they are to take as a reason is the fact that the action will have this effect, not the fact that they have reason to think this.

This reason is the fundamental one, but there are further considerations, flowing from the fact that we are commonly dealing with imperfect information. If any principle that it would not be reasonable to reject would require us to take *C* as a consideration counting strongly against an action, then, since it may not always be obvious to us whether *C* obtains or not, any principles that it would not be reasonable to reject will require us to be on the lookout for *C*, and to take reasonable steps to find out whether or not it obtains. Finally, if *C* counts strongly against an action, any nonrejectable principles will require us to be alert to the possibility that we may be mistaken about *C*, and cautious about acting when our information about it is poor.

Given this account of what is required of us, I think we can account for the "weirdness" of the remark that Thomson imagines being made to *B* in *Day's End*. First, given that the imagined interlocutor (call him *C*) knows that flipping the switch will cause *A* serious injury, it is odd for him to say that he knows something that, *if B knew it*, would count against *B*'s turning on the light. On the contrary, he knows something that *does* count against this action. *C*'s remark is odd because it seems to suggest that *B* would take the fact that he knows about the harm, rather than the harm itself, as counting against turning on the light. If *B* knows about the harm then he should count *it* as a reason against turning on the light. But it is still true that his knowing about it makes an important moral difference. In the original example, the injury to *A* was said to be due to "an extraordinary series of coincidences, unpredictable in advance by anybody." In the modified example, C knows about this effect, and can easily tell B. So the situation is quite different than it was before. But the fact that knowledge makes this difference is quite consistent with the fact that in a situation in which B has this knowledge it is still the fact that is known, not the fact of his knowing it, that he is to take as counting against his action. For these reasons, then, I do not agree with Thomson that the sense of 'ought not' that is directly linked with the moral impermissibility of actions, and in particular with the idea of rights violation, is an objective sense.

Leaving this question aside, let me now turn to some worries about the range of cases in which, on Thomson's account, it would be permissible to kill in self-defense. The first of these worries is that that account seems too narrow, or, to put it more neutrally, to mark the limit of permissible self-defense in a place that seems arbitrary. In *The Realm of Rights*, Thomson suggests that killing in self-defense is permissible in the following case:

> *Innocent Shield of a Threat*: F strapped the innocent E'' onto the front of a computer-controlled tank that he now directs toward D'' to kill him. D'' has only one weapon, an antitank gun. If D'' does nothing, the tank will reach and kill D'' and E'' will have time to escape. D'' can use his antitank gun on the tank, in which case he destroys E'' along with the tank but D'' lives.

She does not mention this case in "Self-Defense," so possibly she has changed her mind about it. Whether one thinks that D'' may kill E'' in this case or not, however, it seems to me that the answer should be the same as in the following case.

> *Hitchhiker*: J is threatened by a car coming down a narrow ramp, out of control. The driver has died from carbon monoxide fumes in the car, and H, a hitchhiker whom he picked up, is unconscious. The only way J can save himself is by causing a heavy steel door to come down, crushing the car and killing H.

It seems to me that we should give the same answer in this case as in *Innocent Shield*, since it does not matter whether the person who will be killed is on the outside of the threatening machine or inside of it. It also seems that it should be decided in the same way as *Innocent Threat*, since it does not matter whether the threat is the person's body or a larger thing in which his body is encased. (In an intermediate case the innocent threat could be wearing a protective metal suit.) On Thomson's analysis, however, these two cases would seem to differ from *Innocent Threat*, since one could not say that if nothing is done the hitchhiker will kill *J* or that the shield will kill *D″*, let alone that either of them will do so by violating a right of *J*'s or *D″*'s. All we can say is that they are attached to or included within objects that will do this.

In "Self-Defense" Thomson says that it is impermissible to save oneself by substituting a bystander (as in *Trolley*), or by using a bystander to stop a threat, or by "running roughshod over a bystander." As to who is a bystander, she offers the following partial characterization: "First, if *Y* is in no way causally involved in the situation that consists in *X*'s being at risk of death, then *Y* is clearly a bystander to it. And second, if *Y* is causally involved in it, and not minimally so—as, for example, when it is *Y* himself or herself who is about to kill *X*—then *Y* is clearly not a bystander to it."[13] It follows from this definition that Thomson's account of permissible killing in self-defense in terms of rights violation does not justify killing a bystander to save one's life. If *Y* is "not causally involved in the situation that consists in *X*'s being at risk of death" then *Y* is not about to violate *X*'s right not to be killed, so (unless there is some other justification), *X*'s killing *Y* to save his own life would violate *Y*'s right not to be killed.

Does it also follow on Thomson's account that if *Y* is *not* merely a bystander in the situation that consists in *X*'s being at risk of death then it is permissible for *X* to kill *Y* in self-defense? This depends on whether it is true that if *Y* is causally involved (or causally involved in a more than minimal way) in *X*'s being at risk of death then, if the threat to *X* is not stopped, *Y* will have killed *X* (in violation of his right not to be killed). The cases just considered bring out an uncertainty about the idea of "causal involvement" that makes it uncertain whether this will always be so. As I said above, it does not seem that the hitchhiker or the shield will kill the people who are threatened in these situations if they do nothing to defend themselves. But it does not seem quite right either to say that the hitchhiker or the shield are mere bystanders. They are not "causally involved" in the threats to the potential victims' lives, if by this one means that they themselves (or their bodies) are involved in making it the case that the victims are so threatened. On the other hand, they are physically related to threatening objects in a way that makes it the case that in acting directly on these objects in the way required to stop them one will also be acting directly on them in a way that will kill them. By contrast, in *Trolley* and other such cases what a person does to protect himself against a threat has the further effect of killing a *mere* bystander who had no previous connection with the threatening object.

One might argue that this difference is morally significant by claiming that a person whose life is (unjustifiably) threatened by some object has a particularly strong claim to be permitted simply to act on that object in a way that will stop it from hitting him, and only a weaker claim to do things that would have further damaging effects on others elsewhere in the world. This would lead to a view rather like the one Thomson defended in "Self-Defense and Rights," where she suggested that permissible killing in self-defense "is limited to cases in which Y is, or shields, a threat to X." (Although she then went on to say that "exactly what constitutes being, or shielding, a threat that it should make this difference is very hard to see.")[14]

It would follow from what I have been arguing that "shields a threat" is too narrow a characterization of the relevant class of cases. I think that "is or is physically part of a threat" comes closer to capturing the relevant class of cases, since it seems to me that *Innocent Threat*, *Innocent Shield*, and *Hitchhiker* should stand or fall together. I have offered a rationale for this distinction, according to which these cases would all stand (as permissible), but this rationale seems to me quite weak. The fact that it is the best rationale for this distinction that I have been able to think of makes me more uncertain about the cases than I was before (but still fairly certain that they should be answered in the same way). So I agree with Thomson's remark that it is very hard to see what explains these cases.

Thomson's later doctrine (based on rights violation) would, as I have said, permit killing in self-defense in *Innocent Shield* but rule it out in the other two cases. It would also permit it in further cases that may seem surprising. Consider first

> *Trolley/Landslide I*: An empty trolley running along a track in a deep cut will kill K unless he detonates an explosive charge, blowing up a section of track. However, if he does so this will cause a landslide, killing L, who is walking along the hillside above the track.

Thomson would hold, I believe, that in this case it is not permissible for K to blow up the track. But consider

> *Trolley/Landslide II*: A situation that is just like *Trolley/Landslide I* except that earlier L, when he was crossing the track before it enters the cut, pushed the button that turns on the warning light to alert trolley drivers to the presence of someone crossing the track. "By virtue of an extraordinary series of coincidences, unpredictable in advance by anybody," this caused the trolley that now threatens K to be set in motion.

If the person who flips the switch in *Day's End* violates a right of the person who is burned as a result, then it would seem that if the trolley is not stopped in this case L will have killed K, in violation of his right not to be killed (although he is in no way at fault in doing this). If so, then Thomson's analysis would imply that it is permissible for K to detonate the charge, killing L, in *Trolley/Landslide II* but not in *Trolley/Landslide I*. This seems odd to me, although I am not certain that it is mistaken. My intuitions about the cases are unclear, but it seems to me somewhat less plausible to claim that K may detonate the charge in *Trolley/Landslide II* but not in *Trolley/Landslide I* than to claim that it is permissible to kill in *Innocent Threat* but not permissible to throw the switch in *Trolley*. This may be because, in *Innocent Threat*, the person against whom force is to be used (or at least that person's body) has a continuing causal involvement in making it the case that the victim is threatened, whereas in *Trolley/Landslide II* L's causal involvement is wholly in the past, and injuring him makes no more difference to the threat to K in this case than it does in *Trolley/Landslide I*. If this is correct, it would support something more like the explanation I suggested above (as a modification of Thomson's suggestion in "Self-Defense and Rights").

Notes

1. See her "Self-defense and Rights," in *Rights, Restitution, and Risk*; her book, *The Realm of Rights*, esp. chapter 14; and, most recently, "Self-Defense," *Philosophy & Public Affairs* 20 (1991), pp. 283–310.
2. I have described this account of right and wrong more fully in *What We Owe to Each Other* (Cambridge, MA: Harvard University Press, 1998).
3. *The Realm of Rights*, p. 33.
4. *The Realm of Rights*, p. 367.
5. For a fuller discussion of this view of choice and responsibility, see *What We Owe to Each Other*, chapter 6, esp. pp. 256–267.
6. *The Realm of Rights*, pp. 371–372.
7. *The Realm of Rights*, p. 367.
8. *The Realm of Rights*, 366.
9. See *The Realm of Rights*, pp. 369–370.
10. "Self-Defense," pp. 300–303.
11. *The Realm of Rights*, p. 229.
12. *The Realm of Rights*, p. 233.
13. "Self-Defense," pp. 298–299.
14. *The Realm of Rights*, p. 371.

Chapter 11

Objectivity without Absolutes

Ernest Sosa

In this essay, I consider whether morality is just a creature of the collective will or whether on the contrary moral claims are objectively true or false.[1] Two main lines of reasoning will be assessed: the Argument from Disagreement, in the first three sections, and the Argument from Naturalism, in the last.

1 The Argument from Disagreement

Do normative questions admit determinately true answers? I focus specifically on questions with yes-or-no answers, questions of the form: whether *p*. Does an objective and determinate fact of the matter determine the right answer to such a question?

I shall consider familiar reasoning, the Argument from Disagreement, which concludes that the normative fails of objective determinacy. Here is a first formulation:

> *The Argument from Disagreement*
> 1. Extensive and irresoluble disagreement over a question *Q* implies the indeterminacy of *Q*.
> 2. Normative questions elicit extensive and irresoluble disagreement.
> 3. Normative questions are indeterminate.

Evidence for premise 2 is plentiful in history and anthropology. Against this, superficial diversity is said to mask underlying agreement. According to E. O. Wilson, for example, altruism is built into our genes. Sociologist Ralph Linton, for his part, had already highlighted "cultural universals" shared by otherwise divergent societies, among them rules against murder and incest, and rules protective of property. Most recently the social theorist James Q. Wilson, in his book *The Moral Sense*, offers a detailed case in favor of extensive underlying human agreement.

Surface diversity is of course compatible with deeper agreement, and may derive just from divergence of circumstances or factual beliefs. The apparent cruelty of the Ik to their young, for example, and of the Eskimos to their elderly, is perhaps explained by the extreme scarcity in which these groups must somehow survive as a people. And disagreement over abortion is perhaps explained largely through deep religious and factual disagreements about ourselves and the world around us.

How plausible is it that all normative disagreement could be traced back to differences in circumstances or underlying factual beliefs? Contemporary controversies conspire to make it doubtful. Some controversies may indeed rest on deeper factual divergence, as perhaps with abortion, gay rights, and capital punishment, but others seem much less likely to do so. Is the distribution of goods and services to be need-based or desert-based? To what extent and in what ways should the state fill the needs of its citizens irrespective of their ability to pay? To what extent can some be required and forced to sacrifice for the sake of others in need? This concerns not only domestic tax policy, but also the extent to which one is morally bound to sacrifice small pleasures, or even just money in the bank never to be used otherwise, for the sake of relieving starvation abroad. Can disagreements over such issues be reduced without remainder to underlying factual disagreement?

How about animal rights versus scientific progress? How does one weigh the suffering inflicted on the furry against scientific progress, including progress that may save innumerable human lives? Thus the certain must be weighed against the uncertain, pain against knowledge, and so on. At first blush it seems unlikely that such disagreements must all yield to increasing factual knowledge. Some conflicts of values may just be fundamental and irresoluble even through deeper and more extensive knowledge of the facts.

What we learn from social science old and new, and from our own reflection on current controversies, gives support to premise 2, therefore, and prompts us to look elsewhere for weakness in the Argument from Diversity. So I turn to premise 1.

2 Disagreement and Competence

Any of three possible attitudes might be taken when one considers a proposition p: one might either believe it, disbelieve it (by believing its negation), or suspend judgment. People "disagree" over a question Q (whether p) when they consider the question and one side believes what the other does not. This is how "disagreement" is to be understood in the Argument from Disagreement.

The argument needs to specify also the relevant group, whose disagreement will imply the indeterminacy of the question. Will *any* group be relevant, regardless of its constitution? Obviously not, since on nearly any question some are too ill positioned (e.g., ill informed) or ill endowed to judge reliably. Their disagreement with the well-positioned and well-endowed would presumably derive from their own deficiencies, not from any indeterminacy in the questions.

Only disagreement among the *competent* might imply the indeterminacy of a question. So we revise the argument as follows.

The Revised Argument from Disagreement
1. If the competent extensively disagree on how to answer a certain question, then that question is indeterminate.
2. The competent extensively disagree on how to answer normative questions.
3. Normative questions are indeterminate.

Contraposing 1, we obtain

1a. If a question is determinate, then the competent, if any, will agree on how to answer it.

And this is notably in harmony with theses emblematic of main philosophies of the last hundred years and more. Recall Peirce's view of the truth as what proper and extensive enquiry would reveal. And compare the logical positivists' verificationism, according to which even just the meaningfulness of a substantive question requires that it be answerable by empirical means. Similar theses have also been defended by contemporary philosophers such as Hilary Putnam, Michael Dummett, and Jürgen Habermas.

Despite its prestigious antecedents, however, to connect the truth thus with the deliverances of human inquiry is a project fraught with difficulties. The truth can be recondite, and this for logical reasons. For example, consider the following:

There are x stars in the universe, but no one (human) so much as considers that there might be exactly that many.

Some such proposition is true, but though true it cannot be believed to be true. So a proposition might be true without being accessible to inquiry.

The kinship between the Revised Argument from Disagreement and emblematic verificationist theses recalls the implausibility of such theses. Perhaps the Revised Argument may be distanced from verificationism through a sharper conception of competence. Is it possible to understand competence in a way that renders defensible the leading premise of the Revised Argument?

Full competence on the question whether p requires perhaps that one be so constituted and so positioned that one *would* get it right on that question: that one *would* believe that p if and only if it were so that p. One must be so endowed with requisite cognitive equipment, and so placed for using it, that one *would believe* that p *if and only if* it were so that p (so that one thereby "mirrors" how it is regarding that question, in the way a mirror reflects how it is in the situation mirrored).

Consider accordingly the following principle:

> (C)   S is fully competent regarding the question whether p *if and only if* S would believe correctly on that question: i.e., S would believe that p if and only if it were so that p (and so S "mirrors" how things stand on that question).

With competence so understood, we can defend premise 1 and its contrapositive. But now it is evidently impossible for the fully competent regarding a question to disagree on that question. Disagreement among the competent will require that some believe a given answer to that question while others do not; and, given (C), that is clearly impossible.

Definition (C) is at best a first approximation, however, since it is too demanding; compare the more relaxed standards of the following.

> (C')   S is competent regarding the question whether p *if and only if* not easily would S fail to believe correctly on that question: i.e., (a) not easily would S believe that p without it being so that p, and not easily would it be so that p without S believing it; and (b) not easily would S disbelieve that p without it being false that p, and not easily would it be false that p without S disbelieving it (i.e., without S believing that not-p).

Unfortunately, this is inadequate if only because despite being in a position to judge correctly, one might yet easily *not* have been so positioned. And if so, then the correct answer to the question might easily have escaped one after all.

A better approach to a relevant conception of competence is perhaps this. With regard to a given question Q, competence is a matter of being endowed with certain cognitive equipment and favored with a certain position, such that those who are so constituted and so positioned *would* not easily fail to answer Q correctly. This is a better approach, but not yet good enough. For it overlooks the fact that there may be several *different* ways to be competent on a certain question. Thus one may be competent to judge the roundness of a billiard ball either by feeling it or by seeing it, and one does not need to do both. So it seems better to think of competence regarding Q as a matter of possessing any of a *range* of equipment + position combinations, such that those so favored regarding Q would not easily fail to answer that question correctly. Thus we arrive at the following.

> (C″) S is competent regarding the question whether p *if and only if* S is so constituted and positioned relative to that question that not easily would S then fail to believe correctly on that question: i.e., (a) not easily would S believe that p while so constituted and positioned without it being so that p, and not easily would it be so that p while S was so constituted and endowed without S believing it; and (b) not easily would S disbelieve that p while so constituted and positioned without it being false that p, and not easily would it be false that p while S was so constituted and endowed without S disbelieving that p.

This is still at best an approximation to the correct account, as more would need to be said about the sort of constitution and positioning that matters for competence on a question, and about how beliefs in answer to that question would need to be related to that constitution and positioning in order to reflect one's *competence* on that question. For our purposes, however, I will work with the present approximation, on the assumption that our reflections would not be affected materially by the required refinements. Of course, any results to be attained here can then, at best, be tentative and conditional.

Our more realistic conception of competence, (C″), makes it possible for people to disagree about a question, whether p, on which they are all nevertheless competent. What is not so clearly possible, however, is that the competent as now defined should disagree *extensively* on that question. For consider: if the competent extensively disagree on that question, could it then be true of them all that they would not *easily* fail to answer it correctly? Take for reductio the population of the competent on a question whether p. Not easily then would any of them fail to get the right answer. Suppose it is true that p. In that case, given the postulated disagreement, there will be an extensive subgroup of the competent who fail to get it right, who fail to believe that p. Suppose it is false that p. In that case, given the postulated disagreement, there will again be an extensive subgroup of the competent who fail to get it right, who fail to disbelieve that p. Suppose finally it is neither true nor false that p. In that case, given the postulated disagreement, there will again be an extensive subgroup of the competent who fail to get it right, either because they believe that p without it being true that p, or because they disbelieve that p without it being false that p.

That argument fails, nevertheless, since the constitution + position combinations at issue, the *ways* of accessing the fact at issue, may be indefinitely many, where at the limit no two of the competent share their relevant combinations, their respective modes of access. This means that even if many fail to get it right, that is no reflection on the competence of the others, which may and does have a different basis. At the same time, for this very reason premise 1 of the Revised Argument from Disagreement is now unconvincing. The fact that the competent as now defined disagree does not entail any indeterminacy in the question at issue, since the disagreement may just reflect the normal slippage allowed by the mere requirement that *not easily* could one with the given constitution + position combination fail to get it right. "Not easily" is different from "not possibly," and what does not easily happen can happen anyhow, within the bounds of normal slippage and with no implication of indeterminacy.

However, we may further revise the argument as follows.

The Further Revised Argument from Disagreement
1. If the homogeneously competent extensively disagree on how to answer a certain question, then that question is indeterminate.
2. The homogeneously competent extensively disagree on how to answer normative questions.
3. Normative questions are indeterminate.

Subjects are homogeneously competent on a certain subject matter if and only if their competence + position combinations are the same in kind. And it seems plausible enough that there is enough homogeneity among the morally and evaluatively competent, favored with modes of access to the relevant subject matter, to induce a problem of determinacy via the likes of the Further Revised Argument.

This saves premise 1, but now we are back with the earlier problem: again it seems impossible for the homogeneously competent extensively to disagree. Disagreement extensive enough to threaten indeterminacy is also thereby extensive enough to threaten no less seriously the relevant lack of homogeneous competence. And the impossibility of extensive disagreement among the homogeneously competent would block the Further Revised Argument. For the second premise could now never be true. It may reasonably be concluded that our framework of competence, defined initially by means of "mirroring," etc., is useless for explicating the familiar line of reasoning that moves from extensive disagreement to indeterminacy and failure of objectivity, or is at least useless for explicating such reasoning in a way that will show it to pose a serious challenge to normative objectivity. But that, I think, would be a premature conclusion.

Here is a further way to understand such reasoning.

The New Argument
1. If, concerning a question Q, there is extensive disagreement not explicable through differential competence, then Q is indeterminate.
2. Questions *in ambit A* elicit extensive disagreement not explicable through differential competence.
3. Questions *in ambit A* are indeterminate.

More explicitly, the argument is as follows.

First, if concerning a given question, there is extensive disagreement not explicable through differential competence on that question, then the parties to the disagreement must be uniformly incompetent on that question.

Second, the incompetence of a subject S concerning a question Q must derive *either* (a) from some lack in S's endowment or some inadequacy in S's position vis a vis Q, *or else* (b) from the indeterminacy of the question.

Third, questions *in ambit A* elicit extensive disagreement not explicable through differential competence.

Fourth, the incompetence of subjects regarding disputed questions *in ambit A* is not explicable through any lack or inadequacy in their endowment or position vis a vis such questions.

Therefore, finally, questions *in ambit A* are indeterminate.

As the sun sets people believe it is nightime in increasing numbers and people disbelieve it is nightime in decreasing numbers, until all are in agreement. The twilight zone thus yields a saddle curve of disagreement (with a valley of suspension), which poses the question of how to understand such disagreement. Again, sometimes disagreement can be explained through differential competence, as when some are able to see a target fact while others are not: those who can see judge accordingly; those who cannot see either suspend judgment or perhaps misjudge. And that is how such disagreement comes about. However, no such explanation is plausible in the twilight zone. There some think it is still daytime, while others think it is no longer so, and others yet suspend judgment. But it is implausible that some should be right while others miss out through incompetence, through some lack in their powers of perception, memory, or reasoning, or through some inadequacy in their position.

How then are we to think of such disagreement? Uniform competence among the parties is logically incompatible with disagreement. And differential competence is implausible in the twilight zone. The only remaining option is that of uniform incompetence. In the twilight zone, according to this option, no one mirrors the truth: no one would be bound to get it right on the question whether p. And why is this? Is it because of some remediable lack that they all suffer? What might they be lacking? Eyesight? Give them all 20/20 sight and perfect color vision. Are they perhaps denied a good view of the ambient light outside? Bring them all outside. Was their conceptual or linguistic development lacking in some relevant way? Replace them with those who enjoy full command of English and of the relevant conceptual repertoire (while also endowed with the best eyesight and placed in the best position to judge). Would we not still expect that given a large enough group in uniform conformity with such requirements, they will *still* spread out in some curve of disagreement over the twilight span?

Uniform incompetence once in the twilight zone is a quite reasonable hypothesis, perhaps the most reasonable. And the incompetence seems irremediable, given our current conceptual repertoire. Twilight disagreement hence seems inexplicable through differential competence. We may thus reasonably conclude that in the twilight zone there *is* no determinate truth as to whether it is daytime or not, or nighttime or not. There being no such facts, it is understandable that no one should be in a position to mirror them, that no one should enjoy such competence.

3 Normative Indeterminacy?

May we now use the twilight model in understanding normative indeterminacy? Consider some relevant normative questions. What should have greater weight:

> a. An unspoiled environment or industrial and commercial progress?
> b. Animal rights or scientific progress through vivisection?
> c. Animal rights or the pleasure of meat eaters?
> d. The life of the fetus or the preferences of the nonbeliever mother?
> e. The needs of all or the desert of those who contribute?

Concerning these issues and other such issues of social policy, disagreement persists despite increasing information and dialogue. More importantly, that is so not only at the present level of abstraction but also when much more concrete issues arise, such as whether a particular vivisection is to be performed. There again opinions differ among parties none of whom can easily be faulted in any relevant respect of information or reasoning. And that should remind us of the twilight zone. Shall we say here again that the spread of disagreement among the relevant parties is best understood on a hypothesis of uniform incompetence? If so, then it seems coordinately plausible that when values come into such conflict there *is* no determinate truth as to how the conflict must be resolved. There being no such facts, finally, it is understandable that no one should be in a position to mirror them.

Normative conflict is the clash of conflicting reasons, which may be couched in the following schemata:

Pro-(reason): That X-ing would have property ϕ is a reason for X-ing.

Con-(reason): That X-ing would have property ψ is a reason against X-ing.

Interestingly, on such pros and cons we are often nearly unanimous. Nearly all agree on what are pros and what are cons at least on fundamentals. But agreement dwindles as we consider how to resolve conflicts. One thing stands out as we stand back: conflicts prompt disagreement not explicable by differential competence, but reveal agreement on the reasons themselves whose clash produces the disagreement.

Our argument from disagreement seems therefore limited in the scope of its conclusion. It shows at best *some* indeterminacy about the normative, which, however, it also reveals to be no peculiar flaw of the normative in particular. After all, the model invoked to introduce the argument in the most plausible light was drawn from the factual realm, not the normative. Twilight phenomena pertain to matters of fact, surely, not to matters of value or norm. Finally, extensive agreement is moreover found on the side of the normative. Extensive systematic disagreement is not restricted to the normative, nor is extensive systematic agreement exceptionally rare therein. We have found reasons to think the normative indeterminate, but none to think *only* the normative indeterminate, nor any to dismiss the normative as pervasively indeterminate.

So far we have discussed a kind of objectivity opposed to indeterminacy. Questions are thus objective if they admit a "determinate fact of the matter." Objective questions are hence unlike the question whether it is night or day, when it is twilight; or whether someone is bald, when he is balding; and so on. We have found no difference in kind between the factual and the normative or evaluative in respect of such indeterminacy or failure of objectivity.

We are wondering whether morality is just a creature of the collective will or whether on the contrary something objective (non-subjective) underlies the truth of moral claims. Arguments from disagreement offer no sufficient reason to deny the objectivity of the moral that would not require denying also the objectivity of daylight. Daylight is no creature of the will despite the disagreement and induced indeterminacy that it may involve at twilight time. Such disagreement and indeterminacy therefore do not sufficiently establish that morality fails of relevant objectivity and is at bottom a creature of the will.

4 Relativism

Suppose competent judges would all agree that killing people for fun is wrong, that inflicting pain for pleasure is evil, and even that someone's action of returning a promised book is right. What could possibly make it true that the killing is wrong, the inflicting evil, the returning right? Are there properties of wrongness, evilness, and rightness that attach to actions the way their location might do so? Anyone skeptical about such properties most likely would be tempted by the following line of thought.

> ### The Argument from Naturalism
> 1. Matters evaluative and normative must be understood without appeal to any properties of "goodness" or "wrongness" attaching to actions the way roundness attaches to our planet.
> 2. *Noncognitivism* (emotivism and prescriptivism), by viewing moral claims on the model of oaths or commands, and hence as neither true nor false, offers such understanding, but faces serious problems that remain unsurmounted.
> 3. *Relativism* appeals as follows to a particular moral code selected in a context of utterance (or thought):
>
>> The utterance (or thought), for example, that "Mary is wrong (morally) to ϕ" is true if and only if Mary's ϕ-ing has some feature F such that the speaker's (thinker's) moral code M categorically prohibits actions with F.
>
> 4. Such relativism offers a way to understand moral discourse (or thought) without appeal to any sui generis moral or evaluative properties; and, as a cognitivist account, it avoids the problems of noncognitivism.

Yasushi may speak truly in saying "Boston is far" although Mary speaks no less truly in saying "Boston is near, not far." Such sentences fail of a kind of objectivity. They cannot be assessed for truth or falsity context-independently. They are true or false not absolutely and objectively but only relative to the location of a subject, the speaker or thinker. According to moral relativism, moral claims too must be assessed relative to the moral code (not just the location) of the speaker or thinker.

Moral claims may thus be true or false without involving any non-natural evaluative or normative properties. This avoids two failures of objectivity, since moral claims come out neither indeterminate nor noncognitivist. For the relativist, plenty of moral claims come out determinately true. Does that yield full moral objectivity? It all depends now on the contents of moral codes. Surely the relativist would view such contents noncognitivistically. That is to say, codes will themselves contain prescriptions and not cognitively true or false claims (since otherwise the problem of truth would recur for the contained claims). If so, then a failure of objectivity may still lie at the bottom of moral relativism, after all. Relativism gives us a way to understand some moral claims as determinately true or false, but it leaves open the status of the underlying moral codes. It is thus left open that these derive from arbitrary volition. (Of course coincident volition, however arbitrary its basis, can be morally efficacious, as with the rules of the road; the question is whether it is *only* such volition that gives content to a moral code.) So it cannot be said that relativism per se would yield all moral objectivity. Nevertheless, relativism may still have an advantage over other naturalist alternatives to moral realism, such as emotivism and prescriptivism: namely, that it gives a way to avoid moral facts writ fundamentally into reality, while still answering an important objection to noncognitivist alternatives, that they do not account well enough for the logical status of moral thought and language.

However, there still remains a problem with such a notion of relativistic moral truth based on underlying codes, the "problem of the prima facie."

Most if not all of our most secure moral convictions take the form of prima facie judgments. Lying is prima facie wrong, but this can be overridden, as presumably it is when a lie saves an innocent life. Much the same idea may be put without the latin: "if to act a certain way would be to lie, that is a reason against so acting," which leaves it open that there may be a counterbalancing and even overriding reason on the other side. What then satisfies the prima facie rule "Don't lie!" when addressed to S? Is it S's *never* lying? S's almost never lying? Rarely lying? Less-often-than-not lying? *None* of these is at all plausible. So how are our moral codes constituted? What do the constituent prescriptions actually require? In that light, how are such prescriptions to be represented? Are they just universal prescriptions? If so, what would *constitute* satisfaction of such prescriptions? What, coordinately, would violate them?

This problem of constitution, though not a problem *especially* for relativism, does bear on a second problem that, if not specific to relativism, is a special worry for it: namely, the problem of the prima facie. For *however* "Lying is prima facie wrong" is to be interpreted and represented within our moral code, it implies no outright prescription against any particular lie, not even given the information that it is a lie. Nor is there any natural feature F such that our moral code logically implies that any lying of sort F is absolutely forbidden. Our moral codes rarely if ever commit to such exceptionless general injunctions, however hedged. Accordingly, our moral codes will generally imply, with regard to any particular act, *neither* that it is definitely obligatory *nor* that it is definitely wrong; nor do they imply this relative to any natural features of that act.

In summary, even the truth of moral relativism would already threaten moral objectivity, since the codes required by the relativist are constituted by mere prescriptions whose status may be that of unconstrained volitions. True, moral relativism would at least explain how moral claims could be determinately true, without appeal to any nonnatural properties of goodness or wrongness, or any such. But we have seen reason to doubt that moral relativism can succeed even here. Our doubt resides in the apparent fact that moral codes imply few if any determinate prescriptions concerning specific acts. Sane moral codes normally shared by actual communities lack the required content. Any code you or I might endorse will contain few if any absolute and exceptionless injunctions of the sort required. The prima facie prescriptions we are willing to endorse will absolutely require or forbid no specific act, even relative to specified features of it. Moral obligation cannot be defined relative to moral codes constituted by such prescriptions, not unless nearly nothing of what anyone does will ever count as morally obligatory. And moral wrongness cannot be so defined either, not unless almost nothing is ever to count as morally wrong.

5 Conclusion

Is morality just a creature of the collective will or does something objective underlie the truth of moral claims?

The Argument from Disagreement argues against objectivity on the basis of disagreement not explicable through differential competence.

My response has been that indeterminacy is quite common in our ordinary factual world, as for example in twilight phenomena, without this showing any pervasive failure of objectivity of the sort charged against the normative. Such disagreement therefore does not constitute a sufficient basis for this charge.

Relativism tries to secure for normative and evaluative claims a status of truth or falsity based on relativity to the moral code of the speaker or thinker. What makes true or false a claim that someone's act is just wrong is whether the act has certain features such that the relevant moral code categorically prohibits the performance of such acts. The problem for such relativism is that no actual moral code will contain any such categorical prohibitions. The injunctions contained in actual codes are never categorical but only prima facie, and these logically imply no categorical prohibition of anything. Moral codes should be understood rather as specifying reasons for and reasons against, but what then might the relativist cite as the source of the truth of such contained specifications?

Neither argument, therefore, is lethal to a positive belief in the objectivity of the normative or evaluative, so long as this is understood to include specifications of reasons for and reasons against, and even all-in claims of moral wrongness or moral obligation. This last may seem surprising, but we must not lose sight of the fact that the main problem posed by conflicts of values and duties lies at the general level, where we try to specify in quite general terms how to weigh one consideration against others that, at that general level, strike us as incomparable, or at least not comparable by us either now or even in foreseeable states of increasing information and apt reflection. This does not stand in the way of our being able to strike a balance quite often in particular cases. So in a particular case it may be clear that the combined weight of the con-reasons outweighs the combined weight of the pro-reasons. And this is compatible with our inability to formulate, even in *foro interno*, the relevant generalization that would sum up our decision and its basis. We may be able to recognize the relevant quantities of the various factors and how they are to be compared, without being able to state or even to entertain in our own thought a generalization that captures those quantities and the right comparison between them.[2,3]

Notes

1. If there is objective moral truth, moreover, we might also wonder how we could ever come to know its content, but that is not our question here.
2. Without claiming exhaustive knowledge of the vast objectivity literature, I mention as especially relevant some very recent work that has impressed me: Gilbert Harman

and Judith Jarvis Thomson, *Moral Relativism and Moral Objectivity* (Blackwell Publishers, 1996); and Russ Shafer-Landau, "Ethical Disagreement, Ethical Objectivism, and Moral Indeterminacy," *Philosophy and Phenomenological Research* 54 (1994): 331–345. I find much to agree with in the way this excellent paper frames the issues and even on some of the positive answers and arguments defended. But there remains important disagreement. For example, it is highly questionable even of ideal reasoners that "... for indeterminate situations, they will all agree that the situation is indeterminate ..." (p. 343). Nevertheless, to Shafer-Landau belongs the credit for making helpful use of the idea of moral indeterminacy and of the comparison with factual indeterminacy. Also important is Ruth Chang (ed.), *Incommensurability, Incomparability, and Practical Reason* (Harvard University Press, 1997).

3. I am delighted to be part of this tribute to Judy Thomson, whose work I have long admired as a model of well-spent lucidity.

Bibliography of Judith Jarvis Thomson

This bibliography includes critical studies, but no book reviews. Starred items are reprinted in *Rights, Restitution, and Risk* (item 49 below).

1. "In Defense of Moral Absolutes." *Journal of Philosophy* 55 (1958): 1043–1053.
2. "Critical Study of *Intention*, G. E. M. Anscombe." *Journal of Philosophy* 56 (1959): 31–41.
3. "Notes on Strawson's Logic." *Mind* 70 (1961): 53–82.
4. "Ethics and *Ethics and the Moral Life*." *Journal of Philosophy* 58 (1961): 65–83.
5. "Definition by Internal Relation." *Australasian Journal of Philosophy* 39 (1961): 125–142.
6. "Professor Stenius on the *Tractatus*." *Journal of Philosophy* 58 (1961): 584–596. Reprinted in Irving Copi and Robert Beard (eds.), *Essays on Wittgenstein's Tractatus* (London: Routledge, 1966); and in John Canfield (ed.), *The Philosophy of Wittgenstein* (New York: Garland, 1986).
7. "Practical Reasoning." *Philosophical Quarterly* 12 (1962): 316–328.
8. "Private Languages." *American Philosophical Quarterly* 1 (1964): 20–31. Reprinted in Stuart Hampshire (ed.), *Philosophy of Mind* (New York: Harper & Row, 1966); and in O. R. Jones (ed.), *The Private Language Argument* (London: Macmillan, 1971).
9. (with James Thomson) "How Not to Derive 'Ought' From 'Is'." *Philosophical Review* 73 (1964): 512–516. Reprinted in Wilfrid Sellars and John Hospers (eds.), *Readings in Ethical Theory*, 2nd ed. (New York: Appleton-Century-Crofts, 1970); W. D. Hudson (ed.), *The Is-Ought Question* (New York: St. Martin's Press, 1979); and in Robert Hoffman and Sidney Gendin (eds.), *Philosophy: A Contemporary Perspective* (Belmont, Calif.: Wadsworth, 1975).
10. "Time, Space, and Objects." *Mind* 74 (1965): 1–27.
11. "Reasons and Reasoning," in Max Black (ed.), *Philosophy in America* (Ithaca, N.Y.: Cornell University Press, 1965).
12. "Grue." *Journal of Philosophy* 63 (1966): 289–309.
13. "More Grue." *Journal of Philosophy* 63 (1966): 528–533.
14. "Introduction," in *Logical Constructions*, John Wisdom. New York: Random House, 1969.
15. "The Identity Thesis," in Sidney Morgenbesser, Patrick Suppes and Morton White (eds.), *Philosophy, Science, and Method: Essays in Honor of Ernest Nagel* (New York: St. Martin's Press, 1969).
16. "Comments on Joseph Agassi, 'Science in Flux: Footnotes to Popper'," in *Boston Studies in the Philosophy of Science*, vol. 3 (Dordrecht: Reidel, 1968).
17. Contribution to the Symposium "Cause and Action," *Proceedings of the Seventh Inter-American Congress of Philosophy* (Québec: Presses de l'Université Laval, 1967).
18. "John Wisdom," in Paul Edwards (ed.), *Encyclopedia of Philosophy* (New York: Macmillan, 1967).

19. "Comments" (on Körner) in Joseph Margolis (ed.), *Fact and Existence: Proceedings of the University of Western Ontario Philosophy Colloquium, 1966* (Oxford: Blackwell, 1969).
20. (Edited with Gerald Dworkin) *Ethics: an Anthology*. New York: Harper & Row, 1968.
21. "The Time of a Killing." *Journal of Philosophy* 68 (1971): 115–132. Reprinted in Roberto Casati and Achille Varzi (eds.), *Events* (Aldershot: Dartmouth, 1996).
22. "Individuating Actions." *Journal of Philosophy* 68 (1971): 774–781.
23. *"A Defense of Abortion." *Philosophy and Public Affairs* 1 (1971): 47–66. Reprinted in Marshall Cohen, Thomas Nagel, and Thomas Scanlon (eds.), *The Rights and Wrongs of Abortion* (Princeton: Princeton University Press, 1974); Joel Feinberg (ed.), *The Problem of Abortion* (Belmont, Calif.: Wadsworth, 1973); James Rachels (ed.), *Moral Problems* (New York: Harper & Row, 1971); Richard Wasserstrom (ed.), *Today's Moral Problems* (New York: Macmillan, 1975); and other anthologies.
24. *"Rights and Deaths." *Philosophy and Public Affairs* 2 (1973): 146–159. Reprinted in Marshall Cohen, Thomas Nagel, and Thomas Scanlon (eds.), *The Rights and Wrongs of Abortion* (Princeton: Princeton University Press, 1974); and other anthologies.
25. *"Preferential Hiring." *Philosophy and Public Affairs* 2 (1973): 364–384. Reprinted in James Rachels (ed.), *Moral Problems* (New York: Harper & Row, 1971); Marshall Cohen, Thomas Nagel, and Thomas Scanlon (eds.), *Equality and Preferential Treatment* (Princeton: Princeton University Press, 1977); and other anthologies.
26. "Molyneux's Problem." *Journal of Philosophy* 71 (1974): 637–650.
27. "Moore's Technique Revisited," in Renford Bambrough (ed.), *Wisdom, Twelve Essays* (Oxford: Blackwell, 1974).
28. "Academic Freedom and Research," in Edmund Pincoffs (ed.), *The Concept of Academic Freedom* (Austin: University of Texas Press, 1975).
29. *"The Right to Privacy." *Philosophy and Public Affairs* 4 (1975): 295–314. Reprinted in Tom Beauchamp and Terry Pinkard (eds.), *Ethics and Public Policy* (Englewood Cliffs, N.J.: Prentice-Hall, 1975); and other anthologies.
30. *"Killing, Letting Die, and the Trolley Problem." *The Monist* 59 (1976): 204–217.
31. "Property-Acquisition" (abstract). *Journal of Philosophy* 73 (1976): 664–666.
32. *"Self-Defense and Rights," 1976 Lindley Lecture, University of Kansas Press. Reprinted in John Kaplan and Robert Weisberg (eds.), *Criminal Law: Cases and Materials* (Boston: Little, Brown, 1986).
33. *Acts and Other Events*. Ithaca, N.Y.: Cornell University Press, 1977.
34. (with Terrance Sandalow) "On Full-Time Non-Tenure-Track Appointments." *AAUP Bulletin* (1978).
35. *"Some Ruminations on Rights." *Arizona Law Review* 19 (1977): 45–60. Reprinted in Jeffrey Paul (ed.), *Reading Nozick* (Oxford: Blackwell, 1982).
36. "Common-Sense Morality" (abstract). *Journal of Philosophy* 76 (1979): 545–547.
37. *"Rights and Compensation." *Noûs* 14 (1980): 3–15.
38. "Philosophical Prospects for a New World," in Peter Caws (ed.), *Two Centuries of Philosophy in America* (Totowa, N.J.: Rowman & Littlefield, 1980).
39. (with Chodosh et al.) "Regulations Governing Research on Human Subjects." *Academe* 67 (1981): 358–370.
40. "Parthood and Identity Across Time." *Journal of Philosophy* 80 (1983): 201–219. Reprinted in Michael Rea (ed.), *Material Constitution* (Lanham, Md.: Rowman & Littlefield, 1997); Jaegwon Kim and Ernest Sosa (eds.), *Metaphysics* (Oxford: Blackwell, 1999); and other anthologies.
41. (with Dreben et al.) "Academic Freedom and Tenure: Corporate Funding of Academic Research." *Academe* 69.6 (1983): 18a–23a.
42. *"Remarks on Causation and Liability." *Philosophy and Public Affairs* 13 (1984): 101–133.

43. *"Some Questions about Government Regulation of Behavior," in Tibor Machan and Bruce Johnson (eds.), *Rights and Regulation: Ethical, Political, and Economic Issues* (Cambridge, Mass.: Ballinger, 1983).

44. *"The Trolley Problem," *Yale Law Journal* 94 (1985): 1395–1415.

45. *"Imposing Risks," in Mary Gibson (ed.), *To Breathe Freely* (Totowa, N.J.: Rowman & Littlefield, 1983).

46. "Causal Priority: A Comment." *Noûs* 19 (1985): 249–253.

47. "A Note on Internalism." *Philosophy and Public Affairs* 15 (1986): 60–66.

48. *"Liability and Individualized Evidence." *Law and Contemporary Problems* 49.3 (1986): 199–219. Reprinted in Tom Campbell (ed.), *Legal Positivism* (Aldershot: Dartmouth, 1999).

49. *Rights, Restitution, and Risk.* William Parent, ed. (Cambridge, Mass.: Harvard University Press, 1986). This volume reprints all the starred items above.

50. "Feinberg on Harm, Offense, and the Criminal Law: A Review Essay." *Philosophy and Public Affairs* 15 (1986): 381–395.

51. (Edited) *On Being and Saying: Essays for Richard Cartwright*. Cambridge, Mass.: The MIT Press, 1987.

52. "Ruminations on an Account of Personal Identity," in *On Being and Saying, op. cit.*

53. "Verbs of Action." *Synthese* 72 (1987): 103–122.

54. "Causation and Rights: Some Preliminaries." *Chicago-Kent Law Review* 63 (1987): 471–521.

55. "The Decline of Cause." (Hart Lecture) *Georgetown Law Journal* 76 (1987–1988): 137–150. Reprinted in William Shaw (ed.), *Readings in Philosophy of Law* (Englewood Cliffs, N.J.: Prentice Hall, 1993).

56. "Morality and Bad Luck." (Metaphilosophy Address) *Metaphilosophy* 20 (1989): 203–221. Reprinted in Daniel Statman (ed.), *Moral Luck* (Albany: State University of New York Press, 1993).

57. "The No Reason Thesis." *Social Philosophy and Policy* 7 (1989): 1–21.

58. *The Realm of Rights.* Cambridge, Mass.: Harvard University Press, 1990.

59. "Ideology and Faculty Selection." *Law and Contemporary Problems* 53.3 (1990): 155–176. Reprinted in William Van Alstyne (ed.), *Freedom and Tenure in the Academy* (Durham: Duke University Press, 1993).

60. "Self-Defense." *Philosophy and Public Affairs* (1991): 283–310.

61. "On Some Ways in Which a Thing Can Be Good." *Social Philosophy and Policy* 9 (1992): 96–117. Reprinted in Ellen Frankel Paul, Fred Miller, and Jeffrey Paul (eds.), *The Good Life and the Human Good* (New York: Cambridge University Press, 1992).

62. (with Matthew Finkin) "Academic Freedom and Church-Related Higher Education: A Reply to Professor McConnell," in William Van Alstyne (ed.), *Freedom and Tenure in the Academy* (Durham: Duke University Press, 1993).

63. "Précis of *The Realm of Rights*." *Philosophy and Phenomenological Research* 53 (1993): 159–162.

64. "Reply to Commentators." *Philosophy and Phenomenological Research* 53 (1993): 187–194.

65. "Goodness and Utilitarianism" (Presidential Address). *Proceedings and Addresses of the American Philosophical Association* 67.2 (1993): 145–159.

66. "Abortion." *Boston Review* 20.3 (1995).

67. "Reply." *Boston Review* 20.4 (1995).

68. "Academic Freedom and Tenure: University of Southern California." *Academe*, November–December (1995): 40–49.

69. (with Gilbert Harman) *Moral Relativism and Moral Objectivity*. Oxford: Blackwell, 1996.

70. "Baier's Carus Lectures on Killing and Letting Die," in J. B. Schneewind (ed.), *Reason, Ethics, and Society* (Chicago: Open Court, 1996).

71. "Killing and Letting Die: Some Comments," in Tom Beauchamp (ed.), *Intending Death* (Englewood Cliffs, N.J.: Prentice Hall, 1995).

72. "Critical Study of Jonathan Bennett's *The Act Itself.*" *Noûs* 30 (1996): 545–557.

73. (with Ronald Dworkin et al.) "Amicus Brief on Assisted Suicide." *The New York Review*, March 27, 1997.

74. "The Right and the Good." *Journal of Philosophy* 94 (1997): 273–298.

75. "People and their Bodies," in Jonathan Dancy (ed.), *Reading Parfit* (Oxford: Blackwell, 1997).

76. "Précis of *Moral Relativism and Moral Objectivity.*" *Philosophy and Phenomenological Research* 58 (1998): 171–173.

77. "Reply to Critics." *Philosophy and Phenomenological Research* 58 (1998): 215–222.

78. "The Statue and the Clay." *Noûs* 32 (1998): 149–173.

79. "Physician-Assisted Suicide: Two Moral Arguments." *Ethics* 109 (1999): 497–518.

80. *Goodness and Advice.* Princeton: Princeton University Press, 2001.

Contributors

Jonathan Bennett is Professor Emeritus of Philosophy at Syracuse University.

Richard L. Cartwright is Professor Emeritus of Philosophy at Massachusetts Institute of Technology.

Joshua Cohen is Professor of Philosophy and Arthur and Ruth Sloan Professor of Political Science at Massachusetts Institute of Technology.

N. Ann Davis is McConnell Professor of Human Relations at Pomona College.

Catherine Z. Elgin is Professor of Philosophy of Education at Harvard University.

Gilbert Harman is Professor of Philosophy at Princeton University.

Barbara Herman is Professor of Philosophy at the University of California, Los Angeles.

F. M. Kamm is Professor of Philosophy and Adjunct Professor of Law at New York University.

Claudia Mills is Associate Professor of Philosophy at the University of Colorado at Boulder.

T. M. Scanlon is Alford Professor of Natural Religion, Moral Philosophy, and Civil Polity at Harvard University.

Ernest Sosa is Romeo Elton Professor of Natural Theology and Professor of Philosophy at Brown University.

Index